POETS' HANDBOOK

NEW RHYMING DICTIONARY AND POETS' HANDBOOK

Printed in the United States of America

Library of Congress catalog card number: 57-9585

84 85 18 17

NEW RHYMING DICTIONARY

AND

POETS' HANDBOOK

By

Burges Johnson, Litt. D.

Author of "Essaying an Essay"; "As I Was Saying"; "Campus vs. Classroom"; "Sonnets from the Pekinese"; "The Lost Art of Profanity," etc.

REVISED EDITION

1817

Harper & Row, Publishers

New York, Hagerstown, San Francisco, London

ACKNOWLEDGMENTS

Lines illustrating the various meters and stanzas, and a number of poems illustrating lyric forms are quoted in this book. The compiler wishes to express grateful acknowledgment to authors or publishers who have allowed the use of copyright material in this way. Following is a list of those who have given such consent:

AUTHOR	LINES FROM	PUBLISHER
William V. Moody	Of Wounds and Sore Defeat	Houghton Mifflin Company
Olive Kilmer	After Grieving	Doubleday, Doran & Company
Sara Teasdale	Spring Night	The Macmillan Company
Austin Dobson	In After Days	Alban Dobson and the Oxford University Press
" "	When I saw you last, Rose	" " "
" "	A Ballad to Queen Elizabeth of the Spanish Armada	" " "
" "	A Ballad of Prose and Rhyme	" " "
" "	On a Nankin Plate	" " "
" "	Rose-Leaves	" " "
" "	In Town	" " "
" "	For a Copy of Theocritus	" " "
" "	"More Poets Yet"	" " "
David Morton	Who Walks with Beauty	G. P. Putnam's Sons
Siegfried Sassoon	Absolution	E. P. Dutton & Co., Inc.
Robert Bridges	And beautiful must be the mountains whence ye come	Oxford University Press
Charles Hanson Towne	The Best Road of All	Doubleday, Doran & Company
Henry Herbert Knibbs	The Sun Worshippers	Houghton Mifflin Company
Florence W. Evans	The Flower Factory	Florence W. Evans
Angela Morgan	Resurrection	Dodd, Mead and Company
Dorothy Parker	Razors pain you	Horace Liveright
Thomas Bailey Aldrich	I would be the lyric	Houghton Mifflin Company
Bret Harte	Plain Language from Truthful James	Houghton Mifflin Company
Thomas Augustine Daly	Wid her basket of apples come Nora McHugh	Harcourt, Brace and Company
" " "	Still we'll be sp'ilin' you	David McKay
D. H. Lawrence	The dawn was apple green	B. W. Huebsch & Co.
" " "	She opened her eyes	" " " " "
Louis Untermeyer	What are those ravens doing in our trees	Harcourt, Brace and Company
Edna St. Vincent Millay	Lethe	Harper & Brothers

AUTHOR	LINES FROM	PUBLISHER
Emily Dickinson	I'll tell you how the sun rose	Little, Brown and Company
" "	To Make a Prairie	" " " "
Alice Meynell	A Dead Harvest	John Lane & Company
Max Michelson	A Hymn to Night	Poetry Magazine
John Gould Fletcher	The Swan	The Macmillan Company
Herman Hagedorn	Broadway	" " "
Harriet Munroe	On the Porch	" " "
Frances Shaw	The Harp of the Wind	Poetry Magazine
Walter Conrad Arensberg	Song of Souls Set Free	Houghton Mifflin Company
Gelett Burgess	There is nothing in afternoon tea	Frederick A. Stokes Company
" "	Chant-Royal of the True Romance	Small, Maynard & Co.
" "	A Daughter of the North	" " "
" "	Rondel of Perfect Friendship	" " "
" "	Sestina of Youth and Old Age	" " "
R. W. Gilder	What is a sonnet?	Century Company
H. C. Bunner	Ready for the Ride	Privately printed
Samuel Minturn Peck	Under the Rose	Frederick A. Stokes Company
Wilfred Wilson Gibson	He's Gone	Macmillan, Ltd.
Don Marquis	The Triolet	Doubleday, Doran & Company
James Branch Cabell	The Conqueror Passes	Robert M. McBride & Company
" " "	Villon Quits France	" " "
Brander Matthews	Les Morts Vout Vite	Privately printed
Arthur Guiterman	Betel Nuts	E. P. Dutton & Co.
James Whitcomb Riley	When the Frost is on the Punkin	Bobbs-Merrill Co.
Frank D. Sherman	Dear Priscilla	Houghton Mifflin Company
Robert Frost	The Tuft of Flowers	Henry Holt & Co.
Jean Starr Untermeyer	The lapping of lake water	B. W. Huebsch
Eugene Field	Seein' things	Chas. Scribner's Sons
Guy Wetmore Carryl	How Jack Found	Harper & Bros.
Charlotte P. S. Gilman	I thought that life	Small Maynard & Co.
Burges Johnson	Alak the Yak	Harper & Bros.
" "	Find first thy meter	" " "
" "	Little things that count	E. P. Dutton & Co.
Sidney Lanier	Marshes of Glynn	Chas. Scribner's Sons
Ogden Nash	"Tomorrow, Partly Cloudy"	Little, Brown & Company
Vachel Lindsay	The Congo	The Macmillan Company

Contents

Introduction

Prose is the language of reason; poetry the language of feeling, the verbal expression of emotional experience. Music is mankind's purest means of expressing emotion, so when he seeks to communicate his message he borrows musical devices such as rhythm, and harmony of word sound, and gives to his words emotional or "poetic" meanings.

Consciousness of rhythm must carry back to the infancy of the human race. The primitive human was conscious of the rhythmic beating of his own heart, and aware that it was affected by external rhythms and was speeded or retarded by hope or fear or joy or anger. Just as children of today, recalling the childhood of our race, will run beside the bass drum in a street parade, feeling their own hearts throbbing in response to its rhythm, so primitive man believed his tom-tom would bring hope to the sick or incite a tribe to war.

Rhyme and rhythm in poetry are two forms of the same thing. Rhythm is the regular beat of accent in successive lines of verse; rhyme is the echoing beat of sound, occurring at regular intervals, according to a pattern. Poetic words are those which when grouped together harmonize in sound; and they are words which have an emotional rather than a literal interpretation. The poet writes that he saw an army of birch trees in their white uniforms marching up a hillside, guarded by a stately sentinel pine. We know there is no army, and no uniforms, and no marching, and no guarding and no sentinel; yet the poet has described the scene more clearly than if he had used prosaically truthful words.

This is a dictionary which brings words together in groups because they "rhyme," and for no other reason. No group can be complete for various reasons: new words are constantly being invented; a local dialect may destroy commonly accepted rhymes or create new ones. Inventive rhymesters may put two or three one-syllable words together so that they rhyme with one word having two or three syllables. (More about that on page 464.)

The greatest value in such a dictionary lies in the fact that it serves as a stimulant to the eager versifier, "activating" all the vocabulary he already possesses, and causing him to accumulate more.

Thought is inner speech. All human thinking is done by the inward use of coined words; so the richer a man's active vocabulary the wider are the range and the effectiveness of his thinking, whether expressed in prose or poetry.

Burges Johnson

POETS' HANDBOOK

Forms of English Versification

Rhythm

Even rhythm by itself, without words, is an effective means of emotional appeal, as is proved by the chanting of primitive tribes when meaningless sounds make varying impressions because of their effect upon the pulse-beat of their hearers.

It is natural for poets to seek new rhythms in order to gain new emotional effects, but an abandonment of all rhythm is an abandonment of poetry.

Poetic art as practiced by the ancients developed certain rigid rhythmic patterns based upon *quantity* and *accent*, but took no account of *rhyming*, as we understand it. Quantity, as the name implies, meant the length of time to be allowed for the pronunciation of a syllable. Poetic feet in classic verse were made up of two or three syllables, some long and some short, in various arrangements. Whether or not a syllable was long or short depended upon certain vowel and consonant combinations.

Quantity

Modern English *rules* of verse consider only accent, but the old quantitative classic names have been transferred to our modern English meter. Quantity, however, still exists as an element in English verse. Syllables are still slow-spoken or quick-spoken, according to the way they are spelled. But nothing would be gained by the user of this handbook if more space were devoted to quantity. The English verse-writer must feel instinctively whether or not his metrical line "sings" well; and it will not sing well if too many of the syllables in the line are long in quantity. Even though there be the right number and they are properly accented, the line will nevertheless seem overcrowded (witness the difference between "The cat that watched" and "The splendor falls"). An ambitious student may find a discussion of classic "prosidy" in any good Latin textbook or in any technical study of poetry.

Feet

In English verse, where accuracy of rhythm depends upon recurrent accents alone, an accented syllable accompanied by one or two unaccented syllables is known as a *foot*; and a definite pattern composed of feet in a fixed and recurrent arrangement is known as *meter*.

The practical verse-writer may wish to go a little further in technical knowledge and learn the ancient names of the four different feet generally used in English verse, and the three others used less frequently. They can be most simply presented in a diagram.

Name of Foot	*Accents*	*Name of Meter*
Iambus	ᴗ –	Iambic
Trochee	– ᴗ	Trochaic
Anapest	ᴗ ᴗ –	Anapestic
Dactyl	– ᴗ ᴗ	Dactylic

Feet used only occasionally in a line

Spondee – –
Pyrrhic ᴗ ᴗ
Amphibrach ᴗ – ᴗ

The word verse *originally meant and still means a single metric line divided into feet. As commonly used it has come to mean metric composition as distinguished from prose; and more loosely still, it has come to mean the lighter forms of poetry in stanza form.*

Meters

Poetic lines, or verses, are classified according to the number of feet in a line. A verse, for instance, containing only a single foot is monometer, two feet dimeter, and so on up to the eight-foot line—trimeter, tetrameter, pentameter, hexameter, heptameter and octameter. The number of feet in a line of English verse rarely exceeds eight; but it is possible for verses to contain more.

The best known and most used foot in English verse is the iambus. Single words illustrating a foot of the iambic meter are

undue, excite, retard, indeed, etc.

Iambic monometer (◡ –) is verse which presents the iambus in a one-foot line. There are few generally known poems written entirely in iambic monometer. Usually, when written, they are mere exercises of verbal trickery. But here is a serious example.

Thŭs Ī
Pass by,
And die:
As one
Unknown
And gone.
I'm made
A shade
And laid
I'th' grave:
There have
My cave
Where tell
I dwell
Farewell.

—*Upon His Departure Hence,* ROBERT HERRICK

Iambic monometer is more often used in refrain lines which belong to poems of other meters:

'Mid pathless deserts I groan and grieve;
In weariest solitudes I leave
  My track;
Bemoaning the fate that has christened me,
In spite of my whiskered dignity,
  A Yak!

O happy child with the epithet
Of Abe or Ike or Eliphalet,
  Or Jack,
You little wot of the blush of shame
That dyes my cheek when I hear the name
  Of Yak!

—*Alack the Yak,* BURGES JOHNSON

Iambic dimeter (⏑ – | ⏑ –) verse is two iambic feet long. Examples are:

Give all | to love
Obey thy heart.

—R. W. Emerson

Who loves | the rain
And loves his home
And looks on life
With quiet eyes . . .

—Frances Shaw

Jim was | my chum
  Up on the bar:
That's why I come
  Down from up yar,
Lookin' for Jim.
  Thank ye, sir! YOU
Ain't of that crew,—
  Blest if you are!

—*Jim,* Bret Harte

Iambic trimeter (⏑ – | ⏑ – | ⏑ –) verse contains three iambic feet:

So fare | well Eng | land old |
  If evil times ensue,
Let good men come to us,
  We'll welcome them to New.

—From *The Simple Cobbler of Aggawam*
Nathaniel Ward

You call | my tale | "Romance,"
  And still the thing may be.
The Jungle Peacocks dance,
  Though none is there to see.

—*Betel Nuts,* Arthur Guiterman

So much | one man | can do,
That does both act and know.

—Andrew Marvell

Of wounds | and sore | defeat
I made my battle stay
Wingèd sandals for my feet
I wove of my delay.
—*Of Wounds of Sore Defeat,* William V. Moody

Iambic tetrameter (◡ – | ◡ – | ◡ – | ◡ –) is four iambic feet long. It is more popular and more generally used than the former meters. Examples are:

When I | was young, | I was | so sad,
I was so sad! I did not know
Why any living thing was glad
When one must some day sorrow so.
—*After Grieving,* Olive Kilmer

The park | is filled | with night | and fog,
The veils are drawn about the world,
The drowsy lights along the path
Are dim and pearled. . . .
—*Spring Night,* Sara Teasdale

What is | this life, | if full | of care
We have no time to stand and stare?
—*Leisure,* W. H. Davies

Iambic tetrameter is particularly adapted to the themes and styles of the French verse forms. Ballades, triolets, rondeaus, and so forth, usually are written in this light meter. A typical and well-known example of French form in iambic tetrameter is the rondeau by Dobson:

IN AFTER DAYS

In after days when grasses high
O'ertop the stone where I shall lie,
Though ill or well the world adjust
My slender claim to honored dust,
I shall not question or reply.

I shall not see the morning sky;
I shall not hear the night-winds' sigh;
I shall be mute, as all men must
In after days!

But, yet, now living, fain were I
That some one then should testify,
  Saying—"He held his pen in trust
  To Art, not serving shame or lust."
Will none?—Then let my memory die
  In after days!

Iambic pentameter (˘ – | ˘ – | ˘ – | ˘ – | ˘ –) verse contains five iambic feet. Probably more English poetry is written in this meter than in any other. The sonnet form is usually written in this measure. Examples of the meter are:

˘ – ˘ – ˘ – ˘ – ˘ –
Who walks | with beau | ty has | no need | of fear.
The sun and moon and stars keep pace with him.

—*Who Walks With Beauty,* David Morton

˘ – ˘ – ˘ – ˘ – ˘ –
The an | guish of | the earth | absolves | our eyes
'Til beauty shines in all that we can see.

—*Absolution,* Siegfried Sassoon

˘ – ˘ – ˘ – ˘ – ˘ –
I lived | with vi | sions for | my com | pany
Instead of men and women, years ago. . . .

—Mrs. Browning

˘ – ˘ – ˘ – ˘ – ˘ –
The learned | reflect | on what | before | they knew:
Careless of censure, nor too fond of fame;
Still pleased to praise, yet not afraid to blame,
Averse alike to flatter or offend,
Not free from faults, nor yet too vain to mend.

—*Criticism,* Pope

˘ – ˘ – ˘ – ˘ – ˘ –
My Rom | ney! Lift | ing up | my hand | in his
As wheeled by seeing spirits toward the east,
He turned instinctively, where faint and far,
Along the tingling desert of the sky
Beyond the circle of the conscious hills,
Were laid in jasper-stone as clear as glass
The first foundations of that new, near day,
Which should be builded out of Heaven and God.

—Mrs. Browning

Iambic hexameter (˘ – | ˘ – | ˘ – | ˘ – | ˘ – | ˘ –) contains six iambic feet. This measure is difficult to handle. Usually only occasional lines are found throughout a poem, in order to vary the meter. Examples are:

> And beau | tiful | must be | the moun | tains whence | ye come.
>
> —Robert Bridges

> We search out dead men's words and works . . .
> And spend | our wit | to name | what most | employ | unnamed.
>
> —Matthew Arnold

> . . . let the ocean dash
> In fiercest tumult on the rocking shore!
> Destroy | this life | or let | earth's fa | bric be | no more.
>
> —*Despair*, Shelley

> Will sleep at midnight o'er the wildered wave.
> Wilt thou | our low | ly beds | with tears | of pi | ty love?
>
> —*Fragment*, Shelley

Iambic heptameter (˘ – | ˘ – | ˘ – | ˘ – | ˘ – | ˘ – | ˘ –) contains seven iambic feet. Examples:

> I like | a road | that wan | ders straight; | the King's | highway |
> is fair,
> And lovely are the sheltered lanes that take you here and there;
> But best of all, I love a road that leads to God knows where.
>
> —*The Best Road of All*, Charles Hanson Towne

> I think | he loved | the spring: | not that | he cared | for flowers— |
> most men
> Think such things foolishment—but we were first acquainted then.
>
> —*The Quaker Widow*, Bayard Taylor

> The husk | y, rust | y rus | sel of | the tos | sels of | the corn,
> And the raspin' of the tangled leaves as golden as the morn;
> The stubble in the furries—kindo' lonesome-like, but still
> A-preachin' sermons to us of the barns they growed to fill;
> The strawstack in the medder, and the reaper in the shed;
> The hosses in theyr stalls below—the clover overhead!—
> O, it sets my hart a-clickin' like the tickin' of a clock,
> When the frost is on the punkin and the fodder's in the shock.
>
> —*When the Frost Is on the Punkin*, James Whitcomb Riley

Iambic octameter (⏑ – | ⏑ – | ⏑ – | ⏑ – | ⏑ – | ⏑ – | ⏑ – | ⏑ –) contains eight iambic feet in each line. Examples:

My lips | would sing | a song | for you, | a soul | ful lit | tle song |
for you

—EDMUND LEAMY

The trail | is high | whereon | we ride, | with all | the world | below |
to see
The cleft of canyon, sweep of range and winter-white of lonely peak;
Lean foothold on the mountain-side, and on, beyond the Mystery
The unattained, the hidden land we may not find, but ever seek.

—*The Sun Worshippers,* HENRY HERBERT KNIBBS

Trochaic.—The trochaic foot contains two syllables. The first is long or stressed; the second short or unstressed. Single words illustrating it are armor, helmet, useful, missile, letter. Because of the lightness of the rhythm which the trochaic meter affects, it is often called the Tripping Measure. It is difficult to find perfect examples of most of the trochaic meters, because the rhythm lends itself so readily to variation. Often hypermetrical verse results from the addition of unaccented syllables to the line. Example:

Tiny | Fea | mitta | nodding | when the | twilight | slips in, | grey

—*The Flower Factory,* FLORENCE W. EVANS

Often unaccented syllables are introduced at the beginning of lines, and the resultant verse is called *anacrusis.* Example:

So! | Mid the | splendor | of e | ternal | spaces!

—*Resurrection,* ANGELA MORGAN

Besides these, truncated lines are often used; that is, lines from which the last unaccented syllables in the final feet have been dropped. Example:

Wept for | me, for | thee, for | all.
When he was an infant small.

Trochaic monometer (– ⏑) combines the one-foot line and the trochee. A complete poem in trochaic monometer is, usually, a rhythmic exercise. A complete poem in four syllables by Strickland

Gillilan, called "Lines on the Antiquity of the Microbe," illustrates this meter:

> – ᴗ
> Adam
> Had 'em.

Trochaic dimeter (– ᴗ | – ᴗ) contains lines which are two trochaic feet in length.

The first, third, fifth, and seventh lines of the following poem are trochaic dimeter; the remaining lines are various metrical lengths:

> – ᴗ – ᴗ
> Razors | pain you;
> Rivers are damp;
> Acids stain you;
> And drugs cause cramp.
> Guns aren't lawful;
> Nooses give;
> Gas smells awful;
> You might as well live.
>
> —Dorothy Parker

Here is an example of truncated trochaic dimeter from which the last unaccented syllable in the second foot has been dropped:

> Welcome, Maids of Honor,
> – ᴗ –
> You do | bring
> – ᴗ –
> In the | spring
> And wait upon her.
>
> —*To Violets,* Robert Herrick

Trochaic trimeter (– ᴗ | – ᴗ | – ᴗ) is three trochaic feet in length:

> – ᴗ – ᴗ – ᴗ
> I would | be the | Lyric
> Ever on the lip
> Rather than the Epic
> Memory lets slip.
>
> —Thomas Bailey Aldrich

Trochaic tetrameter (– ᴗ | – ᴗ | – ᴗ | – ᴗ) contains four trochaic feet in one line. Of all the trochaic meters, the tetrameter seems to lend itself most easily to expression. Longfellow's "Hiawatha" is a well-known example of the rhythm involved:

> Should you | ask me, | Whence these | stories?
> Whence these legends and traditions,
> With the odors of the forest,
> With the dew and damp of meadows,
> With the curling smoke of wigwams,
> With the rushing of great rivers,
> With their frequent repetitions
> And their wild reverberations
> As to thunder in the mountain?

While Longfellow thus carries the trochaic meter perfectly through a whole poem, poets more generally omit the last unaccented syllable from some or all lines. This practice lends a variety which relieves the insistent monotony of the flawless trochaic line. Examples:

> Carol, | every | violet | has
> Heaven for a looking-glass!
> Every little valley lies
> Under many-clouded skies;
> Every little cottage stands
> Girt about with boundless lands.

> Dear Pris | cilla, | quaint and | very
> Like a | modern | Puri | tan,
> Is a modest literary
> Merry young American.
>
> —Frank D. Sherman

Trochaic pentameter (– ⏑ | – ⏑ | – ⏑ | – ⏑ | – ⏑) contains five trochaic feet in each line. Example:

> When the | sunlight | through a | mountain | crevise
> Sends long rays aslant across the desert.

Matthew Arnold's, "Self Dependence" contains some trochaic pentameter lines:

> Weary | of my | self and | sick of | asking
> What I am and what I ought to be.

Trochaic hexameter (– ᴗ | – ᴗ | – ᴗ | – ᴗ | – ᴗ | – ᴗ) contains six trochaic feet in each line.

It is almost impossible to find lines in perfect trochaic hexameter. The six-foot length is unusual in the easier iambic line; it is more unusual in the trochaic.

> Then we | wandered | after | snowfall | in the | darkness,
> Blithe and free,
> But our footprints left a record, that the others
> Laughed to see.
>
> —L. K. K.

The first and third lines of "Epilogue to Asolando" are trochaic hexameter:

> At the | midnight | in the | silence | of the | sleep time
> When you set your fancies free

Trochaic heptameter (– ᴗ | – ᴗ | – ᴗ | – ᴗ | – ᴗ | – ᴗ | – ᴗ) contains seven trochaic feet in each line. Example:

> Stepping | lightly | in their | dancing, | horses | forelegs | skitter |
> Down the driveway, faint staccato as the pebbles pitter
> Like a fall of iron raindrops; and the wind-stopped laughter
> Of the riders send a tinkling alto floating after.

Trochaic octometer (– ᴗ | – ᴗ | – ᴗ | – ᴗ | – ᴗ | – ᴗ | – ᴗ | – ᴗ) contains eight trochaic feet.

Poe's "Raven" exemplifies the meter. The first and third lines of each stanza are good examples of flawless trochaic octameter. The unaccented syllables of the final foot in each of the remaining lines have been dropped:

> Once up | on a | midnight | dreary, | while I | pondered, | weak and |
> weary,
> Over many a quaint and curious volume of forgotten lore
> While I nodded, nearly napping, suddenly there came a tapping
> As of some one gently rapping, rapping at my chamber door.
> "'Tis some visitor,' I muttered, 'tapping at my chamber door,
> Only this and nothing more.'

"Grandmother's Story of Bunker Hill Battle" by Oliver Wendell Holmes is trochaic octometer.

'Tis like | stirring | living | embers | when, at | eighty, one re | members
  All the achings and the quakings of "the times that tried men's
    souls,"
When I talk of Whig and Tory, when I tell the Rebel story,
  To you the words are ashes, but to me they're burning coals.

There's a | woman | like a | dewdrop, | she's so | purer | than the |
    purest;
And her noble heart's the noblest, yes, and her sure faith's the surest;

—*There's a Woman Like a Dewdrop*, Robert Browning

I could | hear their | voices | calling | like an | echo | 'cross the |
    water

Lakeside, A. E. Burnham

The following lines are all truncated:

Then to | side with | Truth is | noble | when we | share her | wretched |
    crust,
Ere her cause bring fame and profit, and 'tis prosperous to be just;
Then it is the brave man chooses, while the coward stands aside,
Doubting in his abject spirit, till his Lord is crucified.

—*Present Crisis*, James Russell Lowell

Anapestic.—The anapestic foot (⌣ ⌣ –) contains three syllables, the first two short and unstressed, the third long and stressed. This trisyllable is difficult to handle and it has not been used as considerably in perfect anapestic lines as the disyllabic foot has been used. The anapest is usually inserted in various other measures for the sake of variance and to relieve monotony. Words and phrases illustrating the meter are:

chiffonier, devotee, luncheonette, violin, to devote, to erase.

The anapestic form in English becomes stilted and artificial because English inflections do not coincide with the form. The effect, however, is musical and some poets have made the form their favorite medium of expression.

Exceptions to the rhythm are usual, and it is rarely that a complete perfect anapestic couplet is found.

Anapestic monometer (⏑ ⏑ –) contains one anapestic foot in each line: several lines in this stanza illustrate:

⏑ ⏑ –
In and out
And round about,
Here you go,
There you go!
Tinkle, tinkle,
Periwinkle!
Here and there,
Everywhere,
Floats the music on the air.

—*Periwinkle,* Julia C. R. Dorr

Often an anapestic foot makes an interesting refrain or a short recurrent line in a poem of a longer and different meter. Oliver Wendell Holmes used the foot effectively in "The Last Leaf":

I know it is a sin
For me to sit and grin
⏑ ⏑ –
At him here;
But the old three-cornered hat,
And his breeches, and all that,
⏑ ⏑ –
Are so queer!

And if I should live to be
The last leaf upon the tree
⏑ ⏑ –
In the spring,
Let them smile as I do now,
At the old forsaken bough
⏑ ⏑ –
Where I cling.

Anapestic dimeter (⏑ ⏑ – | ⏑ ⏑ –) contains two anapestic feet in one line. An example of the meter is contained in the first four lines in each stanza of Bret Harte's "Plain Language from Truthful James":

⏑ ⏑ – ⏑ ⏑ –
Which I wish | to remark,
And my language is plain,
That for ways that are dark
And for tricks that are vain,

The heathen Chinee is peculiar,
Which the same I would rise to explain: . . .
. . . .

In his sleeves, which were long,
He had twenty-four packs—
Which was coming it strong,
Yet I state but the facts;
And we found on his nails, which were taper,
What is frequent in tapers,—that's wax.

⏑ ⏑ – ⏑ ⏑ –
When I saw | you last, Rose,
You were only so high;—
How fast the time goes!

Like a bud ere it blows,
You just peeped at the sky,
When I saw you last, Rose!

—Austin Dobson

Anapestic trimeter (⏑ ⏑ – | ⏑ ⏑ – | ⏑ ⏑ –) contains three anapestic feet in a line:

Hear the drops | on the back | of the roof
As the house crouches low in its pain,
As it sprawls in the clutches of wind,—
Under flickering whips of the rain.

Anapestic tetrameter (⏑ ⏑ – | ⏑ ⏑ – | ⏑ ⏑ – | ⏑ ⏑ –) contains four anapestic feet in each line. Browning's, "How We Carried the News From Ghent to Aix" is an example. Note the galloping rhythm the anapestic meter lends to that, and to Bonny Dundee.

⏑ ⏑ – ⏑ ⏑ – ⏑ ⏑ – ⏑ ⏑ –
To the Lords | of Conven | tion 'twas Clav | er'se who spoke,
"Ere the King's crown shall fall there are crowns to be broke;
So let each Cavalier who loves honor and me,
Come follow the bonnet of Bonny Dundee.

—*Bonny Dundee*, Sir Walter Scott

There comes Em | erson first, | whose rich words, | every one,
Are like gold nails in temples to hang trophies on,
Whose prose is grand verse, while his verse, the Lord knows,
Is some of it pro—no, 'tis not even prose;
I'm speaking of meters; some poems have welled
From those rare depths of soul that have ne'er been excelled;
They're not epics, but that doesn't matter a pin.
In creating, the only hard thing's to begin.

—*A Fable for Critics*, James Russell Lowell

Wid her bas | ket of ap | ples comes No | ra McHugh
  Wid her candies an' cakes an' wan thing an' another,
But the best thing she brings to commind her to you
  Is the smile in her eyes that no throuble can smother.

—Thomas Augustine Daly

Anapestic pentameter (⏑ ⏑ – | ⏑ ⏑ – | ⏑ ⏑ – | ⏑ ⏑ – | ⏑ ⏑ –) contains five anapestic feet in each line. The trisyllabic foot in the pentameter measure gives fifteen syllables to each line. It is a number not easily used in English poetry:

For a mere, | measly snake | in a cy | press our fa | thers went
  wrong.
It was Adam and Eve in vast Eden who met the first fake,
O Satan-sent serpent whose leaf-lurking wiles were so strong
  For a mere measly snake.

Because of the artificial rhythm which results from the use of the perfect anapestic pentameter, poets have generally introduced other feet to vary the meter. A well-known example is from one of Swinburne's roundels:

That the heart | of the hear | er may smile | if to pleas | ure his ear
  A roundel is wrought.

Anapestic hexameter (⏑ ⏑ – | ⏑ ⏑ – | ⏑ ⏑ – | ⏑ ⏑ – | ⏑ ⏑ – | ⏑ ⏑ –) contains six anapestic feet in each line. Some occasional lines of

Swinburne's "Hertha" illustrate the meter: (Although the rhythm is popular, it is rarely that hexameter is found which has not extra syllables, or a number dropped.)

God chan | ges, and man, | and the form | of them bo | dily; I | am
the soul.

Sidney Lanier, in *The Marshes of Glynn*, beautifully varies his meter to suit the mood of his poem. The following example shows anapests in hexameter, many of them truncated:

Ye marsh | es, how can | did and sim | ple and noth | ing with hold
ing and | free
Ye publish yourselves to the sky and offer yourselves to the sea!
Tolerant plains, that suffer the sea and the rains and the sun,
Ye spread and span like the catholic man who hath mightily won
God out of knowledge and good out of infinite pain
And sight out of blindness and purity out of a stain.
As the marsh-hen secretly builds on the watery sod,
Behold I will build me a nest on the greatness of God:
I will fly in the greatness of God as the marsh-hen flies
In the freedom that fills all the space 'twixt the marsh and the skies.

—Sidney Lanier

Anapestic heptameter (⏑ ⏑ – | ⏑ ⏑ – | ⏑ ⏑ – | ⏑ ⏑ – | ⏑ ⏑ – | ⏑ ⏑ – | ⏑ ⏑ –) contains seven anapestic feet in one line. An example:

Hear the sea | rushing co | lour and suds | as it swells | in a vi | olet
ridge | near the sky—
And it rolls, sweeping in, with its fingers curled up at the children
at play on the beach,
It whispers and crashes a song—with a softing refrain that's a sigh—
Then it washes, sinks back, leaving part the sand dry, that the next
rounding wave tries to reach.

—G. F.

From my youth | hath she shown | me the joy | of her bays, that
I crossed, | of her cliffs | that I clomb.

—*In the Water*, Swinburne

When my lips | tried to sing | they were sealed | by the touch |
of a ghost | ly invis | ible hand |

—L. K. K.

Anapestic octameter contains eight anapestic feet in each line. Because it is easier to split eight long feet into two lines of tetrameter length, the rhythm is very rarely found.

So the rid | er went gal | oping on; | as he sped | down the long |
curving high | way, the wind | at his head—
The trees seemed to race with him, dizzily, tall; and the horse ran
on madly, not seeing at all.

—G. F.

Dactylic.—The dactylic foot (– ⏑ ⏑) contains three syllables, the first long or stressed, and the last two short or unstressed. Single illustrating words are anything, terrible, beautiful, anapest, covering.

Like the three-syllable anapest, the dactyl is often used in lines of other meters to vary the form. Because of the artificial meter obtained by using the pure dactylic, poets often leave the last two unaccented syllables from the last foot. (Some of the following examples are characteristic and contain two syllables less than the perfect meter.)

Dactylic monometer (– ⏑ ⏑) contains one dactylic foot in each line. Like other monometers, examples are generally mere rhythmic tricks.

Come to me,
Sing to me,
Cling to me;
Bring to me
Sorrow or
Joy.

Dactylic dimeter (– ⏑ ⏑ | – ⏑ ⏑) contains two dactylic feet in each line of poetry:

Still we'll be | spilin' you,
Blind to the guile in you,
While there's a smile in you,
Nora McHugh!

—Thomas Augustine Daly

– ⏑ ⏑ – ⏑ ⏑
Fast they come, | fast they come;
See how they gather;
Wide waves the eagle plume,
Blended with heather.
Cast your plaids, draw your blades,
Forward each man set!
Pibroch of Donuil Dhu,
Knell for the onset!

—*Pibroch of Donuil Dhu,* SIR WALTER SCOTT

Dactylic trimeter (– ⏑ ⏑ | – ⏑ ⏑ | – ⏑ ⏑) contains three dactylic feet in each line. The line is most unusual when the pure measure is used. The following are some occasional truncated excerpts:

– ⏑ ⏑ – ⏑ ⏑ –
Laughing, dish | eveled and | gay,
Dancing with jubilant feet,
Homeward the children returned
Leaving their books in the school;
Lessons were over till fall.

—*Holidays,* E. T. WILSON

– ⏑ ⏑ – ⏑ ⏑ – ⏑ ⏑
All through the | nighttime a | symphony
Plays on my windowpanes lightfully
Breathing of wind for the instruments—
Thunder for drums coming frightfully;
Chorus ensemble roars mightfully.
Drops on the roof, pianissimo;
Trees, in the lull, singing,—whisper low.

—G. F.

Dactylic tetrameter (– ⏑ ⏑ | – ⏑ ⏑ | – ⏑ ⏑ | – ⏑ ⏑) has four dactylic feet in each line. The following lines are truncated:

– ⏑ ⏑ – ⏑ ⏑ – ⏑ ⏑ – ⏑
Slowly the | mist o'er the | meadow was | creeping,
Bright on the dewy buds glistened the sun,
When from his couch, while his children were sleeping,
Rose the bold rebel and shouldered his gun.

—*Lexington,* OLIVER WENDELL HOLMES

Brightest and | best of the | sons of the | morning;
Dawn on our darkness, and lend us Thine aid;
Star of the east, the horizon adorning,
Guide where our Infant Redeemer is laid!

Bishop Heber

Dactylic pentameter (– ◡ ◡ | – ◡ ◡ | – ◡ ◡ | – ◡ ◡ | – ◡ ◡) contains five dactylic feet in one line: Few examples are to be found.

Crashing in | breakers that | rise in green | washing and | levelly
Sink in dark dizzying swirls, throaty sea-waters sing to us.
Fingers of suds are thrown out of the waves, churning heavily,
Rash in their madness the tempest-teased ocean gods fling to us
All of the whorls and the carvings that hide in the soul of the sea.

—G. F.

Dactylic hexameter (– ◡ ◡ | – ◡ ◡ | – ◡ ◡ | – ◡ ◡ | – ◡ ◡ | – ◡ ◡) contains six dactylic feet in each line. Rarely is the meter used in its perfect form. Syllables are usually added or taken away:

Always it | seems that the | long day is | endless; the | evening is | lonelier.
Night comes and darkness; we wish that the dawn of the day were beginning. . . .

Not of the | princes and | prelates with | periwigged | chario | teers
Riding triumphantly laurelled to lap the fat of the years.

—*A Consecration*, John Masefield

So I am | come to you | now with an | offer and | proffer of | marriage,
Made of a good man and true—Miles Standish, the Captain of Plymouth.

—*John Alden and Priscilla*, Henry Wadsworth Longfellow

Dactylic heptameter (– ◡ ◡ | – ◡ ◡ | – ◡ ◡ | – ◡ ◡ | – ◡ ◡ | – ◡ ◡ | – ◡ ◡) contains seven dactylic feet. Of this meter, too, there are few examples.

Oxen go | trundling through | sod with their | eyes staring | thickly, their | legs stepping | heavily, |

Dumb as the clumps that they walk on, they wabble with dirge-like
and passive persistence.
Fastened to earth which they mutilate, pounding, relentless their
industry—
Swaying and turning, and dragging and beating, not caring nor
counting the distance.

—G. F.

Dactylic octameter (– ◡ ◡ | – ◡ ◡ | – ◡ ◡ | – ◡ ◡ | – ◡ ◡ | – ◡ ◡ | – ◡ ◡ | – ◡ ◡) contains eight dactylic feet. Ordinarily this eight-foot line of twenty-four syllables would be broken into tetrameter lines.

Into the | black and the | swell of the | sea, twenty | men launched
the | lifeboat; the | shouts of en | couragement
Fainted in distance. . . .

Among the "occasional" feet, spondees alone may be said to provide a meter of their own, the spondaic. Tennyson uses the spondee in his line:

Break, break, break on thy cold grey stones, O sea!

Poems cannot easily be written in spondees because any inflected two-syllable word in English mars the meter. An exercise in monosyllabic spondees which attempts to describe the movement of the waves in the even words is this:

Sea, sighs, wash, swish, crash—
Waves, wash, low, wash, back;
Sound, moves, lulls, slows, stops.
Sea, sighs, wash, swish, crash!

Even is come; and from the dark park, hark,
The signal of the setting sun—one gun!
Now puss, while folks are in their beds, treads leads,
And sleepers waken, grumble—"Drat that cat!"

—*A Nocturnal Sketch,* THOMAS HOOD

Other measures have been defined, but practically all poetry can be scanned as pure or varied forms of the meters listed above.

Stanzas

The greatest conceptions of poets, past and present, have usually been in continuous verse, not broken into stanzas. But when the recurrent echoes of sound are used at the ends of lines, stanzas (or fixed groupings of lines) aid in the establishment of a musical pattern. Many patterns are offered in this chapter.

The *couplet*, or *distich*, simplest of stanzas, contains two rhyming lines. A poem containing but a single couplet can be only the vehicle for an epigram, such as

> When I am dead, I hope it may be said,
> His sins were scarlet, but his books were read.
>
> —Hilaire Belloc

> He first deceased, she for a little tried
> To live without him, liked it not, and died.
>
> —*Old epitaph*

The longer poem, made up of successive couplets, is common:

> I went to turn the grass once after one
> Who mowed it in the dew before the sun.
>
> The dew was gone that made his blade so keen
> Before I came to view the leveled scene.
>
> —*The Tuft of Flowers*, Robert Frost

Shakespeare's use of the couplet to round out the blank verse of his dramatic narrative is familiar to everyone:

> Now forth, lord constable and princes all,
> And quickly bring us word of England's fall.

The *triplet*, or three-line stanza, uses only one rhyme sound, (aaa); or may have the first line rhyming with the last (aba). Poems comprised of three-line stanzas (the Villanelle, for example) often alternate the rhyme schemes, as aba, bab, aba, etc. In other forms of triplet the first two lines rhyme, the last line differing throughout the poem, or *vice versa*. Often the triplet is not rhymed.

> a) Youth's for an hour
> a) Beauty's a flower
> b) But love is a jewel that wins the world. . . .
>
> —Moira O'Neil

a) Whoe'er she be,
a) That not impossible she,
a) That shall command my heart and me.

—Richard Crashaw

a) The dawn was apple green,
b) The sky was green wine held up in the sun,
a) The moon was a golden petal between.

a) She opened her eyes, and green
b) They shone, clear, like flowers undone
a) For the first time, now for the last time seen.

—D. H. Lawrenci

a) What are those ravens doing in our trees,
a) Calling on doom and outworn prophecies?
a) Flying in threes. . . .

—Louis Untermeyer

The *quatrain*, or four-line stanza, lends itself easily to verse. The obvious rhyme arrangements are aabb, abab, and abba. The introduction of an unrhymed line makes possible still other forms. Any rhyme scheme is permissible; no rhyme scheme is necessary.

a) The forward youth that would appear,
a) Must now forsake his Muses dear,
b)   Nor in the shadows sing
b)   His numbers languishing.

—A. Marvell

a) His songs were a little phrase
b)   Of eternal song.
a) Drowned in the harping of lays
b)   More loud and long. . . .

—Thomas Macdonagh

a) Black lie the hills, swiftly doth daylight flee,
b) And, catching gleams of sunset's dying smile,
b) Through the dusk land for many a changing mile
a) The river runneth softly to the sea.

—Celia Leighton Thaxter

a) These pearls of thought in Persian gulfs were bred,
b) Each softly lucent as a rounded moon;

a) The diver Omar plucked them from their bed,
a) Fitzgerald strung them on an English thread.

—James Russell Lowell

a) In the cool waves
b) What can be lost?—
b) Only the sorry cost
c) Of the lovely thing, ah, never the thing itself!

a) The level flood that laves
d) The hot brow
e) And the stiff shoulder
d) Is at our temples now. . . .

—Edna St. Vincent Millay

a) A ruddy drop of manly blood
b)   The surging sea outweighs;
c) The world uncertain comes and goes,
d)   The lover rooted stays.

—Ralph Waldo Emerson

a) The lapping of lake water
b) Is like the weeping of women,
c) The weeping of ancient women
d) Who grieved without rebellion.

—Jean Starr Untermeyer

a) I'll tell you how the sun rose—
b) A ribbon at a time.
c) The steeples swam in amethyst
d) The news like squirrels ran.

—Emily Dickinson

a) The innocent, sweet Day is dead.
a) Dark night hath slain her in her bed.
a) O, Moors are as fierce to kill as to wed!
b)   —Put out the light, said he.

—Sidney Lanier

a) In the hush of early even
b) The clouds come flocking over,
a) Till the last wind fell from heaven
c) And no bird cried.

—John Dreeman

A pleasing and distinctive quatrain form is that used in FitzGerald's translation of the "Rubaiyat":

a) Ah, my Belovèd, fill the cup that clears
a) Today of past Regrets and future Fears:
b) Tomorrow!—Why, Tomorrow I may be
a) Myself with Yesterday's Sev'n Thousand Years.

a) Wake! For the Sun, who scatter'd into flight
a) The stars before him from the field of Night,
b) Drives North along with them from Heav'n, and strikes
a) The Sultan's Turret with a Shaft of Light.

Quintet.—Possible arrangements of the five-line stanza are of course still more numerous. The stanza is a varied combination of the couplet and triplet, with the lines usually rhymed in the proportion of two to three, such as aabbb, abbaa, etc. The following are noteworthy illustrations:

a) Here, with one leap,
b) The bridge that spans the cutting; on its back
c) The load
c) Of the main road
b) And under it the railway track.

—*The Bridge,* J. Redwood Anderson

a) Look—on the topmost branches of the world
b) The blossoms of the myriad stars are thick;
b) Over the huddled rows of stone and brick,
c) A few sad wisps of empty smoke are curled
b) Like ghosts, languid and sick.

Sunday Evening In the Common, John Hall Wheelock

a) Along the graceless grass of town
a) They rake the rows of red and brown,—
b) Dead leaves, unlike the rows of hay
b) Delicate, touched with gold and gray,
b) Raked long ago and far away.

—*A Dead Harvest,* Alice Meynell

a) Across the mesa flying,
a) The hawks come swooping, crying;
a) The wind, already dying,
a) Through cedar tops is sighing,—
b) The canyons now are dark.

—C. J.

a) When God at first made man,
b) Having a glass of blessings standing by;
a) Let us (said he) pour on him all we can:
b) Let the world's riches, which disperséd lie,
a) Contract into a span.

—*The Gifts of God,* George Herbert

a) Go, lovely Rose,
b) Tell her that wastes her time and me,
a) That now she knows,
b) When I resemble her to thee,
b) How sweet and fair she seems to be.

—Edmund Waller

a) Stay, stay at home, my heart, and rest,
a) Home-keeping hearts are happiest,
b) For those that wander they know not where
b) Are full of trouble and full of care;
a) To stay at home is best.

—*Song,* Henry W. Longfellow

a) To make a prairie it takes a clover and one bee,—
a) One clover, and a bee,
a) And revery.
b) The revery alone will do
b) If bees are few.

—*To Make a Prairie,* Emily Dickinson

a) Hail to thee, blithe spirit,
b) Bird thou never wert
a) That from heaven, or near it,
b) Pourest thy full heart
b) In profuse strains of unpremeditated art.

—*To a Skylark,* Percy Bysshe Shelley

a) Descend softly on the houses
b) We built with pride,
c) Without worship.
d) Fold them in your veil
e) Spill your shadows.

—*A Hymn to Night,* Max Michelson

The *sestet,* or six-line stanza, uses various combinations of the shorter couplet, triplet, and quatrain. The Petrarchan sonnet closes with a sestet limited to one of the rhyme-schemes, abcabc, ababab; abbaab, ababba, or abbaba.

The following stanzas illustrate some noteworthy forms. There are, obviously, many other possible arrangements:

a) I ain't afraid uv snakes or toads, or bugs or worms or mice,
a) An' things 'at girls are skeered uv I think are awful nice!
b) I'm pretty brave I guess; an' yet I hate to go to bed,
b) For, when I'm tucked up warm an' snug an' when my prayers are said,
c) Mother tells me "Happy Dreams" an' takes away the light,
c) An' leaves me lyin' all alone an' seein' things at night!

—*Seein' Things*, Eugene Field

a) Here room and kingly silence keep
b) Companionship in state austere;
b) The dignity of death is here,
a) The large, lone vastness of the deep.
c) Here toil has pitched his camp to rest:
c) The west is banked against the west.

—*By the Pacific Ocean*, Joaquin Miller

a) Under a wall of bronze,
b) Where beeches dip and trail
c) Their branches in the water;
d) With red-tipped head and wings
b) A beaked ship under sail—
e) There glides a single swan . . .

—*The Swan*, John Gould Fletcher

a) How like the stars are these white, nameless faces—
b) These for innumerable burning coals!
a) This pale procession out of stellar spaces
b) This Milky Way of Souls!
c) Each in its own bright nebulæ enfurled,
c) Each face, dear God, a world!

—*Broadway*, Herman Hagedorn

a) As I lie roofed in, screened in,
b) From the pattering rain,
b) The summer rain—
c) As I lie,
c) Snug and dry,
b) And hear the birds complain.

—*On the Porch*, Harriet Munroe

a) But Jack, no panic showing,
a) Just watched his beanstalk growing,
b)   And twined with tender fingers the tendrils up the pole.
c) At all her words funereal
c) He smiled a smile ethereal,
b)   Or sighed an absent-minded "Bless my soul!"

—*How Jack Found That Beans May Go Back on a Chap,* GUY WETMORE CARRYL

a) Which I wish to remark,
b)   And my language is plain,
a) That for ways that are dark
b)   And for tricks that are vain,
c) The heathen Chinee is peculiar,
b)   Which the same I would rise to explain.

—*Plain Language from Truthful James,* BRET HARTE

a) I thought that life could have no sting
b)   To infant butterflies,
a) So I gazed on this unhappy thing
b)   With wonder and surprise.
a) While sadly with his waving wing
b)   He wiped his weeping eyes.

—*A Conservative,* CHARLOTTE P. S. GILMAN

a) What was he doing, the great god Pan,
b)   Down in the reeds by the river?
a) Spreading ruin and scattering ban,
c) Splashing and paddling with hoofs of a goat,
c) And breaking the golden lilies afloat
b)   With the dragon-fly on the river?

—*A Musical Instrument,* MRS. BROWNING

a) Happy is the man that findeth wisdom,
b) And the man that getteth understanding.
c) For the merchandise of it is better than the merchandise of silver,
d) And the gain thereof than fine gold.
e) She is more precious than rubies:
f) And none of the things thou canst desire are to be compared unto her.

—*Sonnets of Wisdom,* RICHARD MOULTON

a) Thou little bird, thou dweller by the sea,
b)   Why takest thou its melancholy voice,
c)   And with that boding cry

c) Why o'er the waves dost fly?
a) O, rather, with me
b) Through the fair land rejoice!

—*The Little Beach-Bird,* Richard Henry Dana

a) I wandered lonely where the pine trees made
a) Against the bitter East their barricade,
b) And guided by its sweet
c) Perfume, I found, within a narrow dell,
c) The trailing spring flower tinted like a shell,
b) Amid dry leaves and mosses at my feet.

—*The Trailing Arbutus,* John Greenleaf Whittier

a) Wee, modest, crimson-tipped flow'r,
a) Thou's met me in an evil hour;
b) For I maun crush among the stoure
c) Thy slender stem:
b) To spare thee now is past my pow'r,
c) Thou bonie gem.

—*To a Mountain Daisy,* Robert Burns

a) Good-bye, proud world! I'm going home:
b) Thou art not my friend, and I'm not thine:
a) Long through thy weary crowds I roam;
b) A river-ark on the ocean brine,
a) Long I've been like the driven foam;
a) But now, proud world! I'm going home.

—*Good-bye,* Ralph Waldo Emerson

a) Ha! whaur ye gaun, ye crawlin ferlie!
a) Your impudence protects you sairly;
a) I canna say but ye strunt rarely
b) Owre gauge and lace;
a) Tho' faith! I fear ye dine but sparely
b) On sic a place.

—*To a Louse,* Robert Burns

The *septet* may be rhymed in a hundred different ways and is obviously a combination of the shorter forms, couplet, triplet, and quatrain. One famous variation in iambic pentameter or "heroics" is called the *rime royal* (ababbcc), and was used by Chaucer and Spenser and many later English poets. One example is here given, followed by a few of the many other rhyme-schemes of which the septet is capable:

a) So every spirit as it is most pure,
b) And hath in it the more of heavenly light,
a) So it the fairer body doth procure
b) To habit it, and is more fairly dight
b) With cheerful grace and amiable sight;
c) For of the soul the body form doth take
c) For soul is form and doth the body make.

—SPENSER

a) Three corpses lay out on the shining sands
b) In the morning gleam as the tide went down;
a) And the women were weeping and wringing their hands
b) For those who will never come back to the town.
c) For men must work, and women must weep,
c) And the sooner it's over, the sooner to sleep,
d) And good-bye to the bar and its moaning.

—KINGSLEY

a) The flower that smiles today
b) Tomorrow dies;
a) All that we wish to stay
b) Tempts and then flies:
c) What is this world's delight?
c) Lightning that mocks the night,
c) Brief even as bright.

—SHELLEY

a) Swiftly walk o'er the western wave,
b) Spirit of night!
a) Out of the misty eastern cave,
b) Where all the long and lone daylight
c) Thou wovest dreams of joy and fear,
c) Which make thee terrible and dear,—
b) Swift be thy flight!

—*To Night*, PERCY BYSSHE SHELLEY

a) This is the ship of pearl, which, poets feign,
a) Sails the unshadowed main,—
b) The venturous bark that flings
b) On the sweet summer wind its purpled wings
b) In gulfs enchanted, where the Siren sings,
c) And coral reefs lie bare,
c) Where the cold sea-maids rise to sun their streaming hair.

—*The Chambered Nautilus*, OLIVER WENDELL HOLMES

a) Where the bee sucks, there suck I:
a) In a cowslip's bell I lie;
a) There I couch when owls do cry.
a) On the bat's back I do fly
a) After summer merrily.
b) Merrily, merrily, shall I live now
b) Under the blossom that hangs on the bough.

—*The Tempest,* WILLIAM SHAKESPEARE

Octave.—The eight-line stanza is most commonly a combination of the couplet, triplet, and quatrain forms. In the Petrarchan sonnet's detached octave (see p. 39), the rhyme-scheme is abba, abba. Probably each of the many other rhyming combinations that can be formed of eight lines has been used by some poet.

a) Ah, what is love? It is a pretty thing,
a) As sweet unto a shepherd as a king;
b) And sweeter too;
c) For kings have cares that wait upon a crown,
c) And cares can make the sweetest love to frown.
d) Ah then, ah then!
e) If country loves such sweet desires gain,
e) What lady would not love a shepherd swain?

—ROBERT GREENE

a) The spacious firmament on high,
a) With all the blue ethereal sky,
b) And spangled heavens, a shining frame,
b) Their great Original proclaim.
c) Th' unwearied Sun from day to day
c) Does his creator's power display;
d) And publishes to every land
d) The work of an Almighty hand.

—*Hymn,* JOSEPH ADDISON

a) Drink to me only with thine eyes,
b) And I will pledge with mine,
c) Or leave a kiss but in the cup
b) And I'll not look for wine.
a) The thirst that from the soul doth rise
b) Doth ask a drink divine,
c) But might I of Jove's nectar sup,
b) I would not change for thine.

—BEN JONSON

a) Spirit that breathest through my lattice: thou
b) That cool'st the twilight of the sultry day!
a) Gratefully flows thy freshness round my brow;
b) Thou hast been out upon the deep at play,
a) Riding all day the wild blue waves till now,
b) Roughening their crests, and scattering high their spray,
c) And swelling the white sail. I welcome thee
c) To the scorched land, thou wanderer of the sea!

—*The Evening Wind,* WILLIAM CULLEN BRYANT

a) Thou art a female, Katydid!
b) I know it by the trill
c) That quivers through thy piercing notes,
b) So petulant and shrill;
d) I think there is a knot of you
e) Beneath the hollow tree,—
f) A knot of spinster Katydids,—
e) Do Katydids drink tea?

—*To an Insect,* OLIVER WENDELL HOLMES

a) He's gone.
b) I do not understand.
c) I only know
c) That as he turned to go
b) And waved his hand,
d) In his young eyes a sudden glory shone:
c) And I was dazzled by a sunset glow,
a) And he was gone.

-WILFRED WILSON GIBSON

a) Under the greenwood tree
a) Who loves to lie with me,
b) And turn his merry note
b) Unto the sweet bird's throat,
c) Come hither! Come hither! Come hither!
a) Here shall he see
a) No enemy
c) But winter and rough weather!

—*As You Like It,* WILLIAM SHAKESPEARE

The *nine-line stanza* has innumerable possibilities. The most noted form is that used first by Spenser. Its rhyme scheme is exacting: ababbcbcc; the form is written usually in pentameter lines. The last line of the stanza, called the Alexandrine, contains twelve syllables, and ends the stanza with a finish that is rich and distinctive. This Spenserian form has been used in many noted English poems.

Following are two examples, one famous and one infamous:

a) Not vainly did the early Persian make
b) His altar the high places, and the peak
a) Of earth-o'er gazing mountains, and thus take
b) A fit and unwalled temple, there to seek
b) The spirit in whose honour shrines are weak,
c) Upreared of human hands. Come and compare
b) Columns and idol-dwellings, Goth or Greek,
c) With nature's realms of worship, earth and air,
c) Nor fix on fond abodes to circumscribe thy prayer!

—*Childe Harold's Pilgrimage,* Lord Byron

a) Find first thy meter. If the task be hard
b) Consult thy Keats and Shelley—in them is
a) Some measure that will suit a busy bard,
b) ('Twas "Adonais" I used in writing this!).
b) Then, if thy rhymthic feeling run amiss,
c) Heed thou the ticking clock—it may transfer
b) Those beats from out its cranial abyss
c) All choked with wheels, to where thine own works whirr—
c) Then sit thee calmly down before thy typewritér.

Seek next thy subject. Let the matter be
Not as a stranger, but some old, old friend,
As "Death," "A Daisy," "Spring," or "Constancy."
Then for thy rhyming dictionary send,
For oft its echoing columns hap to lend
A few poetic thoughts to him who gleans.
And keep in mind until the very end—
That line is best if none know what it means.
Thus do the poets write their verse for magazines.

—Burges Johnson

Other forms of the nine-line stanza follow:

a) My heart aches and a drowsy numbness pains
b) My sense, as though of hemlock I had drunk,

a) Or emptied some dull opiate to the drains.
b) One minute passed, and Lethe-words had sunk:
c) 'Tis not through envy of thy happy lot,
d) But being too happy in thy happiness,—
e) That thou, light-wingèd Dryad of the trees,
c) In some melodious plot
d) Of beechen green, and shadows numberless,
e) Singest of summer in full-throated ease.

—*Ode to a Nightingale*, JOHN KEATS

a) Fair daffodils, we weep to see
b) You haste away so soon;
c) As yet the early rising sun
b) Has not attained his noon.
d) Stay, stay,
d) Until the hasting day
c) Has run
f) But to the even-song;
a) And, having prayed together, we
f) Will go with you along.

—*To Daffodils*, ROBERT HERRICK

a) My heart leaps up when I behold
b) A rainbow in the sky:
c) So was it when my life began;
c) So is it now I am a man;
a) So be it when I shall grow old
b) Or let me die!
c) The Child is father of the Man;
d) And I could wish my days to be
d) Bound each to each by natural piety.

—WILLIAM WORDSWORTH

Ballad.—The oldest lyric form in English had no rigidity of form, though dependent upon rhythm and rhyme to give it musical character; but both rhyme and rhythm often lacked disciplined regularity. Ballads were sung or chanted, and frequently had a chorus. They always told a story in which characters played a part and action reached a climax.

Kipling's *Barrack-room Ballads* and *Macaulay's Lays of Ancient Rome* furnish examples of the way in which the ballad has been adapted by modern English writers. A fragment of a typical fourteenth-century ballad follows.

CHEVY-CHACE

(Fourteenth Century)

God prosper long our noble king,
  Our lives and safeties all;
A woeful hunting once there did
  In Chevy-Chace befall.

To drive the deer with hound and horn,
  Earl Percy took his way;
The child may rue that is unborn,
  The hunting of that day.

The stout Earl of Northumberland
  A vow to God did make,
His pleasure in the Scottish woods
  Three summer days to take;

The chiefest harts in Chevy-Chace
  To kill and bear away.
These tidings to Earl Douglas came
  In Scotland where he lay:

Who sent Earl Percy present word,
  He would prevent his sport;
The English Earl, not fearing that,
  Did to the woods resort.

. . . .

And of the rest, of small account,
  Did many hundreds die.
Thus endeth the hunting of Chevy-Chace,
  Made by the Earl Percy.

God save the King and bless this land
  With plenty, joy, and peace;
And grant, henceforth, that foul debate
'Twixt noblemen may cease.

Fixed Lyric Forms of Verse

Poets throughout the ages have sung as their fancy pleased them, seeking patterns of rhythm and rhyme which suited their mood and seemed the most appropriate vehicle by which to convey the emotional experience they wished to record.

The Limerick.—Most of these fixed forms which English poets have adopted are native to France; a few came from Italy, and still fewer are English born. Undoubtedly England's oldest and commonest is the humble limerick, popularized by Edward Lear in his Nonsense Books, and called by him "nonsense rhymes,"—the name now generally given them in England. The same verse form, however, appears in ancient Latin, and later in ecclesiastical Latin, and there is at least one sacred hymn found in hymnals of today which follows the pattern exactly. The name "limerick," according to legend, grew out of a custom among Irish mercenaries who fought in all the armies of Europe in the fifteenth century. At parties between battles each would improvise a verse about one of his comrades. All would then join in a chorus: "When we get back to Limerick town 'twill be a glorious morning."

The Lear variety of rhyme usually concerns a person or place, and the rhyming word at the end of the first line is repeated in the last line (see Appendix, p. 457). Examples follow, the first of which is variously quoted. The form used here is certified by a member of the Beecher family.

The Reverend Henry Ward Beecher
Called a hen a most elegant creature.
  The hen, pleased with that,
  Laid an egg in his hat—
And thus did the hen reward Beecher!

—Oliver Wendell Holmes

There was an Old Man who said, "How
Shall I flee from this horrible Cow?
  I will sit on this stile
  And continue to smile
Which may soften the heart of that Cow."

—Edward Lear

W. S. Gilbert has contributed to the world its only limerick thus far in free verse:

There was an old man of St. Bees
Who was stung on the arm by a wasp.
  When asked, "Does it hurt?"
  He replied, "Not at all,
But I thought all the time 'twas a hornet."

There is nothing in afternoon tea
To appeal to a person like me.
  Polite conversation
  Evokes the elation
A cow might enjoy in a tree.

—Gelett Burgess

There was a young man in Schenectady
Who was hit by a brick in the neck today.
  They massaged his thorax
  With coal oil and borax
But now he talks quite disconnectady.

—Anon.

The Sonnet.—Of all the fixed forms, the sonnet properly should come first. It is a form that has been used by English poets of all types and temperaments and abilities since the sixteenth century, though originating in Italy as early as 1294.

That the sonnet must have fourteen lines is beyond dispute. As to other characteristics, there is ancient argument. The most exacting (if not necessarily the most exact) sonnet is that generally called the Petrarchan. Its rhyme scheme is abbaabba cdecde. In this form, which purists have insisted is the only true sonnet, the first eight lines present an argument, and the final six present a conclusion or reflection based upon the first. The only variation from this form of "true" sonnet permitted by its defenders is in the final sestet; cdcdcd, or cddccd, or any other arrangement of two or three rhyme sounds is allowable so long as the sonnet does not end with a couplet.

The fact that Shakespeare wrote a great number of fourteen-line poems which ignore several of these restraints, and called them sonnets, has encouraged many to refuse to accept the rigid Petrarchan definition. Charles Lamb referred to Shakespeare's sonnets as "fourteeners," refusing to grant them the name; but other great poets have used the irregular or Shakespearean pattern,—ababcdcdefefgg.

Between these two extremes of definition there are forms of the sonnet with a different arrangement of the octave—ababbaba—and a couplet at the end of the sestet. Examples of several forms follows:

The Petrarchan Sonnet (abbaabbacdecde):

I lift mine eyes, and all the windows blaze,
With forms of Saints, and holy men who died,
Here martyred and hereafter glorified;
And the great Rose upon its leaves displays
Christ's Triumph, and the angelic roundelays,
With splendor upon splendor multiplied;
And Beatrice again at Dante's side
No more rebukes, but smiles her words of praise.
And then the organ sounds, and unseen choirs
Sing the old Latin hymns of peace and love
And benedictions of the Holy Ghost;
And the melodious bells among the spires
O'er all the house-tops and through heaven above
Proclaim the elevation of the Host!

—*Divina Comedia, V,* H. W. Longfellow

What is a sonnet? 'Tis a pearly shell
That murmurs of the far-off murmuring sea;
A precious jewel carved most curiously;
It is a little picture painted well.

What is a sonnet? 'Tis the tear that fell
From a great poet's hidden ecstasy;
A two-edged sword, a star, a song—ah me!
Sometimes a heavy-tolling funeral bell.

This was the flame that shook with Dante's breath,
The solemn organ whereon Milton played.
And the clear glass where Shakespeare's
shadow falls:

A sea this is—beware who ventureth!
For like a fiord the narrow floor is laid
Deep as mid-ocean to sheer mountain walls.

—R. W. Gilder

Two variant forms (abbaabbacdcdcd and abbaaccadedeff):

Sonnets from the Portuguese
(No. XXII.)

When our two souls stand up erect and strong,
Face to face, silent, drawing nigh and nigher,
Until the lengthening wings break into fire
At either curved point,—what bitter wrong
Can the earth do to us, that we should not long
Be here contented? Think. In mounting higher,
The angels would press on us and aspire
To drop some golden orb of perfect song
Into our deep, dear silence. Let us stay
Rather on earth, Beloved,—where the unfit
Contrarious moods of men recoil away
And isolate pure spirits, and permit
A place to stand and love in for a day,
With darkness and the death-hour rounding it.

—Elizabeth Barrett Browning

Scorn not the Sonnet; Critic, you have frowned,
Mindless of its just honours; with this key
Shakespeare unlocked his heart; the melody
Of this small lute gave ease to Petrarch's wound;
A thousand times this pipe did Tasso sound;
With it Camoens soothed an exile's grief;
The Sonnet glittered a gay myrtle leaf
Amid the cypress with which Dante crowned
His visionary brow; a glow-worm lamp,
It cheered mild Spenser, called from Faery-land
To struggle through dark ways; and, when a damp
Fell round the path of Milton, in his hand
The Thing became a trumpet, whence he blew
Soul-animating strains—alas, too few!

—William Wordsworth

Shakespearean Sonnets:

BRIGHT STAR!

Bright Star! would I were steadfast as thou art—
Not in lone splendour hung aloft the night,
And watching, with eternal lids apart,

Like Nature's patient, sleepless Eremite,
The moving waters at their priest-like task
Of pure ablution round earth's human shores,
Or gazing on the new soft fallen mask
Of snow upon the mountains and the moors—

No—yet still steadfast, still unchangeable,
Pillowed upon my fair love's ripening breast
To feel for ever its soft fall and swell,
Awake for ever in a sweet unrest,
Still, still to hear her tender-taken breath,
Half-passionless, and so swoon on to death.

—John Keats

SONNET XVIII

Shall I compare thee to a summer's day?
Thou art more lovely and more temperate;
Rough winds do shake the darling buds of May,
And summer's lease hath all too short a date:
Sometime too hot the eye of heaven shines,
And often is his gold complexion dimm'd;
And every fair from fair sometime declines,
By chance or nature's changing course untrimm'd;
But thy eternal summer shall not fade,
Nor lose possession of that fair thou owest;
Nor shall Dcath brag thou wander'st in his shade,
When in eternal lines to time thou grow'st:
So long as men can breathe, or eyes can see,
So long lives this, and this gives life to thee.

—William Shakespeare

Fixed Forms from France

If this were a historical study of English verse it would be profitable to trace the development of the French forms in the land of their birth, and the dates and fashions of their English adoption. Such study is well worth while, and there are several books that make it easy and delightful. For the purposes of this handbook it is sufficient to give examples of ballade, rondeau, rondel, roundel, villanelle, triolet, sestina and pantoum in their most generally accepted English forms, and name a few less familiar types.

The ballade, as perhaps the earliest in origin, and the oldest by English adoption, comes first. Its similarity in name to the English ballad is no accident. Originally it too was intended to be sung. Its period of growth and change extended over four centuries, but only those forms are given here into which it finally crystallized. A noteworthy characteristic is the "envoy" addressed to some prince or power, patron or lady-love.

Ballade, type I, (ababbcbc, ababbcbc, ababbcbc, bcbc).—Three stanzas of eight lines each, and an envoy of four lines. There are only three rhyme-sounds in all. The final line of the first stanza is repeated at the end of the three following stanzas:

A BALLAD TO QUEEN ELIZABETH

of the Spanish Armada

King Philip had vaunted his claims;
  He had sworn for a year he would sack us;
With an army of heathenish names
  He was coming to fagot and stack us;
  Like the thieves of the sea he would track us,
And shatter our ships on the main;
  But we had bold Neptune to back us,—
And where are the galleons[1] of Spain?

His carackes were christened of dames
  To the kirtles whereof he would tack us;
With his saints and his gilded stern-frames,
  He had thought like an egg-shell to crack us;
  Now Howard may get to his Flaccus,
And Drake to his Devon again,
  And Hawkins bowl rubbers to Bacchus,—
For where are the galleons of Spain?

Let his Majesty hang to St. James
  The axe that he whetted to hack us;
He must play at some lustier games
  Or at sea he can hope to out-thwack us;
  To his mines of Peru he would pack us
To tug at his bullet and chain;
  Alas! that his Greatness should lack us!—
But where are the galleons of Spain?

[1] Pronounced *galyons*.

ENVOY

Gloriana!—the don may attack us
Whenever his stomach be fain;
He must reach us before he can rack us, . . .
And where are the galleons of Spain?

—Austin Dobson

BALLADE OF THE LITTLE THINGS THAT COUNT

The furrow's long behind my plow—
My field is strewn with stones of care,
And trouble gathers thick enow
As years add silver to my hair.
Could I an easier path prepare
For baby feet that start to mount?—
Save them a bit of wear and tear,—
And show the little things that count?

I see a tiny maiden bow
O'er slate and pencil, in her chair:
A little pucker on her brow,
A little tousle in her hair.
And one wee tear has fallen where
The crooked figures grin and flount;
My heart goes reaching to her there—
I love the little things that count!

Arithmetic is such a slough—
A pilgrim's swamp of dull despair,
But Discipline will not allow
My hand to point a thoro'fare.
Harsh figures face us everywhere,
O'erwhelming in their vast amount;
Must she so soon their burden bear?—
I love the little things that count!

Stern Teacher, must she ever fare
Alone to Learning's chilly fount?
There is so much I long to share—
I *love* the Little Things That Count!

—Burges Johnson

Ballade, type II, (ababbccdcd, ababbccdcd, ababbccdcd, ccdcd).—Three stanzas of ten lines each, and an envoy of five lines. There are four rhyme-sounds, and a refrain-line appears at the end of each stanza:

VILLON QUITS FRANCE

"*Demain tous nous mourrons; c'est juste notre affaire.*"
—*Theodore Passerat*

We hang tomorrow then? That doom is fit
For most of us, I think. Yet, harkee, friend,
I have a ballad here which I have writ
Of us and our high ending. Pray you, send
The scrawl to Cayeux, bidding him commend
Francois to grace. Old Colin loves me well,
For no good reason, save it so befell
We two were young together . . . when I am hung,
Colin will weep—and then will laugh, and tell
How many pranks we played when we were young.

Dear lads of yesterday! . . . We had no wit
To live always so we might not offend,
Yet—how we laughed! I marvel now at it,
Because that merry company will spend
No more mad nights together. Some are penned
In abbeys, some in dungeons, others fell
In battle . . . Time assesses Death's *gabelle,*—
Salt must be taxed, eh?—well, we ranked among
The salt of earth, once, who are old and tell
How many pranks we played when we were young.

Afraid to die, you ask?—Why, not a whit.
Ah, no! whole-heartedly I mean to wend
Out of a world I have found exquisite
By every testing. For I apprehend
Life was not made all lovely to the end
That life ensnare us, nor the miracle
Of youth devised but as a trap to swell
Old Legion's legions; and must give full tongue
To praise no less than prayer, when bidden tell
How many pranks we played when we were young.

Nay, cheerily, we of the Cockle-shell,
And all whose youth was nor to stay nor quell,
Will dare foregather when earth's knell is rung,
And Calvary's young conqueror bids us tell
How many pranks we played when we were young.

—James Branch Cabell

The Double Ballade [ababbcbc, ababbcbc, ababbcbc, ababbcbc, ababbcbc, ababbcbc (bcbc); or ababbccdcd, ababbccdcd, ababbccdcd, ababbccdcd, ababbccdcd, ababbccdcd (ccdcd)].—Six stanzas of either eight or ten lines each, similar in rhyme-scheme to the ballade, but with or without an envoy:

DOUBLE BALLAD

Of the Singers of the Time

I

Why are our songs like the moan of the main,
  When the wild winds buffet it to and fro,
(Our brothers ask us again and again)
  A weary burden of hopes laid low?
  Have birds ceased singing or flowers to blow?
Is Life cast down from its fair estate?
  This I answer them—nothing mo'—
Songs and singers are out of date.

II

What shall we sing of? Our hearts are fain,
  Our bosoms burn with a sterile glow.
Shall we sing of the sordid strife for gain,
  For shameful honour, for wealth and woe,
  Hunger and luxury,—weeds that throw
Up from one seeding their flowers of hate?
  Can we tune our lutes to these themes? Ah no!
Songs and singers are out of date.

III

Our songs should be of Faith without stain,
  Of haughty honour and deaths that sow
The seeds of life on the battle-plain,
  Of loves unsullied and eyes that show
  The fair white soul in the deeps below.
Where are they, these that our songs await
  To wake to joyance? Doth any know?
Songs and singers are out of date.

IV

What have we done with meadow and lane?
  Where are the flowers and the hawthorn-snow?
Acres of brick in the pitiless rain,—
  These are our gardens for thorpe and stow!
  Summer has left us long ago,
Gone to the lands where the turtles mate
  And the crickets chirp in the wild-rose row.
Songs and singers are out of date.

V

We sit and sing in a world in pain;
  Our heartstrings quiver sadly and slow:
But, aye and anon, the murmurous strain
  Swells up to a clangour of strife and throw,
  And the folk that hearken, or friend or foe,
Are ware that the stress of the time is great
  And say to themselves, as they come and go,
Songs and singers are out of date.

VI

Winter holds us, body and grain:
  Ice is over our being's flow;
Song is a flower that will droop and wane,
  If it have no heaven towards which to grow.
  Faith and beauty are dead, I trow
Nothing is left but fear and fate:
  Men are weary of hope; and so
Songs and singers are out of date.

—John Payne

Ballade with a double refrain (ababbcbc, ababbcbc, ababbcbc, bbcc).—Three stanzas of eight lines each, with an envoy of 4 lines; the lines 4, 12, 20 and 26 are alike; and 8, 16, 24 and 28:

THE BALLADE OF PROSE AND RHYME
(Ballade a double refrain)

When the roads are heavy with mire and rut,
  In November fogs, in December snows,
When the North Wind howls, and the doors are shut,
  There is place and enough for the pains of prose;—
  But whenever a scent from the whitethorn blows,
And the jasmine-stars to the casement climb,
  And a Rosalind-face at the lattice shows,
Then hey!—for the ripple of laughing rhyme!

When the brain gets dry as an empty nut,
  When the reason stands on its squarest toes,
When the mind (like a beard) has a "formal cut,"
  There is place and enough for the pains of prose;—
  But whenever the May-blood stirs and glows,
And the young year draws to the "golden prime,"—
  And Sir Romeo sticks in his ear a rose,
Then hey!—for the ripple of laughing rhyme!

In a theme where the thoughts have a pedant-strut
  In a changing quarrel of "Ayes" and "Noes,"
In a starched procession of "If" and "But,"
  There is place and enough for the pains of prose;—
  But whenever a soft glance softer grows,
And the light hours dance to the trysting-time,
  And the secret is told "that no one knows,"
Then hey!—for the ripple of laughing rhyme!

ENVOY

In the work-a-day world,—for its needs and woes,
There is place and enough for the pains of prose;
But whenever the May-bells clash and chime,
Then hey!—for the ripple of laughing rhyme!

—Austin Dobson

Chant royal (ababccddede, ababccddede, ababccddede, ababccddede, ababccddede, ddede).—Five stanzas of eleven lines each, with an envoy of five lines. Only five rhyme-sounds are permitted. The final line of the first stanza is repeated as a refrain at the end of each following stanza and envoy:

CHANT-ROYAL OF THE TRUE ROMANCE

Romance is dead, say some, and so, to-day,
  Honour and Chivalry are faint and cold;
And now, Adventure has no modern way
  To stir the blood, as in the days of old.
They mourn the times of Gallantry as done,
Knighthood has seen the setting of its sun,
And fairy, nymph and genie, grown too shy,
No more, in these new lands, hold revel high;
  There lives no mystery, now, and they cry woe
To this old world, so twisted and awry!
  Romance is dead, say some; but I say No!

Haroun-al-Raschid, so the sceptics say,
  Would seek in vain for sights his book has told—
Crusoe could find no island far away
  Enough, his life with glamour to enfold—
Ulysses now might rove, nor fear to run
The risks of perils Homer's fable spun—
And Hiawatha's white canoe would try
In vain to find some beach, whence to descry
  The hunting-grounds where once he bent his bow.
Gone are the Halcyon Days, they sadly sigh;
  Romance is dead, say some; but I say No!

Not while the ancient sea casts up its spray
  Upon the laughing beach, and I behold
The myriad dancing ripples of the bay
  Speed out to meet the sunset's robe of gold;
Not till the last ship's voyage has begun;
Not till the storm god's lightnings cease to stun!
Not till the mountains lift no more to sky
Their secret fastnesses, and forests vie
  No more with winds and mists, with sun and snow,
And rustling fields no more to streams reply!
  Romance is dead, say some; but I say No!

Not while the Night maintains her mystic sway,
  And conjures, in the haunted wood and wold,
Her eerie shadows, fanciful and fey,
  With priests of Darkness, pale and sombre-stoled;
Not while upon the Sea of Dreams are won
Strange ventures, escapades, and frolic fun;
Where tricksy phantoms, whimsically sly,
Order your deeds, you know not how nor why;
  Where Reason, Wit, and Conscience drunken go.
Have you e'er dreamed, and still can question? Fie!
  Romance is dead, say some; but I say No!

Not while Youth lives and Springtime bids be gay!
  Not while love blooms, and lovers dare be bold!
Not while a poet sings his roundelay,
  Or men by maiden's kisses are cajoled!
You have not seen her, or you, too, would shun
The thought that in this world Romance there's none;
For oh, my Love has power to beautify

My whole life long, and all its charm supply;
  My bliss, my youth, my dreams, to her I owe!
And so, ye scornful cynics, I deny;
  Romance is dead, say some; but I say No!

ENVOY

God, keep my youth and love alive, that I
May wonder at this world until I die!
  Let sea and mountain speak to me, that so,
Waking or sleeping, I may fight the lie;
  Romance is dead, say some; but I say No!

—Gelett Burgess

Villanelle (aba, aba, aba, aba, aba, abaa).—Five stanzas of three lines each, and a final stanza of 4 lines. Only two rhyme-sounds are permitted throughout. The first and third lines in the first stanza are refrain lines. Line 1 reappears at the end of the second and fourth stanzas and as the third line in the sixth stanza; line 3 reappears at the end of the 3rd, 5th and 6th stanzas.

Ingenious and musical, this form has been a vehicle throughout four centuries for light and dainty fancies, with a few notable examples of verses with a serious, mystical or religious purport:

ON A NANKIN PLATE

"Ah me, but it might have been!
Was there ever so dismal a fate?"—
Quoth the little blue mandarin.

"Such a maid as was never seen!
She passed, tho' I cried to her, 'Wait,'—
Ah me, but it might have been!

"I cried, 'O my Flower, my Queen,
Be mine!' 'Twas precipitate,"—
Quoth the little blue mandarin,—

"But then . . . she was just sixteen,—
Long-eyed,—as a lily straight,—
Ah me, but it might have been!

"As it was, from her palankeen,
She laughed—'You're a week too late!'"
(Quoth the little blue mandarin.)

"That is why, in a mist of spleen,
I mourn on this Nankin Plate.
Ah me, but it might have been!"—
Quoth the little blue mandarin.

—Austin Dobson

FOR A COPY OF THEOCRITUS

O singer of the field and fold,
Theocritus! Pan's pipe was thine,—
Thine was the happier Age of Gold.

For thee the scent of new-turned mould,
The bee-hives, and the murmuring pine,
O Singer of the field and fold!

Thou sang'st the simple feasts of old,—
The beechen bowl made glad with wine . . .
Thine was the happier Age of Gold.

Thou bad'st the rustic loves be told,—
Thou bad'st the tuneful reeds combine,
O Singer of the field and fold!

And round thee, ever-laughing, rolled
The blithe and blue Sicilian brine . . .
Thine was the happier Age of Gold.

Alas for us! Our songs are cold;
Our Northern suns too sadly shine:—
O Singer of the field and fold,
Thine was the happier Age of Gold!

—Austin Dobson

Rondel, type I, [ABab; baAB; ababAB (the capitals indicate identical lines)]. A poem of fourteen lines in which a two-line refrain appears three times. Various rhyme orders may be followed so long as only two rhyme-sounds are used, and the two refrain-lines.

"Rondel" is an earlier form of the word rondeau, just as the final crystallized forms of these two French lyrics are closely allied. Originally the rondel was a song for a round dance, and it is as ancient as the ballade. Both the rondel and the rondeau have undergone many changes, and only the final forms are illustrated here. In 1597 the rondeau was actually banished from French literature by a papal bull, in favor of the sonnet. But it returned to become a vehicle of the graceful fancies of some of the greatest French and English poets:

READY FOR THE RIDE—1795

Through the fresh fairness of the Spring to ride,
As in the old days when he rode with her,
With joy of Love that has fond Hope to bride,
One year ago had made her pulses stir.
Now shall no wish with any day recur
(For Love and Death part year and year full wide),
Through the fresh fairness of the Spring to ride,
As in the old days when he rode with her.

No ghost there lingers of the smile that died
On the sweet pale lip where his kisses were—
Yet still she turns her delicate head aside,
If she may hear him come, with jingling spur—
Through the fresh fairness of the Spring to ride,
As in the old days when he rode with her.

—H. C. Bunner

Rondel, type II, [ABba, abAB, abbaA (the capitals indicate identical lines)].—Thirteen lines in which a two-line refrain appears twice in the first eight lines; and the first line reappears, generally with new meaning, as a final line. Only two rhyme-sounds may be used.

RONDEL OF PERFECT FRIENDSHIP

Friend of my soul, forever true,
What do we care for flying years,
Unburdened all by doubts or fears,
Trusting what naught can e'er subdue?

Fate leads! Her path is out of view;
Nor time nor distance interferes!
Friend of my soul, forever true,
What do we care for flying years?

For, planted when the world was new,
In other lives, in other spheres,
Our love today a bud appears—
Not yet the blossom's perfect hue,
Friend of my soul, forever true!

—Gelett Burgess

THE WANDERER

Love comes back to his vacant dwelling,—
The old, old Love that we knew of yoreel!
We see him stand by the open door,
With his great eyes sad, and his bosom swling.

He makes as though in our arms repelling,
He fain would lie as he lay before;—
Love comes back to his vacant dwelling,—
The old, old Love that we knew of yore!

Ah, who shall help us from over-spelling
That sweet, forgotten, forbidden lore!
E'en as we doubt in our heart once more,
With a rush of tears to our eyelids welling,
Love comes back to his vacant dwelling.

—Austin Dobson

Rondeau, type I, aabba, aabC, aabbaC (C indicates a repeated unrhymed refrain)]. Fifteen lines in which the first part of the first line serves as an unrhymed refrain, lines 9 and 15. Only two rhyme-sounds and refrain, which generally contains a play on meaning:

LES MORTS VONT VITE

Les morts vont vite: The dead go fast!
So runs the motto France has cast.
To nature man must pay his debt;
Despite all struggle, despite all fret,
He journeys swift to the future vast.

It needs no ghost from out the past,
To make mere mortals stand aghast,—
To make them dream of death—and yet
Les morts vont vite.

Although the sails (bellowed by blast)
Of Charon's bark may strain the mast—
The dead are not dead while we regret;
The dead are not dead till we forget;
But true the motto, or first or last:
Les morts vont vite.

—Brander Matthews

RONDEAU

Thou fool! if madness be so rife,
That, spite of wit, thou'lt have a wife,
I'll tell thee what thou must expect—
After the honeymoon neglect,
All the sad days of thy whole life;

To that a world of woe and strife,
Which is of marriage the effect—
And thou thy woe's own architect,
Thou fool!

Thou'lt nothing find but disrespect,
Ill words i' th' scolding dialect,
For she'll all tabor be, or fife;
Then prythee go and whet thy knife,
And from this fate thyself protect,
Thou fool!

—Cotton (17th Cent.)

Rondeau, type II, [abbaabC; abbaC (C indicates a one-word refrain, which also appears as the first word in the first line)]. Twelve lines, but the 7th and 12th lines are but a single word, which was the first word in the poem. Here also a play on meanings is desired:

A RONDEL OF MYSTERY

Blood on the moon, and the breakers roar—
And a villa near where a ship was wrecked—
And a diagram by its architect—
And sets of footprints along the shore.
An old man guarding his golden store—
And eager readers who all expect
Blood.

A stain—a grain of sand on the floor—
A hearth with curious ashes flecked;
Clues that only His eyes detect.
WHAT'S THAT CREEPING BENEATH THE DOOR?
BLOOD!

—B. J.

Rondeau Redoublé [abab baba abab baba abab baba c (c indicates the first phrase of the first line)].—Six stanzas of four lines each, with a reappearance, as a refrain, at the end of the poem, of the first words of the opening line. Only two rhyme-sounds may be used:

A DAUGHTER OF THE NORTH

Who wins my hand must do these three things well:
Skate fast as winter wind across the glare;
Swim through the fiord, past breaker, rip and swell;
Ride like the Storm Fiend on my snow-white mare!

Shall a maid do what Viking may not dare?
I wed no lover I can aught excel—
Skate, swim and ride with me, and I declare,
Who wins my hand must do these three things well!

Bind on your skates, and after me pell-mell;
Follow me, Carles, and catch my streaming hair!
(Keep the black ice—O Bolstrom, if you fell!)
Skate fast as winter wind across the glare!

Thrice have I swum from this grey cliff to where
On the far side, the angry surges yell;
(Into the surf! O Bolstrom, have a care!)
Swim through the fiord, past breaker, rip and swell!

Bring out my Frieda, none but I can quell;
(Watch her eye, Bolstrom, when you mount—beware!)
Ride bareback now and find the master-spell;
Ride like the Storm Fiend on my snow-white mare!

Skohl! Vikings, Skohl! Am I not bold and fair?
Who would not barter Heaven, and venture Hell,
Striving the flower of my love to wear?
(Mind my words, Bolstrom, hark to what I tell!)
Who wins my hand?

—Gelett Burgess

Roundel [abaB; bab; abaB (capital letter indicates repeated line)].—The *roundel*, as distinct from *rondel*, uses as a refrain the first part of the first line, but it must have the rhyme-sound of b. Swinburne favored a line of six feet with frequent anapaests:

NORTH-EASTER

The north wind blows; the air is filled with spray,
The light within the beacon ebbs and glows,
A sailor's wife stops from her work to pray;
The north wind blows.

The night is bitter cold, and no one knows
What happenings will come when winters flay
The windward coast. Hark! how the tempest throws
The waves against the shore in cruel play;
Waves mountain high in endless, foamy rows.
Invader, screaming in his lust to slay,
The north wind blows.

—C. J.

A ROUNDEL

I love to write these little Gallic things;
They do not call for matter erudite,
And though the words be crude, the meter sings
I love to write.
But when some pleasing fancy *does* alight
Upon my pen, what happiness it brings!
Swift thoughts rush out to meet it, phrased aright;
Each after each in rhythmic order swings.
Until my form's complete,—all poised for flight,
Then all my words are lifted up on wings.
I love to write!

—Burges Johnson

HATE

Hate is a cruel thing,
Cometh it soon or late,
Nought of joy doth it bring,
Hate.

Dark as the Nordic Fate,
Black as the raven's wing,
Hidden it lies in wait;

Only death can it bring
To the heart insensate
Sinfully sheltering
Hate!

—C. J.

Triolet [ABaAabAB (capital letters indicate the "refrain" or duplicated lines)].—One stanza of eight lines, in which lines 1 and 2 are repeated in 7 and 8. Line 1 also is repeated as line 4:

ROSE-LEAVES

"Sans peser.—Sans rester."

A KISS

Rose kissed me to-day.
Will she kiss me to-morow?
Let it be as it may,
Rose kissed me to-day.
But the pleasure gives way
To a savour of sorrow;—
Rose kissed me to-day,—
Will she kiss me to-morrow?

CIRCE

In the School of Coquettes
Madam Rose is a scholar:—
O, they fish with all nets
In the School of Coquettes!
When her brooch she forgets
'Tis to show her new collar;
In the School of Coquettes
Madam Rose is a scholar!

A TEAR

There's a tear in her eye,—
Such a clear little jewel!
What *can* make her cry?
There's a tear in her eye.
"Puck has killed a big fly,—
And it's *horribly* cruel";

There's a tear in her eye,—
  Such a clear little jewel!

A GREEK GIFT

Here's a present for Rose,
  How pleased she is looking!
Is it verse?—is it prose?
Here's a present for Rose!
"*Plats*," *Entrées*," and "*Rots*,"—
  Why, it's "Gouffe on Cooking"!
Here's a present for Rose,
  How pleased she is looking!

"URCEUS EXIT"

I intended an Ode,
  And it turned to a Sonnet.
It began *à la mode*,
I intended an Ode;
But Rose crossed the road
  In her latest new bonnet;
I intended an Ode;
  And it turned to a Sonnet.

—Austin Dobson

UNDER THE ROSE

HE (*aside*)

If I should steal a little kiss,
  Oh, would she weep, I wonder?
I tremble at the thought of bliss,—
If I should steal a little kiss!
Such pouting lips would never miss
  The dainty bit of plunder;
If I should steal a little kiss,
  Oh, would she weep, I wonder?

SHE (*aside*)

He longs to steal a kiss of mine—
  He may, if he'll return it:
If I can read the tender sign,
He longs to steal a kiss of mine;

"In love and war"—you know the line
Why cannot he discern it?
He longs to steal a kiss of mine—
He may if he'll return it.

BOTH (*five minutes later*)
A little kiss when no one sees,
Where is the impropriety?
How sweet amid the birds and bees
A little kiss when no one sees!
Nor is it wrong, the world agrees,
If taken with sobriety.
A little kiss when no one sees,
Where is the impropriety?

—SAMUEL MINTURN PECK

Oh, that men would praise the Lord
For his goodness unto men!
Forth he sends his saving word,
—Oh, that men would praise the Lord!—
And from shades of death abhorred
Lift them up to life again;
Oh, that men would praise the Lord
For his goodness unto men.

—GEORGE MACDONALD

THE TRIOLET

Your triolet should glimmer
Like a butterfly;
In golden light, or dimmer,
Your triolet should glimmer,
Tremble, turn, and shimmer,
Flash, and flutter by;
Your triolet should glimmer
Like a butterfly.

—DON MARQUIS

Sestina (ababab, bababa, ababab, bababa, ababab, bababa, bab).—This ingenious form was first "invented" in the twelfth century. Its distinguishing characteristic is a rearrangement of the final words of the six lines of the first stanza as the final words in succeeding stanzas, but no two arrangements are alike. Numbering the final words of the first stanza 1 to 6, the final word schemes of each of the six stanzas must be as follows:

1–2–3–4–5–6
6–1–5–2–4–3
3–6–4–1–2–5
5–3–2–6–1–4
4–5–1–3–6–2
2–4–6–5–3–1

The envoi (or tornada) contains all of these ending-words, arranged as follows: 2 in middle of first line; 5 at end of first line; 4 in middle of second line, and 3 at end; 6 in middle of third line and 1 at end. The sestina is frequently unrhymed, though with perfect rhythm:

SESTINA OF YOUTH AND AGE

My father died when I was all too young,
And he too old, too crowded with his care,
For me to know he knew my hot fierce hopes;
Youth sees wide chasms between itself and Age—
How could I think he, too, had lived my life?
My dreams were all of war, and his of rest.

And so he sleeps (please God), at last at rest,
And, it may be, with soul refreshed, more young
Than when he left me, for that other life—
Free, for a while, at least, from that old Care,
The hard, relentless torturer of his age,
That cooled his youth, and bridled all his hopes.

For now I know he had the longing hopes,
The wild desires of youth, and all the rest
Of my ambitions ere he came to age;
He, too, was bold, when he was free and young—
Had I but known that he could feel, and care!
How could I know the secret of his life?

In my own youth I see his early life
So reckless, and so full of flaming hopes—
I see him jubilant, without a care,
The days too short, and grudging time for rest;
He knew the wild delight of being young—
Shall I, too, know the calmer joys of age?

His words come back, to mind me of that age
When, livingly, he watched my broadening life—
And, dreaming of the days when he was young,
Smiled at my joys, and shared my fears and hopes.
His words still live, for in my heart they rest,
Too few not to be kept with jealous care!

Ah, little did I know how he could care!
That, in my youth, lay joys to comfort age!
Not in this world, for him, was granted rest,
But as he lived, in me, a happier life,
He prayed more earnestly to win my hopes
Than ever for his own, when he was young!

ENVOI

He once was young; I too must fight with Care;
He knew my hopes, and I must share his age;
God grant my life be worthy, too, of rest!

—Gelett Burgess

THE CONQUEROR PASSES

"Non dormatz plus! les messatges de douz pascor"

—Raimbaut de Vaqueiras

Awaken! for the servitors of Spring
Proclaim his triumph! oh, make haste to see
With what tempestuous pageantry they bring
The victor homeward! haste, for this is he
That cast out Winter, and all woes that cling
To Winter's garments, and bade April be!

And now that Spring is master, let us be
Content, and laugh as anciently in spring
The battle-wearied Tristan laughed, when he
Was come again Tintagel-ward, to bring
Glad news of Arthur's victory—and see
Ysoude, with parted lips that waver and cling.

Not yet in Brittany must Tristan cling
To this or that sad memory, and be
Alone, as she in Cornwall; for in spring
Love sows against far harvestings,—and he
Is blind, and scatters baleful seed that bring
Such fruitage as blind Love lacks eyes to see.

Love sows, but lovers reap; and ye will see
The loved eyes lighten, feel the loved lips cling,
Never again when in the grave ye be
Incurious of your happiness in spring,
And get no grace of Love there, whither he
That bartered life for love no love may bring.

No braggart Heracles avails to bring
Alcestis hence; nor here may Roland see
The eyes of Aude; nor here the wakening spring
Vex any man with memories; for there be
No memories that cling as cerements cling,
No force that baffles Death, more strong than he.

Us hath he noted, and for us hath he
An hour appointed; and that hour will bring
Oblivion,—Then laugh! Laugh, dear, and see
The tyrant mocked, while yet our bosoms cling,
While yet our lips obey us, and we be
Untrammeled in our little hour of spring!

Thus in the spring we jeer at Death, though he
Will see our children perish, and will bring
Asunder all that cling while love may be.

—James Branch Cabell

Double Sestina: twelve stanzas of twelve lines each, with a six-line envoy. This is a *tour de force* so elaborate and difficult that few poets other than Swinburne have attempted it. Obviously, twelve final words rather than six are required, and are found in twelve different arrangements in the successive stanzas. Swinburne, in "The Complaint of Lisa," not only accomplishes this, but does it with the added complication of rhyme. Because of its length, the example will not be reprinted here.

The *pantoum* (also *pantun*) is a fixed verse form originating in the Malay Peninsula as a song or chanty, and coming to England by way of France, where Victor Hugo gave it dignity in his *Orientales.*

The pantoum has an indefinite number of stanzas. Its rigidity lies in the fact that the final line of the poem is identical with the opening line. Stanzas are of four lines each, and the second and fourth line of each stanza become the first and third of the next. In the final stanza the fourth line is identical with the first line of the first stanza. "In Town" by Austin Dobson is a sufficient illustration. Other worthwhile examples are equally long.

Toiling in Town is "horrid,"
  (There is that woman again!)
June in the zenith is torrid,
  Thought gets dry in the brain.

There is that woman again:
  "Strawberries! fourpence a pottle!"
Thought gets dry in the brain;
  Ink gets dry in the bottle.

"Strawberries! fourpence a pottle!"
  Oh for the green of a lane!—
Ink gets dry in the bottle;
  "Buzz" goes a fly in the pane!

Oh, for the green of a lane,
  Where one might lie and be lazy!
"Buzz" goes a fly in the pane;
  Bluebottles drive me crazy!

Where one might lie and be lazy,
  Careless of Town and all in it!—
Bluebottles drive me crazy:
  I shall go mad in a minute!

Careless of Town and all in it,
  With some one to soothe and to still you;—
I shall go mad in a minute;
  Bluebottle, then I shall kill you!

With some one to soothe and to still you,
  As only one's feminine kin do,—
Bluebottle, then I shall kill you:
  There now! I've broken the window!

As only one's feminine kin do,—
  Some muslin-clad Mabel or May!—
There now! I've broken the window!
  Bluebottle's off and away!

Some muslin-clad Mabel or May,
  To dash one with eau de Cologne;—
Bluebottle's off and away!
  And why should I stay here alone!

To dash one with eau de Cologne,
  All over one's eminent forehead;—
And why should I stay here alone!
  Toiling in Town now is "horrid."

—Austin Dobson

Other Fixed Forms

The various fixed lyric forms illustrated on preceding pages, though originating in France and Italy, have become naturalized. They are English forms. Interest in them has waxed and waned throughout the centuries and one may safely assert that it will continue to do so. Each one provides a certain "melody" which may add to the beauty or charm of the poetic thoughts which the poet has fitted into it.

On the other hand it is possible for the poet to choose a form or a rhythm which does not harmonize with his poetic mood. Some meters dance in jig time and do not harmonize with solemn thoughts. Dactylic lines are too rollicking for dirges, as one must realize when reading Hood's

"Take her up tenderly, lift her with care,
Fashioned so slenderly, young and so fair."

Or O. W. Holmes's

Slowly the mist o'er the meadow was creeping,
  Bright on the dewy buds glistened the sun,
When from his couch, while his children were sleeping,
  Rose the bold rebel and shouldered his gun.

The fact that although many of these forms are centuries old, our children are still reciting poems set to their measure, and poets are still making good use of them, gives assurance that they will not die. Other forms from the literature of Spain and Portugal have now and then been put to English use, and enthusiastic versifiers may yet popularize them in English; a few less common forms from the French also deserve place here.

The *rondelet* has been used by many poets, but the form is so obviously a simplification of the rondel and the rondeau that it lacks their distinction.

RONDELET

I wish I knew
  Which dress I want to wear tonight!
I wish I knew
Whether to wear the pink or blue.
  Does pink look well by evening light?
  He said he liked me best in white.
I wish I knew!

CONSTANCE JOHNSON

Another form, even more simple, is the *lai.* This is a series of three-line stanzas, as many as desired, but in the entire poem there are but two rhyme-sounds. Each stanza is composed of a couplet and a short line two syllables in length.

LE LAI

La grandeur humaine
Est une ombre vaine
  Qui fuit;
Une ame mondaine,
A perte d'haleine
  La suit.

LAI

Success is a folly,—
Come, let us be jolly,
  Content!
Go hence, Melancholy,
Though we haven't, by golly,
  A cent!

The *virelai* is more elaborate, yet it is so natural a form that it has often appeared without the author's consciousness that he was following a classic model.

A VIRELAY

  Thou cruel fair, I go
To seek out any fate but thee,
Since there is none can wound me so,
Nor that has half thy cruelty;
  Thou cruel fair, I go.

  Forever, then, farewell,
'Tis a long leave I take, but oh!
To tarry with thee here is hell,
And twenty thousand hells to go;
  For ever, then, farewell.

CHARLES COTTON (17th Cent.)

All of the lyric forms thus far illustrated have a certain perfection and dignity due to their ancient tradition. But there is nothing to prevent our modern poets from arranging new forms to suit a mood, and many have done so.

It is evident, for instance, that the possible varieties of the sextet are many, and of the septet and octet, and the possible varieties of the nine-line stanza seem numberless. Any verse writer who wishes to combine a sextet and an octet so as to make a unified whole with a limited number of rhyme sounds is not prevented from doing so merely because the sonnet has given the dignity of tradition to one and another combination of that sort.

Gelett Burgess had especial praise for one twelve-line form which he chose to call the *douzet.* Here is an approved example contributed to Franklin P. Adams's column. The rhyme scheme is abba cddc abdc.

A STANZA

Into Chapala, when, with banners streaming,
  Day's leader stood triumphant on the hills,
Duquesne rode laughing. When the valley fills
These dawns of March with slow white fountains steaming
Out of the yellow lake, could I forget
  How he rode down between the gloomy boulders
  Where crookedly the quartz vein gleams and smoulders
Like topaz? Dancing rawhides twinkle wet—
Star grass has caught his stirrup—lather creaming
  Over the girths—a West of daffodils,
    And dazzling as the heron's crystal shoulders
    The teeth that hold a fainting cigarette.

—Marian Storm

Inner Rhymes

Future poetasters may find names for some of those forms which depend for their novelty and individuality upon inner rhymes. Thomas Hood offered proof of his skill as a rhymester in this field when he wrote "A Nocturnal Sketch," quoted here in part:

Even is come; and from the dark Park, hark,
The signal of the setting sun—one gun!

. . . .

Now thieves do enter for your cash, smash, crash,
Past drowsy Charley in a deep sleep, creep,
But frightened by Policeman B 3, flee,
And while they're going, whisper low, "No go!"

Rhyme and rhythm are musical devices of equal value to the poet or rhymester who wishes his words to sing. But it seems to be a fact that our present-day verse writers have applied their ingenuity even more to rhyme than to inventing new patterns of rhythm. Inner rhymes, rhymes suddenly injected as pleasant surprises, skillfully manufactured rhymes where any rhyme at all seems impossible—these are characteristic of the light verse of today.

Ogden Nash, for instance, substitutes enormity for conformity and wins the allegiance of lovers of nonsense. As, for instance, the following:

"TOMORROW, PARTLY CLOUDY"[1]
(incomplete)

Rainy vacations
Try people's patience.
To expect rain in the autumn
Experience has tautumn,
And rain in the spring and winter
Makes no stories for the printer,
But rain on summer colonies
Breeds misdemeanors and felonies.
Summer cottages are meant just to sleep in,
Not to huddle all day in a heap in,
And whether at sea level or in higher places
There are not enough fireplaces,
And the bookcase stares at you starkly
And seems to be full of nothing but Volume II
of the life of Rutherford B. Hayes, and The
Rosary, by Florence M. Barclay . . .

On the other hand, Vachel Lindsay, a few years earlier, has a debauch of pure rhythm in his *Congo and Other Poems*. Both ignore the stanza.

Fat black bucks in a wine-barrel room,
Barrel-house kings with feet unstable,
Sagged and reeled and pounded on the table,
Pounded on the table,
Beat an empty barrel with the handle of a broom,
Hard as they were able,
Boom, boom, BOOM,
With a silk umbrella and the handle of a broom,
Boomlay, boomlay, boomlay, BOOM.

[1] Copyright 1942 by Ogden Nash.

NEW RHYMING DICTIONARY

Part I	One-syllable rhymes
Part II	Two-syllable rhymes
Part III	Three-syllable rhymes
Appendix	Suggestions for amusing exercises in verse writing.

Editor's Note: This dictionary is complete insofar as a sincere effort has been made to include all common rhyme-sounds, and to suggest technical vocabularies as well as words in common use. But the compiler well knows that no such collection could include all possible rhymes. For new words are added to our language from day to day in unknown numbers. They come in through the front door from other languages and from the laboratories of science and from factories where new foods and garments and gadgets are created and from the Patent Office; and also through the back door as one slang term after another becomes socially acceptable. There is no authoritative list of the new words added to our language in the past quarter century.

Nor is this dictionary a final authority as to true and false rhymes, since usage alone is the final authority, and pronunciation rather than spelling is the deciding factor as to rhyme. Where English and American usages differ, the American has been followed or else both are indicated. Where a rhyme is included which is not a legitimate dictionary word, but might be useful in any informal verse, it has been enclosed within quotation marks.

A few "manufactured" rhymes have been included by way of suggestion. By this term is meant the building of a rhyme such as "fail her" to rhyme with "sailor." Such rhymes are numberless and are found oftenest in humorous verse, such as the writings of W. S. Gilbert and Lewis Carroll and the *Ingoldsby Legends* (which provide a treasury of them), and in the verse of such outstanding rhymesters of today as Ogden Nash and Dorothy Parker. Even Browning and Swinburne found them useful.

But a rhyming dictionary must be as complete as possible to cut down the labors of a busy poet.

APOLOGY

I'd rather do rhymes of a morning betimes
Than anything else on the gamut of crimes.
Discursing with versing began with my nursing,
And chasing a metrical thought as it climbs
Is sweet, I repeat—why, e'en as I eat
The chewing I'm doing quite lyric'ly chimes.
Alas, what a pass! My head's a morass
Of singular jingular meters en masse.

Nor do they retreat at the noise of the street,
But tread through my head to the beat of my feet,
The while each particular ruption auricular
(Jars of the cars, or a hubbub vehicular)
Falls into line, as though by design,
To act as a dactyl or trochee of mine.
Ah me, you can see by the force of my plea,
How troublesome bubblesome meter may be.

One hint is enough for some stuff in the rough,
And I promptly advert to my shirt-sleeve or cuff;
A word I have heard that is odd, or a name
That's odder, is fodder for feeding the flame.
Also the vernacular adds a spectacular
Shine to a line that were otherwise tame.
This shows, I suppose, as far as it goes,
A skill with the quill quite unsuited to prose.

And so, when I'm hit by a rhythmical fit,
I rhyme against time, and I don't, I admit,
Disturb with a curb any verbular bit,
But build up upon it a sonnet or skit.
I never expect its course to direct,
But let it express its excesses unchecked.
'Tis better than drinking, to my way of thinking,
For others, not I, must endure the effect.

Forgive this smug praise of my ways, but for days
I've itched to be rich in reward for my lays;
And maybe I might, so much I indite,
If only I had some ideas when I write.

ONE-SYLLABLE RHYMES

A (*as in* ah)

ah	la	hurrah	shah
baa	ma	huzza	spa
fa	aha	mamma	pah
hah	faux pas	papa	

A (*as in* call), *see* Aw

A (*as in* say), *see* Ay

Ab

bab	contab	gab	nab
bedab	crab	grab	scab
blab	dab	lab	slab
cab	drab	jab	stab
confab	frab	mab	tab

Abe

abe	babe	astrolabe	outgrabe

Ac, Ack, Ak, Ach

alack	pack	aback	elegiac
arrack	pickaback	attack	cul-de-sac
back	rack	jimcrack	good-lack
black	ransack	knickknack	monomaniac
brack	sac	almanac	Union-jack
claque	sack	bric-a-brac	wool-back
crack	shack	cardiac	thrack
hack	slack	maniac	mocaque
hatchmatack	smack	zodiac	symposiac
haversack	snack	demoniac	ladybrack
huckaback	stack	hypochondriac	seawrack
jack	tack	salammoniac	tick-tack
knack	thwack	ammoniac	quack
lac	track	bivouac	wrack
lack	whack	chack	dipsomaniac
clack	repack	hysteriac	haystack
Polack	calpack	dionysiac	ipecac
shellac	iliac	slapjack	anzac
Sassenach	Frontenac	megalomaniac	yak
natterack	cognac	kayak	stickleback
anglomaniac	holdback	hunchback	skipjack
theriac	iliac	sumoniac	champak
kleptomaniac	Slovak	Cluniac	dyak
hogback	blackjack	*bootjack*, etc.	*knapsack*, etc.

Ace

ace
base
bass
brace
case
chase
dace
face
grace
lace
mace
pace
place
plaice
race
space
trace
abase
apace
debase
deface
misplace
outface
outpace
replace
disgrace
displace
efface
embrace
grimace
unlace
interlace
interspace
populace
rebrace
unbrace
enchase
discase
encase
erase
retrace
underbrace
commonplace
vase
thrace
carapace
anelace
begrace
boniface
chariot-race
footpace
fortlace
idocrase

Ach, Atch

batch
catch
hatch
latch
match
patch
ratch
scratch
smatch
snatch
thatch
attach
bandersnatch
detach
dispatch
unlatch
unattach
cratch
scratch
slatch
swatch
mismatch
overmatch
reattach
brach
butterhatch
tach

Ache, *see* Ake

Act

act
backed (*and past of verbs ending* Ack)
fact
fract
intact
contract (verb)
entr'acte
retroact
interact
matter-of-fact
precontract (verb)
pact
tact
tract
attract
co-act
compact (adj.)
contact
detract
abstract (verb)
re-enact
redact
distract
enact
epact
exact
extract
impact (verb)
infract
react
protract
unbacked
transact
retract
diffract
subact
subtract
transact
cataphract
cataract
counteract
incompact
interact
anteact

Ad

add
bad
bade
marinade
superade
dad
mad
pad
plaid
winterclad
yclad
bedad

AD—(*Cont.*)

brad
cad
clad
egad
ivy-clad
pine-clad, etc.
fad
gad
glad
had
lad
forbade
rad
sad
shad
unclad
"undergrad"
ironclad
olympiad
scad
englad
footpad

AD (*as in* wad), *see* OD

ADE (*French*)

psha'd
baa'd
chamade
estrade
façade
couvade
fougade
roulade
pomade
promenade
dragonnade
lancepesade
huzzaed
estanfade
noyade
pavesade

ADE (*English*)

aid
blade
braid
bayed (*and past of verbs ending* AY)
cade
dade
fade
glade
grade
jade
lade
laid
made
maid
paid
raid
shade
spade
staid
enfilade
fanfaronade
camisade
cassonade
old maid
mermaid
slade
alcaid
pesade
plantigrade
trade
wade
afraid
arcade
blockade
brigade
brocade
cascade
cockade
crusade
decade
degrade
dissuade
evade
grenade
inlaid
invade
obeyed
parade
milkmaid
croupade
Damascus-blade
persuade
escalade
galiconnade
co-aid
pomade
harlequinade
sacrade
pervade
relaid
repaid
tirade
unlade
unpaid
unmade
upbraid
accolade
ambuscade
barricade
bastinade
cannonade
cavalcade
centigrade
esplanade
defilade
flanconnade
glissade
colonnade
fusillade
gasconade
lemonade
marmalade
escapade
gallopade
stockade
parade
ready-made
rodomontade
charade
masquerade
overlaid
pasquinade
renegade
retrograde
serenade
underlaid
abraid
ambassade
arquebusade
balustrade
bejade
passade
pistolade
promenade

ADZE, ADS

adze
adds (*add s to nouns and verbs ending* AD)

AFE

chafe
safe
waif
unsafe
vouchsafe
enchafe

AFF, APH (*either flat or broad* a)

chaff
gaff
staff
carafe
calf
half
laugh
quaff
distaff
giraffe
riffraff
tipstaff
cenotaph
behalf
epitaph
paragraph
quarterstaff
actinograph
agraffe
anagraph
autograph
chronograph
cryptograph
draff
flagstaff
heliograph
idiograph
telegraph
phonograph
photograph
cinematograph
dictograph
lithograph
monograph
penny-gaff
shandygaff
stenograph

AFT (*either flat or broad* a)

aft
craft
daft
draft
draught
graft
haft
raft
shaft
waft
abaft
ingraft
handicraft
fellow-craft
overdraft
river craft
sea craft
chaffed (*and past of verbs ending in* AFF *and* APH)

AG

bag
brag
crag
drag
fag
flag
gag
hag
jag
lag
nag
quag
rag
sag
scrag
shag
slag
snag
stag
swag
tag
wag
rag-tag
zigzag
battle-flag
bullyrag
cag
fishfag
knag
mag
saddle-bag
scallowag
shrag
sprag

AGE

age
cage
gage
gauge
sage
stage
wage
assuage
presage (verb)
disengage
discage
foot-page
mid-age
outrage
swage
weather-gauge

AGE—(*Cont.*)

page	engage	mage	*cortège*
rage	enrage		

AGE (*French*)

barage	menage	equipage	appanage

AGE (*as* idg)

appanage	parentage	pilgrimage	anchorage
equipage	parsonage	villanage	arbitrage
foliage	pasturage	vicarage	average
heritage	patronage	concubinage	baronage
hermitage	personage	acreage	cartilage
beverage	brigandage	alienage	sacralage

AIL, ALE

ale	entail (verb)	swale	detail (verb)
bail	mail	tail	exhale
brail	male	tale	impale
dale	nail	trail	prevail
fail	pale	vale	regale
flail	pail	veil	retail (verb)
frail	quail	wail	unveil
gale	rail	wale	*wholesale*
gaol	sail	whale	countervail
grail	sale	assail	farthingale
hail	scale	avail	nightingale
hale	shale	*blackmail*	they'll
jail	snail	bewail	aventaile
kail	stale	curtail	bale
bepale	camail	canaille	engaol
countervail	death-pale	divale	martingale
engrail	*entrail*	fairy-tale	unveil
grisaille	inhale	interpale	vail
paravail	sliding-scale	taille	

AIM, AME

ashame	dame	shame	exclaim
disfame	fame	tame	inflame
entame	flame	acclaim	misname
hame	frame	aflame	*nickname*
melodrame	game	became	proclaim
aim	lame	declaim	reclaim
blame	maim	defame	surname

Aim, Ame—(*Cont.*)

came
claim
name
same
disclaim
overcame

Ain, Ane

aëroplane
alecampane
allophane
ativain
bestain
bower-thane
bridle-rein
compane
chamberlain
chatelaine
chicain
cocaine
counterpane
Dane
delaine
demain
diaphane
frangipane
germane
humane
hurricane
hydroplane
inane
inurbane
bane
blain
brain
cain
chain
crane
deign
drain
fain
fane
feign
gain
grain
lain
lane
main
mane
pain
pane
plain
plane
rain
reign
rein
profane
restrain
entertain
sane
skein
slain
sprain
stain
strain
swain
ta'en
thane
train
twain
refrain
retain
vain
vane
vein
wain
wane
abstain
amain
arraign
attain
campaign
champagne
complain
regain
sustain
constrain
detain
disdain
distrain
domain
enchain
explain
henbane
maintain
obtain
ordain
pertain
remain
appertain

Aint

ain't
faint
feint
mayn't
paint
plaint
quaint
saint
taint
acquaint
attaint
complaint
constraint
distraint
restraint
bepaint
besaint
daint
straint

Air, Are, Aire

air
bare
bear
blare
care
chair
dare
lair
mare
mayor
ne'er
pair
pare
pear
tear
their
there
ware
wear
were
where
vin-ordinaire
forswear
howe'er
impair
prepare
repair
whate'er

AIR, ARE, AIRE—(*Cont.*)

e'er	*prayer*	yare	whene'er
ere	rare	affair	where'er
fair	scare	armchair	debonair
fare	share	aware	howsoe'er
flair	snare	beware	solitaire
flare	spare	co-heir	unaware
gare	square	compare	whatso'er
glair	stair	declare	millionaire
hair	sware	*elsewhere*	commissionaire
hare	swear	ensnare	concessionaire
heir	tare	forbear	anywhere
agre	backstair	bêche-de-mer	arrière
chargé d'affaires	cockle-stair	mal de mer	capillaire
	etagère	devil-may-care	doctrinaire
earthenware	outstare	jardinère	laissez-faire
maidenhair	sedan-chair	outwear	parterre
proletaire	underwear	thoroughfare	*threadbare*
unfair			

AIRD

laird	haired	bared (*and past of verbs ending in* ARE, AIR)

AIRS, ARES

theirs	unawares	airs (*and add s to nouns and verbs ending in* AIR, etc.)

AISE, AZE

chrysoprase	amaze	appraise	glaze
blaze	sideways	mayonnaise	craze
braise	paraphrase	daze	maize
graze	braze	laze	phase
haze	marseillaise	naze	raise
mays	chaise	praise	ablaze
phrase	maze	gaze	crase
rays (*and add s to nouns and verbs ending* AY, etc.)		paraphrase	raze

AIT, ATE (*long*)

bait	fate	great	plate
bate	freight	hate	prate
crate	gait	late	rate
date	gate	mate	sate
eight	grate	pate	skate

AIT, ATE (*long*)—(*Cont.*)

slate
spate
desecrate
dictate
execrate
fluctuate
glaciate
immigrate
liberate
navigate
obviate
percolate
proximate
state
straight
strait
wait
weight
abate
await
belate
collate
create
cremate
debate
dilate
elate
estate
frustrate
ingrate
innate
irate
migrate
narrate
orate
designate
dominate
fabricate
fulminate
graduate
implicate
liquidate
modulate
operate
permeate
punctuate
placate
prostrate
rebate
relate
sedate
translate
vacate
abdicate
abrogate
advocate
decorate
aggravate
agitate
alienate
animate (verb)
demonstrate
annotate
antedate
arbitrate
arrogate
aspirate (verb)
cachinnate
devastate
emanate
fascinate
fumigate
granulate
inficate
lubricate
mutilate
opiate
populate
relegate
calculate
candidate
captivate
castigate
celebrate
circulate
congregate
consecrate
contemplate
dedicate
cultivate
delegate
deprecate
derogate
decimate
desolate (verb)
dislocate
dissipate
educate
elevate
emigrate
emulate
deviate
excavate
flood-gate
germinate
gravitate
irrigate
masticate
obligate
osculate
procreate
abnegate
absinthiate
aërate
antiquate
compensate
consummate
criminate
saturate
situate
stimulate
supplicate
triturate
validate
venerate
estimate (verb)
generate
immolate
instigate
magistrate
perforate
potentate
reprobate (verb)
syndicate (verb)
titivate
ciolate
accommodate
anticipate
capitulate
communicate
contaminate
degenerate (verb)
discriminate
equivocate
exasperate
facilitate
importunate (verb)
invalidate
participate
premeditate
regenerate
excommunicate
acclamate
aggregate
approximate
concentrate
coronate
culminate
scintillate
speculate
stridulate
syncopate
undulate
variate

AIT, ATE (*long*)—(*Cont.*)

ventilate
extricate
hestitate
intimate (verb)
nominate
perpetrate
predicate
stipulate
temperate (verb)
tolerate
abominate
accumulate
articulate (verb)
coagulate
compassionate (verb)
co-operate
deliberate (verb)
elaborate (verb)
eradicate
expectorate
felicitate
initiate
investigate
precipitate (verb)
prevaricate
reiterate
incapacitate
emaciate
incriminate
actuate
alternate
cogitate
confiscate
correlate
renovate
segrate
spoliate
stylobate
syndicate
vaccinate
vassalate
verberate
formulate
hibernate
imprecate
irritate
oscillate
personate
propagate
subjugate
terminate
accelerate
adulterate
assassinate
commemorate
confederate (verb)
corrobate
denominate
emancipate
evaporate
expostulate
illuminate
intimidate
matriculate
predestinate (verb)
procrastinate
reverberate
candidate
illustrate
adulate
amputate
comminate
conjugate
corrugate
runagate
simulate
stellulate
sublimate
tabulate
vacillate
vegetate
vitiate
fornicate
imitate
innovate
inundate
penetrate
postulate (verb)
regulate
suffocate
tête-à tête
vindicate
accentuate
annihilate
capacitate
commiserate
congratulate
debilitate
depopulate
emasculate
exaggerate
exterminate
impersonate
intoxicate
necessitate
predominate
recriminate
subordinate (verb)
reprobate
depreciate
manipulate
orginate
prognosticate
recuperate
rejuvenate
retaliate
substantiate
abbacinate
acuminate
ameliorate
appreciate
associate
circumstantiate
delineate
deteriorate
disintegrate
ejaculate
cnumerate
exhilarate
habituate
inaugurate
infatuate
inoculate
invigorate
negociate
perambulate
promulgate
refrigerate
remonstrate
reverberate
abbreviate
affiliate
annunciate
asphyxiate
authenticate
disseminate
eliminate
episcopate
expatiate
humiliate
incarcerate
infuriate
insinuate
irradiate
obliterate
perpetuate
recalcitrate
renumerate

AIT, ATE (*long*)—(*Cont.*)

somnambulate
vituperate
ablaqueate
asseverate
binoculate
consolidate
differentiate
dissociate
elucidate
evacuate
extenuate
hypothecate
incorporate
ingerminate
interpolate
luxuriate
officiate
preponderate
reciprocate
regurgitate
repudiate
sophisticate
vociferate
acidulate
agglutinate
apostolate
assimilate
captivate
decapitate

ATE (*short, as in* obstinate). *Sometimes used either as rhymes to* AIT, ATE (*long*) *or* IT

accurate
adequate
advocate (noun)
animate (adj.)
aspirate (noun)
temperate (adj.)
syndicate (noun)
affectionate
subordinate
intemperate
celibate
delicate
desolate (adj.)
estimate
fortunate
confederate (adj.)
considerate
degenerate (adj.)
articulate (adj.)
unfortunate
intimate (adj.)
intricate
literate
moderate (adj.)
desperate
passionate
illiterate
immoderate
importunate (adj.)
deliberate (adj.)
chalybeate
postulate (noun)
predicate (noun)
profligate
obstinate
separate (adj.)
precipitate (adj.)
predestinate (adj.)
inaminate
insatiate
disconsolate
triumverate
inveterate
inviolate
undenominate
invertebrate
certificate
duplicate
inadequate
intermediate
obdurate
inarticulate
insubordinate
commensurate
chocolate
federate
inveterate
compassionate (adj.)
legitimate
determinate
agglomerate
antepenultimate
appropriate
collegiate
immaculate
inconsiderate
laureate
regenerate
effeminate
elaborate (adj.)
baccalaureate
conglomerate
immediate
inebriate

AITH

baith
faith
wraith
rathe
snathe

AKE

ache
bake
brake
break
cake
drake
fake
flake
hake
aslake
johnnycake
lake

Ake—(*Cont.*)

make
quake
rake
sake
shake
slake
snake
spake
crake
outbreak
stake
steak
take
wake
awake
bespake
betake
corn-crake
forsake
daybreak
keepsake
mandrake
mistake
namesake
opaque
partake
snowflake
overtake
undertake
heartbreak
wedding-cake
stomach-ache
back-ache, etc.

Al (*flat*)

mall
pal
banal
corral
shall
morale
cabal
canal
"musicale"
madrigal

Al (*short ending*), *false rhymes, sometimes used with either* Al *or* All

trivial
animal
annual
arsenal
cannibal
capital
cardinal
carnival
clinical
comical
conical
conjugal
corporal
aboriginal
allodial
arborial
conditional
conventional
dramatical
electrical
aerial
caracal
communal
cynical
ethical
firical
logical
matinal
mythical
optical
punctual
rhythmical
spherical
virtual
zodiacal
pictorial
precautional
recessional
sensational
empirical
fanatical
harmonical
hysterical
inaugural
memorial
nonsensical
perennial
economical
intellectual
reciprocal
satirical
hypocritical
decimal
festival
funeral
general
genial
hospital
inimical
initial
interval
liberal
literal
littoral
madrigal
magical
mareschal
medical
mineral
academical
alluvial
baccharal
confessional
devotional
dynamical
elliptical
cardinal
copal
destinal
faldernall
functional
lyrical
matronal
nautical
patronal
quizzical
ritual
stoical
visional
piratical
primordial
remedial
sophistical
ephemeral
fantastical
heretical
identical
industrial
mercurial
numerical
allegorical
energetical
oratorical
oratical
hypercritical
national
natural
pastoral

AL (*short ending*)—(*Cont.*)

pedestal
personal
physical
principal
prodigal
rational
seneschal
several
temporal
terminal
tragical
whimsical
asthmatical
colloquial
accentual
antiphonal
botanical
congressional
didactical
ecstatical
emotional
biblical
doctrinal
forcical
geminal
marginal
metrical
nominal
pictural
radical
sceptical
synchronal
visual
perpetual
platonical
professional
residual
symbolical
ethereal
funeral
heroical
illogical
intentional
methodical
occasional
architectural
immaterial
periodical
tyrannical
rheumatical
dogmatical
equinoctial
equivocal
hymeneal
hexagonal
imperial
impersonal
intellectual
municipal
octagonal
orginal
pentagonal
poetical
political
pragmatical
problematical
prophetical
affectional
antipodal
conclusional
conjectural
dilurial
effectual
admiral
boreal
clerical
cosmical
epical
federal
jovial
marital
mutual
notional
pivotal
retinal
scriptual
virginal
vortical
phenomenal
pontifical
pyramidal
sartorical
symmetrical
eventual
habitual
historical
imaginal
ironical
monarchical
pathetical
diabolical
individual
puritanical
rhetorical
schismatical
reciprocal
rhetorical
rheumatical
musical
oratorical
satirical
cortical
tyrannical
hypercritical
hypocritical
criminal
mystical
diaconal
diagonal

ALC

talc
catafalque

ALD

bald
balled
bawled (*and verbs ending in* ALL)
piebald
scald
so-called

ALE, *see* AIL

ALF, *see* AFF

ALK, AUK, AWK

auk
balk
baulk
calk
awk
chalk
gawk
hawk
mawk
Mohawk
stalk
talk
walk
tomahawk
pawk
squawk

ALL, AUL, AWL

all
all-in-all
awl
ball
bawl
befall
bemawl
Bengal
brawl
call
caterwall
caul
crawl
drawl
dwaul
evenfall
fall
footfall
forestall
gall
Gaul
hall
haul
kraal
mall
maul
pall
recall
scrawl
sea-wall
shawl
snowball
small
spawl
sprawl
squall
stall
tall
thrall
trawl
wall
wherewithal
yawl
appal
enthral
football
install
overhaul
waterfall
windfall
blackball
baseball
basket-ball
volley-ball, etc.

ALM

alm
balm
calm
palm
psalm
qualm
becalm
salaam

ALMS

alms
psalms (etc.) *See* ALM

ALSE

false
valse
waltz
salts (*and add* s *to nouns and verbs in* ALT)

ALT (*short*)

alt
asphalt
shalt

ALT (*long*), **AULT**

fault
halt
malt
salt
vault
assault
cobalt
default
exalt
basalt
envault
gault
somersault
spalt
asphalt

ALVE (*silent L*)

calve
halve
enclave
Slav
salve
suave
Zouave

ALVE (*L sounded*)

salve valve

AM

am	jam	diagram	cham
cam	jamb	diaphragm	ma'am
clam	lam	epigram	nizam
cram	lamb	monogram	shram
dam	pram	oriflamb	slam
damn	ram	telegram	tram
dram	sham	parallelogram	yam
drachm	swam	*ad nauseam*	dithyramb
flam	anagram	auriflamme	gambe
gramme	cryptogam	cablegram	madame
ham	cryptogram	caimacam	salaam

AME, *see* AIM

AMP

camp	gamp	stamp	encamp
champ	lamp	tramp	Davy's-lamp
clamp	ramp	vamp	samp
cramp	scamp	decamp	tamp
damp			

AMP (*as in* swamp) *see* OMP

AN (*accented*)

an	japan	trepan	pavane
ban	rattan	unman	pecan
bran	sedan	anan	redan
can	pan	inspan	trapan
clan	plan	*merman*	caravan
fan	ran	van	also-ran
man	scan	flan	Castellan
began	span	khan	Catalan
divan	tan	superman	catamaran
foreran	than	orang-utan	

AN (*short*), questionable rhymes, often used either with AN or UN

alderman	clergyman	journeyman	oppidan
anglican	countryman	lighterman	ortolan
artisan	courtesan	merchantman	Ottoman
barbican	highwayman	midshipman	overman
barracan	husbandman	Mussulman	partisan
charlatan	juryman	nobleman	pelican

AN (*short*)—(*Cont.*)

publican	diocesan	liveryman	sacristan
puritan	African	Mohammedan	talisman
suffragan	Alcoran	Parmesan	Vatican
veteran	echinidan	American	republican
waterman	kaimakan	pemmican	

AN (*as in* swan and wan), *see* ON

ANCE, ANSE (*long*)

chance	stance	expanse	complaisance
dance	trance	intrance	perchance
glance	advance	mischance	entrance
lance	askance	romance	finance
manse	*elegance*	seance	bechance
prance	enhance	circumstance	

ANCE, ANSE (*short*); *questionable rhymes used with* ANCE, ENCE *or* UNCE

ambulance	temperance	concomitance	irrelevance
arrogance	utterance	continuance	luxuriance
consonance	vigilance	conversance	ordinance
countenance	deliverance	dominance	precipitance
dissonance	exorbitance	furtherance	preponderance
ignorance	extravagance	heritance	protruberance
maintenance	exuberance	impuissance	radiance
ordinance	inheritance	incogitance	suppliance
petulance	intemperance	incognisance	tolerance
sufferance	significance	inhabitance	variance
sustenance	appurtenance	intolerance	

ANCH

blanch	ganch	stanch	carte-blanche
branch	ranche	scranch	avalanche
flanch			

AND

and	land	disband	withstand
band	rand	expand	caravaned
bland	sand	fairyland	contraband
fanned	stand	aband	countermand
gland	strand	ampersand	deodand
grand	command	brand	reprimand
hand	demand	fatherland	understand

AND—(*Cont.*)

wonderland, lotus-land, remand, banned, *and past of verbs in* AN
four-in-hand, multiplicand, sarabande

AND (*as in* wand), *see* OND

ANE, *see* AIN

ANG

bang	pang	swang	*mustang*
clang	rang	tang	boomerang
fang	sang	twang	sprang
gang	slang	harangue	orang-autang
hang	stang	meringue	zamang

ANGE

change	range	arrange	exchange
grange	strange	estrange	interchange
mange			

ANK

bank	disrank	mountebank	slank
blank	drank	plank	spank
brank	enrank	point-blank	stank
cank	franc	prank	swank
chank	frank	rank	tank
clank	flank	sank	thank
crank	hank	shank	twank
dank	lank	shrank	

ANSE, *see* ANCE

ANT (*short*)

ant	displant	confidant-e	*cormorant*
bant	decant	dilettant	*covenant*
cant	discant	extant	*disputant*
chant	enchant	gallivant	*dissonant*
grant	gallant	germinant	*dominant*
pant	implant	gratulant	*elegant*
plant	levant	habitant	*elephant*
rant	recant	romant	*ignorant*
slant	supplant	*arrogant*	*jubilant*
scant	transplant	*combatant*	*militant*
tant	adamant	*complaisant*	*petulant*
aslant	commandant	*consonant*	*recreant*

ANT (*short*)—(*Cont.*)

recusant
ruminant
termagant
vigilant
visitant
exorbitant
extravagant
exuberant
inhabitant
significant
insignificant
abdicant
adultenant
altivalant
annuitant
anticipant
applicant
appurtenant
communicant
concomitant
congratulant
corposant
corroborant
corybant
courant
determinant
emigrant
excommunicant
executant
figurant
flagellant
fulminant
hesitant
hierophant
illuminant
imaginant
immigrant
impuissant
incogitant
incognisant
inhabitant
intolerant
intoxicant
irradiant
irrelevant
undulant
irritant
itinerant
litigant
luminant
luxuriant
mendicant
occupant
odorant
penetrant
postulant
precipitant
predominant
preponderant
procreant
protuberant
pursuivant
variant
recalcitrant
recusant
reiterant
relevant
resonant
resuscitant
reverberant
scintallant
sibilant
stimulant
suppliant
supplicant
sycophant
tintinnabulant
tolerant
vaciverant

ANT (*long*), *see also above*

chant
grant
aunt
can't
debutante
shan't

ANT (*as in* want), *see* ONT

AP

cap
chap
clap
dap
flap
gap
hap
jap
lap
map
nap
pap
rap
sap
scrap
slap
snap
strap
tap
trap
wrap
yap
entrap
enwrap
mayhap
mishap
afterclap
flip-flap
foolscap
frap
genappe
handicap
heel-tap
"Jap"
knap
nightcap
overlap
rattletrap
shoulder-strap
unlap
unwrap
wapp

APE

ape
cape
chape
crape
drape
gape
grape
jape

APE—(*Cont.*)

pape
rape
scape
escape
undrape
scrape
agape
crêpe
jackanape
landscape
red-tape
seascape
shipshape
trape

APES

traipse
apes (*and add s to nouns and verbs in* APE)

APH, *see* AFF

APSE, APS

caps (*add s to nouns and verbs in* AP)
apse
flaps
lapse
elapse
relapse
perhaps
relaps
collapse
schnapps

APT

capped (*and past of verbs in* AP)
apt
rapt
adapt
inapt

AQUE, *see* ACK

AR (*long*)

are
bar
car
char
far
jar
mar
par
scar
parr
spar
star
tar
afar
bazaar
catarrh
cigar
debar
disbar
felspar
guitar
hussar
unbar
avatar
caviare
cinnabar
gnarr
jaguar
afar
ajar
bizarre
cymar
czar, tzar
Exalibar
registrar
saddle-bar
shooting-star
evening-star, etc.

AR (*short*); *all questionable rhymes sometimes used with either* AR *or* ER

angular
calendar
popular
regular
secular
scimitar
similar
singular
titular
vinegar
dissimilar
irregular
particular
perpendicular
animalcular
annular
binocular
circular
consular
crepuscular
funicular
globular
hospodar
insular
jemidar
jocular
jugular
peninsular
scapular
somnambular
spectacular
stellular

Ar (*short*)—(*Cont.*)

tabernacular	triangular	uvular	zemindar
tabular	tutelar	vernacular	

Ar (*as in* war) (*see* Or)

Arb

barb	garb	*rhubarb*	"yarb"

Arc, *see* Ark

Arce, Arse

farce	sparse	parse	"sarse"

Arch (*soft*)

arch	outmarch	starch	inarch
larch	parch	countermarch	

Arch (*hard*) *see* Ark

Ard

bard	shard	retard	milliard
card	yard	disregard	placard
guard	blackyard	interlard	sard
hard	bombard	boulevard	shard
lard	discard	brocard	barred (*also*
mard	petard	canard	*past tense of*
pard	regard	foulard	*verbs in* Ar)

Ard (*as in* ward) *see* Ord (*short*)

Are, *see* Air

Arf

dwarf	wharf	corf

Arf (*as in* scarf); *no rhymes except dialect, as* "larf"

Arge

barge	marge	enlarge	surcharge
charge	targe	o'ercharge	sparge
large	discharge	recharge	

Ark

arc	hark	park	genearck
ark	flood-mark	shark	knark
bark	footmark	spark	remark
barque	lark	stark	hierarch
dark	mark	embark	obligarch

ARK—(*Cont.*)

heresiarch	cark	marc	sark
bedark	disembark	patriarch	

ARL

carl	marl	snarl	jarl
gnarl	parle	harl	

ARM

arm	charm	harm	disarm
barm	farm	alarm	gendarme

ARM (*as in* warm), *see* ORM

ARN

barn	darn	tarn	incarn
yarn	imbarn		

ARN (*as in* warn), *see* ORN

ARP

carp	monocarp	pericarp	sharp
escarp	harp	scarp-e	counterscarp

ARS

Mars (*and plural nouns and verbs ending in* AR)

ARSE (*hard*), *see* ARCE

ARSH

harsh	marsh

ART

art	counterpart	smart	depart
cart	lion-heart	start	dispart
carte	heart	sweetheart	impart
chart	mart	tart	indart
dart	part	apart	upstart
hart	sart		

ART (*as in* wart), *see* ORT

ARTH

hearth	garth	swarth

ARVE

carve	starve	larve

AS

as	has	*topaz*	whereas

As (*short*); *questionable rhymes often used with* **Us**

candlemas	Michaelmas	erysipelas

Ase, *see* **Ace** *and* **Aise**

Ash (*as in* ash)

ash	calabash	smash	rash
bash	*lache*	abash	trash
brash	sabretache	*brache*	sash
cash	dash	calash	splash
clash	flash	mountain-ash	moustache
crash	gash	squabash	*cache*
slash	gnash	mash	fash
thrash	hash	pash	patache
balberdash	lash	plash	tache

Ash (*as in* wash), **Osh**

bosh	debosh	splosh	swash
gosh	troche	musquash	tosh
josh	losh	goloshe	bervash
wash	quash	squash	mackintosh

Ask

ask	casque	antimask	mask
bask	cask	masque	immask
task	flask	hask	Pasch

Asm

spasm	phasm	iconoclasm	bioplasm
chasm	miasm	plasm	metaplasm
enthusiasm	phantasm	sarcasm	pleonasm
demoniasm	protoplasm	cataplasm	

Ass

ass	paillasse	bonnilass	surpass
bass	sassafras	damasse	hippocras
brass	en-masse	isinglass	kavass
class	grass	*paterfamilias*	overpass
crass	glass	tarantass	rubasse
gas	lass	amass	demi-tasse
unclass	mass	cuirass	*declasse*
balass	pass	morass	Khyber Pass, etc.
crevasse	alas	outclass	
hour-glass	"coup de grâce"	repass	
looking-glass			

Ast

blast
cast
caste
fast
hast
aghast
contrast (verb)
ecclesiast
idoloclast
paraphrast
steadfast
last
bombast
forecast (verb)
past
vast
enthusiast
devast
elegiast
jury-mast
protoplast
symposiast
avast
metaphrast
overcast
outcast
repast
iconoclast
downcast
flabbergast
metaplast
scholiast
classed (*also past tense of verbs in* Ass)

Aste

baste
chaste
haste
paste
taste
unchaste
foretaste
distaste
waist
waste
impaste
raced (*also past of verbs in* Ace)

At

at
bat
brat
cat
chat
fat
that
cushat
flat
gat
gnat
hat
mat
pat
vat
polecat
plait
rat
sat
spat
sprat
tat
cravat
acrobat
aristocrat
civet-cat
democrat
habitat
proletariat
autocrat
commissariat
diplomat
heliostat
plutocrat
slat
caveat
dandiprat
drat
monocrat
secretariat
thermostat

Atch, *see* Ach

Ate, *see* Ait

Ath

bath
hath
lath
math
aftermath
snath
path
rath
scath
pilomath

Athe

bathe
swathe
lathe
unswathe
scathe

Aub

daub
"baub"

Aud

bawd	gaud	laud	cawed, (*and past tense of verbs in* Au)
broad	fraud	abroad	
applaud	defraud	maraud	

Augh, *see* Aff

Aught (*as in* laught), *see* Aft

Aught (*as in* taught)

aught	*forethought*	bethought	wrought
bought	fraught	methought	besought
brought	naught	overwrought	distraught
caught	nought	taught	over-thought
fought	ought	taut	argonaut
maut	sought	thought	

Auk, Aulk, *see* Alk

Aun, *see* Awn

Aunch

haunch	launch	paunch	craunch

Aunt, (*see also* Ant)

daunt	haunt	romaunt	vaunt
gaunt	jaunt	taunt	avaunt
flaunt			

Aur, *see* Or

Ause, Auze

cause	hawse	pause	saws (*and add s to verbs and nouns in* Au)
clause	because	applause	
gauze			

Aust

exhaust	lost	tossed (*and past of verbs in* Oss)	
holocaust	frost		

Ave

brave	margrave	pave	belave
cave	augusticlave	rave	beslave
crave	drave	save	galley-slave
gave	encave	shave	slave
grave	impave	snave	stave
knave	lave	engrave	they've
deprave	nave	outbrave	wave

AVE—(*Cont.*)

behave	architrave	eleve	thrave
conclave	concave	glaive	waive
forgave			

AW

awe	gnaw	macaw	guffaw
caw	haw	scaw	overawe
chaw	jaw	thraw	braw
claw	law	seesaw	haw
craw	maw	saw	*pawpaw*
daw	paw	squaw	slaw
draw	pshaw	straw	tau
flaw	raw	thaw	overdraw
jackdaw	withdraw	yaw	oversaw
usuquebaugh	begnaw	foresaw	underjaw
shah	faugh	heehaw	
taw			

AWL, *see* ALL

AWN

awn	drawn	impawn	yawn
bawn	faun	pawn	indrawn
brawn	fawn	prawn	sawn
dawn	lawn	spawn	*gone*

AX

axe	zax	parallax	tax
flax	lax	almanacs	relax
lacs	wax	(*and add* s *to*	climax
thorax	*borax*	*nouns and*	pax
		verbs in AC)	

AY

aye (ever)	Chevrolet	pay	stay
bay	foray	play	stray
bray	holiday	pray	sway
clay	inveigh	prey	they
gay	Milky Way	ray	repay
may	prepay	say	survey
assegai	nay	matinée	disarray
bey	née	slay	runaway
caroway	neigh	spray	day

Ay—(*Cont.*)

dray
eh?
fay
hay
agley
bobsleigh
castaway
estray
galloway
heyday
horseplay
leeway
outlay
missay
sachet
tray
tway
way
weigh
whey
affray
allay
array
shay
astray
away
betray
bewray
convey
waylay
disobey
roundelay
flay
fray
jay
gray
lay
alackaday
bouquet
drey
footway
highway
crossway
interplay
mainstay
malay
popinjay
decay
defray
denay
dismay
display
essay (*verb*)
gainsay
hooray
inlay (*verb*)
assay
obey
outweigh
portray
purvey
relay (*verb*)
belay
stowaway
subway
tramway
déjeuner
cabriolet, *and French endings such as*
employé
reveille
toupet
tourniquet
habitué
negligée
papier maché
au fait
distrait
passée
protégé
soirée
auti-de-fé
coupé
gourmet
outré
resumé
sobriquet
visé

Aze, *see* Aise

E, Ea, Ee

be
bee
dree
fee
flea
flee
gee
free
levee
spree
tea
tee
thee
three
tree
we
wee
aborigine
reveille
rupee
scotfree
settee
trustee
absentee
apogee
assignee
bargainee
employe
toupet, *and other English adaptations of French words with final* e
he
key
knee
lea
lee
me
pea
plea
quay
sea
she
oversea
pedigree
recipe
repartee
animalculæ
felo-de-se
recognizee
addressee
apostrophe
bel-esprit
bourgeoisie
calorie
chimpansee
diablerie

E, Ea, Ee—(*Cont.*)

fiddle-de-dee
Gethsemane
licensee
mobee
pot-pourri
systole
glee
ye
agree
bawbee
bohea
decree
degree
donee
foresee
fusee
grandee
grantee
lessee
on dit
oversee
perigee
referee
simile
covenantee
facsimile
agapomene
anemone
appointee
blea
bumblebee
catastrophe
Cybele
dominie
fleur-de-lis
goatee
maravedi
Penelope
sesame
Terpsichore
facsimile
cap-a-pie
cognisee
coterie
debauchee
devotee
disagree
eau-de-vie
filigree
guarantee
jubilee
jeu d'esprit
mortgagee
nominee
patentee
presentee
refugee
vis-à-vis
extempore
hyperbole
abandonee
antistrophe
bailee
Bon Ami
calliope
chickadee
debris
ennui
fricassee
interrogatee
marquee
Pharisee
topee
vertebræ

Words ending in Y (short) are also freely used by poets as rhymes in E

Eace (*hard*)

cease
crease
fleece
geese
grease
lease
chersonese
masterpiece
cantatrice
griece
semese
niece
peace
piece
apiece
caprice
decease
Siamese
Buonese
Singalese
Chinese, etc.
chimneypiece
verdigris
coulisse
mease
valise
decrease
increase
obese
police
release
surcease
frontispiece
afterpiece
esquisse
pelisse
creese

Each, Eech

beach
beech
bleach
breach
each
leech
peach
reach
screech
speech
teach
impeach
outreach
leach
overreach
sleetch
beseech
queach

Ead (*long*), Ede, Eed

bead
bleed
breed
cede
creed
deed
feed
heed

EAD (*long*), EDE, EED—(*Cont.*)

keyed	read	gleed	stampede
knead	rede	indeed	succeed
lead	reed	retrocede	antecede
mead	seed	concede	intercede
supersede	speed	exceed	aniseed
brede	steed	impede	Ganymede
glede	weed	misdeed	God-speed
greed	accede	linseed	interbreed
meed	centipede	precede	swede
need	velocipede	proceed	tweed
plead	djereed	recede	

treed (*and past participle of verbs in* E)

EAD (*short*), *see* ED

EAF (*short*), EF

deaf	chef	clef

EAF (*long*), *see* EEF

EAGUE, IGUE

league	teague	*colleague*	enleague
fatigue	intrigue		

EAK, EEK, IQUE

beak	cleek	bespeak	streak
bleak	fleak	chic	teak
cheek	physique	antique	tweak
cliquc	leak	cacique	weak
creak	leek	*clinique*	antique
creek	meek	gluk	critique
eek	peak	*relique*	after-peak
eke	peek	Sikh	apeak
freak	pique	shriek	caïque
week	reek	sleek	comique
bezique	seek	sneak	meak
oblique	sheik	speak	Salique
aleak	wreak	squeak	unique
areek			

EAK (*as in* steak), *see* AKE

EAL, EEL

deal	eel	heal	keel
deil	feel	heel	leal

EAL, EEL—(*Cont.*)

meal	seal	Kabyle	reveal
profile	squeal	postille	*deshabille*
cochineal	steal	sheal	she'll
we'll	sweal	tweel	automobile
barleymeal	teal	weal	chenille
creel	veal	wheal	enseal
interdeal	repeal	wheel	mercantile
ne'er-do-weel	commonweal	zeal	real
seel	he'll	anneal	teel
peal	alquazil	conceal	vakeel
peel	Bastile	congeal	Camile, etc.
reel	difficile	genteel	

EALD, IELD

field	yield	afield	healed (*and past tense of verbs in* EAL, EEL)
weald	enshield	harvest-field (etc.)	
battlefield	wield		
shield			

EALM, ELM

elm	realm	overwhelm	dishelm
helm	whelm	unhelm	Anselm

EALTH

health	stealth	wealth	commonwealth

EAM, EEM

beam	hareem	supreme	theme
bream	moonbeam	academe	beseam
cream	ream	daydream	blaspheme
deem	scheme	ice-cream	misdeem
dream	scream	reem	disesteem
gleam	seam	riem	fleam
esteem	seem	stream	leam
redeem	steam	team	regime
abeam	extreme	teem	weather-gleam
centime			

EAMT, EMPT

dreamt	attempt	pre-empt	unkempt
tempt	contempt	exempt	undreamt
kempt			

EAN, EEN, ENE, INE

been
bean
clean
dean
e'en
glean
green
keen
careen
demesne
marine
routine
sardine
serene
shagreen
unclean
unseen
aniline
bombazine
advene
aquamarine
atween
barkentine
brigantine
carrogeen
coralline
damascene
eglantine
fascine
fourteen
gradine
indigene
libertine
mazarine
miocene
opaline
peen
poteen
quinine
sappharine
serene
squireen
subrene
trephine
lean
mean
mien
quean
queen
scene
screen
seen
convene
foreseen
obscene
contrabene
crinoline
evergreen
gabardine
gelatine
guillotine
go-between
intervene
velveteen
algerine
Argentine
baleen
Beguine
cadene
chagrine
crystalline
dene
eighteen
fifteen
galantine
heterogene
infantine
lien
mesne
moreen
palanquin
petaline
protein
ravine
sateen
serpentine
stein
supervene
vespertine
Jean
shean
spleen
teen
wean
ween
yean
between
canteen
demean
machine
tambourine
toureen
misdemean
nectarine
nicotine
overseen
overween
quarantine
saccharine (*noun*)
ultramarine
atropine
bandoline
bottine
caffein
codeine
cuisine
ean
epicene
Florentine
gozogene
incarnadine
lateen
magazine
mezzanine
pean
pistareen
preen
routine
scalene
sibylline
subterrene
terreen
Wolverine

EAND, IEND, etc.

fiend
cleaned (*and past of verbs above*)

EANT, *see* ENT

EAP, EEP

cheap
cheep
clepe
creep
deep
heap
beweep
overleap
adeep
chimneysweep
keep
leap
neap
peep
reap
sheep
outleap
oversleep
bo-peep
estrepe
sleep
steep
sweep
threap
weep
asleep
outsleep
unasleep
chepe
seep
swepe

EAR, EER, ERE, EIR, IER

beer
bier
blear
cere
cheer
clear
dear
deer
drear
ear
sincere
fleer
gear
here
hear
jeer
leer
mere
near
peer
pier
queer
chanticleer
cordelier
engineer
gondolier
hemisphere
mountaineer
mutineer
pamphleteer
ameer
bayadere
caravaneer
circuiteer
electioneer
financier
garreteer
harpooneer
Indianeer
mir
planisphere
reappear
specksioneer
rear
sear
seer
sere
shear
sheer
skeer
smear
sneer
spear
fear
steer
tear
veer
tier
weir
year
adhere
appear
arrear
austere
besmear
chevalier
disappear
fusilier
grenadier
insincere
muleteer
overhear
aërosphere
arear
belvedere
carbineer
crotcheteer
ensphere
fineer
gaselier
heer
madrier
muffineer
sermoneer
tabasheer
brevier
career
cashier
cohere
compeer
endear
inhere
rehear
revere
severe
sphere
uprear
veneer
auctioneer
atmosphere
bandolier
bombardier
brigadier
buccaneer
cannoneer
cavalier
chandelier
chiffonier
domineer
gazetteer
halberdier
interfere
musketeer
overseer
affeer
asmear
canceleer
chimere
cuirossier
fakir
frontier
gonfalonier
indear
meer
pistoleer
putpiteer
souvenir
targeteer

EAR, EER, ERE, EIR, IER—(*Cont.*)

teer	privateer	sonneteer	persevere
Tyr	timbestere	volunteer	carabinier
vizier	underpeer	timoneer	charioteer
pioneer	walleteer	undersphere	*congé d'élire*

EARCH, ERCH, IRCH, URCH

birch	lurch	search	smirch
church	perch		

EARD (*short*), ERD, IRD, URD

bird	sherd	begird	storm-bird
curd	surd	third	verd
heard	word	engird	occurred (*and past tense of verbs ending in* ER *or* RE)
herd	absurd	ungird	
gird	Kurd	ladybird	
love-bird	mocking-bird	sea-bird	
snow-bird	song-bird		

EARD (*long*), EIRD

beard	weird	feared (*and past of verbs ending* EER, EAR, ERE)

EARL, IRL, URL

churl	furl	merle	unfurl
curl	girl	swirl	kerl
earl	hurl	pearl	querl
whirl	uncurl	purl	thurl
burl	impearl	twirl	

EARN, ERN, URN, OURN

burn	erne	turn	stern
churn	inurn	urn	fern
dern	learn	eterne	intern
discern	quern	lucerne	return
concern	spurn	yearn	extern
hern	earn	adjourn	pirn
kerne	tern	astern	taciturn

EARSE, *see* ERCE

EART, *see* ART

EARTH, ERTH, IRTH

birth	dearth	girth	worth
berth	earth	mirth	unearth
firth	*hearth*		

EARTH (*as in* hearth), *see* ARTH

EASE (*hard*), *see* EACE

EASE (*soft*), EESE, EEZE

bees (*and add s to nouns and verbs in* E)
breeze
cheese
drees
ease
freeze
he's
leas
mise
pease
please
overseas
these
trapeze
chevaux-de-frise
friese
heeze
ambergris
antipodes
bise
congeries
syntheses
valise
seize
she's
sneeze
squeeze
tease
wheeze
appease
bawbees
boheas
chemise
presentees
covenantees
feaze
hypotheses
indices
analyses
antitheses
Bolognese
obsequies
rabies
vortices
demise
disease
displease
donees
houris
forseize
heart's ease
journalese
anterides
balize
cerise
parentheses
remise
tweeze

Plurals of words ending in Y (short) are also legitimate rhymes.

EAST, IEST

beast
east
feast
fleeced
least
priest
yeast
artiste
ceased (*and past tense of verbs in* EACE, etc.)

EAST (*as in* breast), *see* EST

EAT (*long*), EET, ETE, EIT

beat
beet
bleat
greit
accrete
bittersweet
cleat
country-seat
facete
judgment-seat
maltreat
preconceit
meat
secrete
meet
mete
neat
peat
pleat
escheat
sheet
sleet
street
cheat
eat
feat
heat
afrete
carte-de-visite
cleet
dead-beat
geat
leat
overeat
receipt
retreat
suite
sweet
teat
treat
wheat
complete
seat
concrete
deceit
defeat
feet
fleet
greet
leet
athlete
cheet
compete
deplete
guerite
lorikeet

EAT (*long*), EET, ETE, EIT—(*Cont.*)

parrakeet	discreet	élite	estreat
vegete	discrete	entreat	repeat
weet	effete	conceit	replete
delete			

EAT (*as in* great), *see* AIT

EAT (*as in* sweat), *see* ET

EATH (*long*)

heath	teeth	unsheath	bequeath
neath	wreath	underneath	sneath
beneath	sheath		

EATH (*short*)

breath	death	saith	Seth

EATHE

inbreathe	ensheathe	enwreathe	sneathe
seethe	teethe	bequeathe	

EAVE, EIVE, IEVE, EVE

beeve	conceive	reive	receive
cleave	deceive	we've	relieve
eave	perceive	achieve	reprieve
eve	greave	aggrieve	disbelieve
grieve	heave	unweave	preconceive
lieve	leave	interweave	deev
reeve	retrieve	breve	Khedive
sleeve	interleave	keeve	naïve
thieve	undeceive	misconceive	recitative
weave	engrieve	reave	sheave
believe	make-believe	seave	steeve
bereave	qui vive	solive	vive

EB, EBB

ebb	web	keb	Seb
cubeb	neb	sub-deb	

ECK

beck	henpeck	peck	speck
check	trek	reck	wreck
cheque	fleck	bewreck	bedeck
deck	neck	spec	kneck

Ect

sect
analect
correct
exsect
interject
porrect
aspect
pandect
bisect
collect
confect
conject
connect
deflect
deject
direct
defect
dissect
detect
traject
dialect
indirect
intersect
adject
annect
disconnect
genuflect
misdirect
prelect
effect
elect
erect
expect
infect
inflect
inject
insect
inspect
introspect
neglect
object (*verb*)
architect
disaffect
intellect
retrospect
affect
arrect
disinfect
indirect
non-elect
resurrect
trisect
perfect (*verb*)
prefect
project
prospect
protect
refect
reflect
reject
respect
select
subject (*verb*)
suspect
circumspect
disrespect
incorrect
recollect
decked
deckt (*and past tense of verbs in* Eck)

Ed, Ead (*short*)

bed
bled
bread
bred
dead
led
pled
read
red
said
stead
thread
tread
wed
zed
dread
fed
fled
head
lead
instead
unread
loggerhead
adread
bespread
deadhead
foresaid
highbred
outspread
redd
thoroughbred
unthread
shed
shred
sled
sped
spread
misled
unsaid
maidenhead
arrowhead
blunderhead
dunderhead
go-head
homebred
overfed
surbed
underbred
woolly-head
abed
ahead
behead
bestead
inbred
o'erspread
gingerbread
trucklebed
bettle-head
breviped
embed
watershed
jolter-head
quadruped
ted
unwed
trundlebed
visited
spirited (*and all preterites and past participles ending in* ed *when the* e *is not silent are possible rhymes*)

Edge

edge
dredge
fledge
hedge
sacrilege
kedge
ledge
pledge

EDGE—(*Cont.*)

sedge	sledge	allege	tedge
cledge	wedge	privilege	unedge

EE, *see* E

EECE, *see* EACE

EECH, *see* EACH

EED, *see* EAD

EEF, IEF

beef	neckerchief	handkerchief	relief
brief	grief	unbelief	bas-relief
chief	leaf	shereef	misbelief
fief	lief	thief	interleaf
feof	sheaf	belief	hief
disbelief	reef	enfeof	

EEK, *see* EAK

EEL, *see* EAL

EEM, *see* EAM

EEN, *see* EAN

EER, *see* EAR

EESE, EEZE, *see* EASE

EET, *see* EAT

EF, *see* EAF

EFT

cleft	heft	theft	unbereft
deft	left	weft	wheft
eft	reft	aleft	bereft

EG, EGG

beg	keg	skeg	philabeg
egg	peg	tegg	unpeg
leg	seg	*nutmeg*	

EGE, *see* EDGE, *also* IDGE

EGM, *see* EM

EIGN, *see* AIN

EIN, *see* AIN

EINT, *see* AINT

EIT, *see* EAT

EL

Astrophel
bechamel
bel
bonnibel
brocatel
caravel
chanterelle
chaumontelle
cockle-shell
cordelle
coronel
crenelle
dameisel
damoiselle
death bell
dentelle
dinner-bell
fricandel
gabelle
horebell
heather-bell
hydromel
immortelle
insbell
intermell
jargonelle
Jezebel
kell
lapel
locustelle
mademoiselle
mongorel
nonpareil
pennoncelle
personnel
petronel
pimpernel
propel
pucelle
refel
sea-shell
snell
tourelle
treille
vielle
zel
bell
belle
cell
dell
dwell
ell
fell
hell
jell
knell
mell
quell
sell
shell
smell
spell
swell
tell
well
yell
befell
compel
dispel
excel
expel
farewell
foretell
gazelle
hotel
impel
pell-mell
rebel (verb)
repel
rondel
asphodel
bagatelle
calomel
caramel
citadel
cockerel
doggerel
infidel
mackerel
muscatel
parallel
philomel
sentinel
undersell
villanelle

ELD

seld
unbeheld
unquelled
upheld
weld
withheld
eld
geld
held
beheld
belled (*and past tense of verbs in* ELL)

ELF

delf
elf
pelf
ourself
self
shelf
myself
itself
thyself
himself
herself
mantel-shelf

ELM, *see* EALM

ELP

help	whelp	skelp	self-help
kelp	yelp		

ELT

belt	felt	pelt	swelt
celt	gelt	smelt	welt
dealt	knelt	spelt	veldt
dwelt	melt	svelte	

ELVE

delve	shelve	twelve	elve
helve			

EM

clem	them	requiem	bediadem
gem	condemn	*theorem*	Bethlehem
hem	contemn	*stratagem*	protem
phlegm	apothegm	anadem	em
stem	diadem	adbominem	"mem"

EME, *see* EAM

EMPT, *see* EAMT

EN

den	wen	oxygen	endogen
fen	when	nitrogen	equestrienne
glen	wren	waterhen	fountain pen
hen	again	aldermen	Parisienne
ken	amen	ben	*regimen*
men	*citizen*	brevipen	*specimen*
pen	*denizen*	cayenne	tragedienne
ten	hydrogen	cyclamen	tren
then			

ENS

lens   cleanse   dens (*and add s to nouns and verbs above*)

ENCE, ENSE

cense	sense	condense	incense
dense	tense	defence	intense
fence	thence	dispense	offence
hence	whence	expense	nescience
pence	commence	immense	pretence

ENCE, ENSE—(*Cont.*)

prepense
propense
suspense
nonsense
abstinence
accidence
affluence
audience
competence
condolence
conference
confidence
confluence
consequence
continence
corpulence
crapulence
deference
difference
diffidence
negligence
diligence
eloquence
eminence
evidence
excellence
exigence
feculence
frankincense
fraudulence
imminence
impotence
impudence
incidence
indigence
indolence
inference
influence
innocence
insolence
opulence
penitence
permanence
pertinence
pestilence
prescience
preference
prevalence
prominence
providence
prurience
recompense
redolence
reference
residence
reverence
sapience
subsidence
truculence
inconvenience
blandiloquence
dissidense
grandiloquence
incompetence
maleficence
salience
supereminence
turbulence
vehemence
violence
beneficence
benevolence
circumference
circumfluence
coincidence
concupiscence
convenience
equivalence
expidence
expedience
experience
impenitence
impertinence
improvidence
incongruence
inexpedience
breviloquence
flocculence
imprevalence
incomprehense
percipience
quantivalence
somnolence
inconsequence
incontinence
indifference
insipience
intelligence
irreverence
magnificence
malevolence
mellifluence
munificence
obedience
omnipotence
omniscience
pre-eminence
resilience
subservience
transilience
disobedience
inexperience
commonsense
fructescence
incoincidence
magniloquence
plenipotence
reticence
succulence

ENCH

bench
blench
clench
drench
bedrench
quench
stench
trench
retrench
tench
wench
wrench
intrench
flench
monkey-wrench
squench

END

bend
blend
end
fend
friend
lend
mend
propend
rend
send
spend
tend
trend
vend
wend
amend

End—(*Cont.*)

append
ascend
attend
befriend
commend
compend
contend
defend
depend
descend
distend
expend
forefend
impend
intend
misspend
obtend
offend
perpend
pretend
portend
transcend
minuend
supend
vilipend
unbend
apprehend
comprehend
condescend
discommend
dividend
re-ascend
recommend
reprehend
reverend
pitch-blende
unfriend
weather-fend
misapprehend
superintend
an-end
amend
forelend
forespend
forewend
gable-end
Godsend
interblend
subtend
upsend
penned (*and past tense of verbs in* En)

Ene, *see* Ean

Enge

Avenge
revenge
Stonehenge

Ength

length
strength

Ense, *see* Ence

Ent

bent
blent
brent
cent
fent
gent
lent
meant
pent
rent
scent
sent
spent
tent
vent
went
absent (verb)
acquent
anent
ascent
assent
attent
augment
besprent
cement
comment (verb)
consent
content
descent
dissent
event
extent
ferment
foment
frequent (verb)
indent
intent
invent
lament
discontent
circumvent
coaugment
malcontent
accent (verb)
detent
forewent
leant
overspent
sprent
stent
unkent
unmeant
underwent
misrepresent
misspent
o'erspent
ostent
present
prevent
relent
repent
resent
torment (verb)
unbent
represent
abstinent
accident
affluent
aliment
ambient
argument

ENT—(*Cont.*)

armament
banishment
battlement
blandishment
chastisement
competent
complement
compliment
condiment
confident
confluent
congruent
consequent
continent
corpulent
decrement
deferent
detriment
different
diffident
diligent
document
effluent
element
eloquent
eminent
esculent
evident
excellent
excrement
measurement
merriment
mollient
monument
muniment
negligent
nourishment
nutriment
occident
opulent
orient
exigent
feculent
filament
firmament
flatulent
fraudulent
fundament
government
gradient
immanent
imminent
implement
impotent
impudent
incident
increment
indigent
indolent
innocent
insolent
instrument
languishment
lenient
ligament
liniment
management
ornament
parliament
pediment
penitent
permanent
pertinent
pestilent
precedent
prescient
president
prevalent
prisonment
prominent
provident
prurient
punishment
ravishment
redolent
regiment
resident
reticent
abandonment
abolishment
accipient
admeasurement
affamishment
affranchisement
babblement
bedevilment
bedizenment
betterment
bewilderment
blazonment
blemishment
botherment
brabblement
cherishment
dazzlement
decipherment
demolishment
development
devilment
diffluent
diminishment
dimplement
disablement
disarmament
disobedient
dispiritment
dissident
distinguishment
embattlement
embitterment
emblazonment
embodiment
empannelment
enablement
encompassment
endeavourment
enfeeblement
enlightenment
envelopment
environment
envisagement
expedient
extinguishment
flacculent
foreanent
fosterment
dissonent
franchisement
garnishment
gracilent
grandiloquent
harassment
ignipotent
imperilment
impoverishment
incipient
incongruent
inexpedient
influent
ingredient
insentient
insipient
inveiglement
lavishment
luculent
magniloquent
obedient
percipient
pesterment
portent
prattlement
premonishment
presentiment
refluent
replenishment
somnolent
thercanent
tremblement

ENT—(*Cont.*)

vaniloquent
vanishment
vanquishment
veriloquent
vinolent
wanderment
wilderment
worriment
reverent
rudiment
sacrament
salient
sapient
sediment
sentient
sentiment
settlement
subsequent
succulent
supplement
tegument
tenement
testament
tournament
transient
truculent
turbulent
vehement
violent
virulent
wonderment
accompaniment
accomplishment
accoutrement
acknowledgment
admonishment
advertisement
aggrandizement
aperient
apportionment
arbitrament
armipotent
astonishment
belligerent
bellipotent
beneficent
benevolent
circumfluent
coincident
concupiscent
constituent
convenient
discouragement
disfigurement
disfranchise-ment
disparagement
divertisement
embarrassment
embellishment
embezzlement
emolient
emolument
encompassment
encouragement
enfranchise-ment
ennoblement
enravishment
entanglement
equivalent
establishment
esurient
experiment
habiliment
impediment
impenitent
impertinent
imprisonment
improvident
incompetent
inconsequent
incontinent
indifferent
integument
intelligent
irreverent
lineament
magnificent
maleficent
malevolent
medicament
mellifluent
misgovernment
mismanagement
munificent
omnipotent
parturient
plenipotent
predicament
pre-eminent
recipient
relinquishment
resilient
subservient
temperament
circumambient
hereditament
impoverishment
inconvenient
pre-establish-ment
re-establishment
supereminent

EP

nep
repp
skep
step
steppe
demirep
"rep"

EPT

crept
kept
pept
sept
slept
wept
accept
adept
except
yclept
overslept
intercept
inept
unkept
leapt
swept
stepped

Er, Err, Ir, Ur, Re

aberr
astir
befur
chirr
concur
confer
defer
incur
infer
occur
per
recur
refer
shirr
amateur
chauffeur
connoisseur
hauteur
blur
burr
cur
err
fir
fur
her
knur
myrrh
purr
sir
slur
spur
stir
whir
aver
bestir
demur
deter
douceur
disinter
inter
prefer
transfer
arbiter
armiger
barrister
canister
chorister
conjurer
cottager
cylinder
dowager
flatterer
forager
foreigner
gardener
grasshopper
harbinger
islander
lavender
loiterer
lucifer
mariner
massacre
messenger
minister
murderer
officer
passenger
pillager
presbyter
prisoner
provender
register
slanderer
sophister
sorcerer
terrier
thunderer
traveler
usurer
villager
victualer
voyager
wagoner
administer
adulterer
artificer
astronomer
astrologer
idolater
interpreter
philosopher
admonisher
adventurer
baluster
bannister
banterer
bargainer
barometer
biographer
blunderer
calender
carpenter
caterer
chronicler
comforter
commoner
coroner
customer
determiner
diameter
disparager
distributer
driveler
enlightener
examiner
forester
forfeiter
gossamer
harvester
hexameter
jabberer
languisher
lavender
lecturer
measurer
milliner
murmurer
nourisher
posturer
perjurer
pesterer
photographer
plasterer
plunderer
polisher
profferer
publisher
punisher
rioter
riveter
roisterer
saunterer
scimiter
sepulchre
sinister
stenographer
sufferer
thermometer
treasurer
trumpeter
vanquisher
venturer
vintager
visiter
wagerer
wanderer
whimperer
widower
worshiper
cheerier
merrier (etc.)
(and comparative of adjectives for other doubtful rhymes)

Ers, Errs, Irs, Urze

furze	refers	errs	stirs (*and add s to nouns and verbs above*)

Erb, Urb

curb	serb	reverb	gerb
herb	verb	*suburb*	perturb
kerb	disturb	superb	

Erce, Erse, Urse, Earse

curse	accurse	diverse	reverse
erse	adverse	imburse	sesterce
hearse	amerce	immerse	subverse
nurse	asperse	inverse	transverse
herse	averse	perverse	traverse
purse	coerce	reimburse	intersperse
terse	converse	*universe*	terce
verse	*commerce*	submerse	burse
worse	disburse	precurse	excurse
abterse	disperse	rehearse	

Erch, *see* Earch

Erd, *see* Eard

Ere, *see* Ear

Erf, Urf

scurf	serf	surf	turf

Erge, Irge, Urge, Ourge

dirge	submerge	immerge	deterge
gurge	scourge	tharematurge	diverge
merge	serge	verge	demurge
purge	surge	converge	berge
emerge	urge		

Erk, Irk, Urk

burke	yerk	quirk	stirk
dirk	kirk	handiwork	Turk
firk	lurk	derk	work
irk	murk	shirk	cirk
jerk	perk	smirk	mirk

Erm, Irm

firm	derm	affirm	infirm
sperm	term	germ	misterm
squirm	worm	confirm	pachyderm

ERN, *see* EARN

ERSE, *see* ERCE

ERST, *see* IRST

ERT, IRT, URT

blurt
cert
curt
dirt
flirt
girt
hurt
pert
shirt
skirt
spurt
ungirt
disconcert
malapert
chert
exsert
extrovert
introvert
squirt
vert
wert
wort
advert
alert
assert
avert
concert (verb)
convert (verb)
desert (verb)
unhurt
inexpert
animadvert
engirt
gurt
preconcert
syrt
dessert
divert
exert
expert (adj.)
inert
sea-girt
insert (verb)
invert
obvert
pervert (verb)
revert
subvert
controvert
intersert
begirt
evert
intervert
retrovert
transvert

ERTH, *see* EARTH

ERVE, URVE

curve
nerve
serve
swerve
conserve
deserve
disserve
observe
preserve
reserve
subserve
incurve
unnerve
verve

ES, ESCE, ESS

bless
cess
chess
cress
dress
address
caress
baroness
covoless
egress
frondesce
jess
quiesce
turgesce
redress
possess
princess
profess
progress (verb)
recess
mayoress
overdress
poetess
prepossess
prioress
sorceress
ambassadress
fesse
guess
less
mess
press
agress
compress (verb)
canoness
deliquesce
evanesce
ingress
obsolesce
regress
confess
prophetess
digress
distress
duress
express
excess
impress
largess
noblesse
obsess
oppress
underdress
proprietress
stress

Es, Esce, Ess—(*Cont.*)

tress	effloresce	repress	coalesce
yes	finesse	success	dispossess
abscess	intermesce	suppress	effervesce
access	opalesce	transgress	*giantess*
assess	transgress	unless	*adulteress*
accresce	depress	acquiesce	nevertheless
conqueress	repossess		

also comfortless, happiness *and any compounds in* Less *and* Ness *in which the accent is not on the penultimate syllable. There are over a thousand of these.*

Ese, *see* Eace *and* Ease

Esh

flesh	mesh	enmesh	afresh
fresh	nesh	thresh	"secesh"
refresh			

Esk, Esque

desk	grotesque	arabesque	picturesque
burlesque	Romanesque		

Est

best	arrest	behest	manifest
blest	invest	detest	acquest
breast	*interest*	obtest	divest
chest	nest	reinvest	ingest
crest	rest	anapest	unbreast
guest	divest	furest	dressed (*and past tense of verbs in* Ess, Esce.)
inquest	suggest	vest	
hest	unblest	bequest	
lest	unrest	digest	
quest	*incest*	protest	answerest
west	infest	*disinterest*	troublest (*and other third person sing. of two syllable verbs*)
wrest	molest	cest	
yest	jest	geste	
zest	pest	attest	
abreast	contest (verb)	congest	
	test	request	

Et, Ette

et	fret	let	pet
bet	get	met	set
debt	jet	net	sweat

ET, ETTE—(*Cont.*)

threat
vet
wet
whet
yet
abet
beget
beset
martinet
minuet
overset
pirouette
summerset
wagonette
aigrette
angelet
annulet
banquet
brochette
castoret
croquette
estafette
formeret
lacunette
Lett
medalet
revet
somerset
vedette
bewet
brunette
cadet
coquet
coquette
curvet
duet
forget
gazette
lunette
piquet
quartet
quintet
regret
rosette
roulette
sestet
serviette
upset
vignette
mignonette
novelette
parapet
rivulet
suffragette
quodlibet
alette
amourette
backset
bassinet
calumet
clarionet
crossett
facette
genet
landaulet
barquette
silhouette
sunset
vergette
alphabet
amulet
anchoret
banneret
baronet
bayonet
cabinet
canzonette
cigarette
coronet
coverlet
epaulette
epithet
etiquette
falconette
floweret
leveret
marionette
marmoset
minaret
omelette
parroquet
sarcenet
violet
allumette
anisette
baguet
benet
carcaret
corvette
egrette
flet
globulet
lorgnette
planchette
soubrette
tabouret
zonulet
tourniquet

ETCH

etch
fetch
vetch
retch
sketch
outstretch
stretch
wretch

ETE, *see* EAT

EVE, *see* EAVE

EUD, *see* UDE, *and also* OOD *for imperfect rhymes*

EUM, *see* OOM

EW, *see* OO *and* UE

Note: the vowel in Ew is pronounced sometimes as a diphthong (eu) and sometimes with the single sound of oo. The two sounds are so nearly alike that they are often rhymed; yet a precise speaker or writer should be conscious of the distinction.

Ex, Ecks

sex	ex	circumflex	henpecks
annex	specs	reflex	checks (*and*
complex	*apex*	kex	*add s to*
index	convex	vex	*nouns and*
vortex	perplex	codex	*verbs in* Eck)

Ext

next	text	annexed (*and past of verbs in* Ex)
vext	pretext	

Ey, *see* Ay

Ez

fez	says	Cortez	"oyez"

I, *see* Y (*long*)

Ib

bib	fib	o'ersib	sib
crib	glib	nib	quib
drib	jib	rib	gib
squib			

Ibe

bribe	interscribe	prescribe	subscribe
gibe	ascribe	superscribe	transcribe
kibe	describe	gybe	circumscribe
scribe	imbibe	proscribe	diatribe
tribe	inscribe		

Ic, Ick

brick	arithmetic	wick	*choleric*
chick	bailiwick	politic	*empiric*
click	flick	*turmeric*	fiddlestick
crick	rick	impolitic	heretic
lick	sic	benedick	lunatic
candlestick	sick	kinnikinic	rhetoric
nick	slick	*picnic*	archbishopric
pick	thick	arsenic	impolitic
prick	kick	bishopric	*chivalric*
quick	tic	stick	snick
plethoric	tick	catholic	stick
splenetic	trick		

Ics, *see* Ix

ICE (*short*), *see* IS

ICE (*long*), ISE (*hard*)

bice	gneiss	entice	bespice
dice	sice	paradise	concise
ice	rice	gnice	precise
mice	slice	syce	sacrifice
nice	spice	trice	lice
price	splice	twice	thrice
device	thrice	vice	vise
suffice	tice	advice	

ICH, *see* ITCH

ICK, *see* IC

ICKS, *see* IX

ICT, ICKED

pict	addict (verb)	afflict	derelict
convict (verb)	conflict (verb)	constrict	maladict
depict	evict	inflict	licked (*and past of verbs in* ICK)
predict	relict	restrict	
benedict	contradict	interdict	
strict	astrict		

ID

bid	mid	forbid	outdid
brid	quid	outbid	skid
chid	rid	underbid	pyramid
cid	slid	fordid	fid
did	squid	katydid	invalid
hid	thrid	scrid	overdid
"grid"	amid	overbid	unbid
kid	bestrid	cid	undid
lid	*eyelid*	gid	

IDE, IED

bide	confide	Whitsuntide	eyed
gride	divide	alongside	guide
nide	misguide	hyde	pride
side	provide	lapicide	slide
tide	Christmastide	outride	wide
arride	eventide	riverside	aside
backslide	matricide	uxoricide	beside
betide	stillicide	bride	*broadside*

IDE, IED—(*Cont.*)

decide
elide
outside
reside
decide
fratricide
parricide
subdivide
infanticide
barmecide
hillside
liberticide
parenticide
sororicide
vaticide
chide
herpicide
glide
hide
ride
stride
abide
astride
bestride
collide
deride
inside
preside
subside
Eastertide
homicide
regicide
suicide
tyrannicide
foreside
insecticide
noontide
patricide
unbetide
vermicide
vulpicide
cried (*and past of verbs in* Y (E), IGH, IE)

IDES

ides
besides
tides (*and add s to nouns and verbs above*)

IDGE

bridge
fidge
sacrilege
midge
ridge
enridge
abridge
privilege
nidge

See also AGE (*short*)

IDST

amidst
bidst
chidst
didst
hidst
kidst
midst
ridst
slidst
overbidst
bestridst
forbidst
outbidst
underbidst

IE, *see* Y

IEF, *see* EEF

IEGE

liege
besiege
siege
assiege
prestige

IELD, *see* EALD

IEN, *see* EAN

IEND, *see* EAND *and* END

IER, *see* EAR

IERCE

fierce
pierce
impierce
tierce
transpierce

IES, *see* IS *and* ISE

IEST, *see* EAST

IEVE, *see* EAVE

IF, IFF, YPH

cliff	glyph	tiff	hieroglyph
if	sniff	griff	hippogriff
skiff	stiff	whiff	miff

IFE

fife	life	*fishwife*	strife
knife	rife	*goodwife*	wife

IFT

drift	snowdrift	sniffed	whiffed
gift	shift	uplift	adrift
lift	shrift	thrift	miffed
rift	sift	tiffed	spindrift

IG

big	rig	snig	twig
dig	jig	whirligig	whig
fig	pig	thingumajig	wig
gig	prig	sprig	brig
grig	rig	swig	trig
periwig	thimblerig		

IGE

oblige	tige

IGH, *see* Y (*long*)

IGHT, *see* ITE

IGUE, *see* EAGUE

IKE

dike	fyke	mislike	belike
like	shrike	"bike"	unlike
pike	spike	tyke	*oblique*
dislike	strike	alike	tike

IL, ILL

bill	drill	frill	grille
brill	dill	gill	hill
chill	fill	grill	fulfill

IL, ILL—(*Cont.*)

quadrille	quill	upfill	downhill
uphill	rill	volatile	freewill
domicile	shrill	squill	instil
bestill	sill	still	until
kiln	skill	swill	daffodil
'twill	spill	thill	befrill
vill	stockstill	thrill	cill
ill	codicil	till	jill
kill	watermill	trill	spadille
mill	chrysophyll	will	*versatile*
pill	enthrill	distil	whippoorwill
nil	prill		

ILD (*short*), ILLED

build	gild	billed (*and past of verbs in* ILL)
begild	guild	

ILD (*long*), ILED

aisled	child	guiled	filed (*and past of verbs in* ILE)
mild	styled	wild	

ILE

aisle	style	rile	juvenile
bryle	taille	smile	peristyle
erstwhile	tile	stile	versatile
"spile"	vile	domicile (verb)	anglophile, etc.
enisle	erewhile	pentastyle	bibliophile
meanwhile	exile	reconcile	wile
vibratile	*gentile*	isle	awhile
ensile	pensile	mile	camomile
resile	while	beguile	crocodile
bile	revile	compile	diastyle
chyle	aquatile	defile	infantile
file	pile	edile	mercantile
guile			

ILK

bilk	silk	ilk	milk

ILM

bilm	film

ILT

built	guilt	wilt	jilt
begilt	hilt	unspilt	kilt

ILT—(*Cont.*)

milt	lilt	tilt	unbuilt
quilt	spilt	twilt	silt
atilt	stilt		

ILTH

bilth	illth	spilth	tilth
filth			

IM

brim	betrim	interim	whim
dim	lym	seraphim	bedim
glim	limb	enlimn	*pilgrim*
grim	limn	shim	pseudonym
him	prim	swim	synonym
hymn	rim	trim	"gym"
cherubim	skim	vim	zimb
sanhedrim	slim	Jim	

IME

chime	lime	thyme	pantomime
chyme	mime	time	I'm
climb	prime	begrime	berhyme
clime	rhyme	sublime	*meantime*
crime	rime	*sometime*	beslime
dime	maritime	*aforetime*	upclimb
aftertime	slime	overtime	paradigm
grime			

IMES

betimes	ofttimes	sometimes	chimes (*and add s to nouns and verbs above*)

IMP

crimp	imp	limp	"simp"
gimp	jimp	pimp	tymp
shrimp	primp	skrimp	blimp

IMPSE

glimpse	crimps (*and add s to nouns and verbs above*)

IN, INN, INE (*short*)

bin
chin
din
djinn
fin
gin
glynn
grin
Berlin
maudlin
wherein
agrin
baudekin
bulletin
gelatine
saccharine
cannakin
capuchin
culverin
discipline
feminine
finickin
harlequin
peregrine
in
inn
kin
lin
pin
shin
sin
skin
chagrin
therein
within
alizarine
bearskin
cherubin
francolin
gyn
tourmalin
heroine
jacobin
javelin
jessamine
kilderkin
libertine
mandarin
ravelin
spin
thin
tin
twin
whin
win
akin
begin
herein
unpin
baldachin
baldaquin
been
chinkapin
genuine
jinn
opaline
whin
mandolin
mannikin
masculine
minikin
origin
paladin
palanquin
violin
widdershin

INCE

mince
prince
convince
quince
rinse
evince
since
wince
unprince
chintz

INCH

cinch
finch
inch
clinch
winch
flinch
chinch
bepinch
pinch
linch
lynch

INCT, INKED

tinct
extinct
succinct
depinct
instinct
indistinct
distinct
precinct
procinct
blinked (*and past of verbs in* INK)

IND (*short*), **INNED**

tind
rescind
wind
disciplined
tamarind
abscind
chinned (*and past of verbs in* IN)

IND (*long*), INED

bind
grind
mind
behind
remind
gavelkind
humankind
blind
hind
rind
mankind
unkind
womankind
inbind
find
kind
wind
purblind
unwind
crined
rynd
dined (*and past of verbs in* INE)

INE (*French*), *see* EAN

INE (*long*)

brine
chine
dine
eyne
fine
kine
line
mine
nine
pine
shine
sign
sine
shrine
swine
syne
thine
trine
twine
vine
whine
crystalline
interline
palatine
saturnine
underline
wine
assign
calcine
canine
carbine
carmine
combine
compline
condign
confine
consign
decline
define
design
divine
enshrine
feline
entwine
incline
indign
moonshine
disincline
intertwine
porcupine
superfine
undermine
"opine"
outline
outshine
recline
refine
repine
saline
sunshine
supine
woodbine
untwine
alkaline
aquiline
asinine
brigantine
byzantine
columbine
celandine
concubine
coralline
countermine
eglantine
leonine
saccharine (adj.)
turpentine
uterine
valentine
adulterine
almandine
anserine
barkantine
caballine
countersign
ensign
hyaline
leonine
matutine
propine
resupine
spine
trephine
vespertine
agatine
aniline
appenine
benign
capitoline
dessiatine
fescennine
infantine
libertine
opaline
quarantine
serpentine
spline
ursuline
viperine
incarnadine
align
anonyne
ashine
bine
carabine
dyne
Florentine
langsyne
malign
pavonine
resign
sibylline
sycamine
vaticine
vuturine

ING

bring
cling
ding
fling
ging
king
ling
ring
sing
chitterling
underling
sting
scatterling (*and other nouns with German diminutive*)
enring
spring
string
swing
thing
wing
wring
unsling
unstring
ping
sling
murmuring
offering
scaffolding
breakfasting
christening
coloring
reasoning
scattering
seasoning
uttering
covering
wondering (*and any other participles ending in* ING *with the accent on the antepenultimate*).
entering
evening
gardening
gathering
issuing
chambering
muttering
opening
reckoning
smoldering
westering

INGE

cringe
dinge
fringe
hinge
singe
syringe
mindge
springe
stinge
swinge
tinge
twinge
unhinge
scringe
astringe
attinge
befringe
impinge
infringe
constringe
perstringe

INK

blink
brink
chink
drink
rink
kink
wink
link
mink
pink
ink
shrink
sink
zinc
skink
slink
stink
think
tink
twink
bethink
enlink
interlink
bobolink
forethink
cinque
jink
hoodwink
appropinque
trink
"gink"
tiddledewink

INT (*short*)

dint
flint
hint
mint
reprint
septuagint
lint
sprint
print
quint
splint
squint
calamint
footprint
mezzotint
vint
stint
tint
asquint
imprint
peppermint
glint
misprint
"soda mint"

INT (*long*)

pint
ahint (*Scotch*)

INTH

plinth	colocynth	labyrinth	terebinth
hyacinth			

INX, INKS

lynx	minx	*larynx*	blinks (*and add s to nouns and verbs in* INK)

IP

chip	whip	jip	outstrip
clip	atrip	trip	unrip
dip	quip	pip	battleship
drip	rip	grippe	hip
flip	scrip	kip	tip
gip	shrip	ship	nip
grip	sip	equip	dog-whip
gyp	skip	*horsewhip*	hyp
strip	slip	inship	outstrip
lip	snip	landslip	

fellowship, horsemanship (*and all words with prefix* SHIP *with accent on antepenultimate*).

IPE

gripe	electrotype	*tintype*	antitype
pipe	tripe	guttersnipe	linotype
ripe	type	stipe	stereotype
snipe	wipe	*windpipe*	daguerreotype
stripe	*bagpipe*	unripe	kipe
monotype	*hornpipe*	archetype	swipe
autotype	prototype		

IPSE, IPS

eclipse	ellipse	apocalypse	chips (*and add s to nouns and verbs in* IP)

IQUE, *see* EAK

IR, *see* ER

IRCH, *see* EARCH

IRD, *see* EARD

IRE

briar
buyer
byre
choir
crier
dire
drier
dyer
fire
flier
friar
gyre
hire
higher
ire
liar
lyre
mire
nigher
require
sapphire
suspire
untier
beautifier
deifier
falsifier
spitfirc
applier
complier
plyer
prior
pryer
pyre
quire
sigher
shire
shyer
sire
slyer
skier
spire
squire
tire
trier
tyre
wire
acquire
admire
respire
satire
transpire
wildfire
certifier
dignifier
afire
swire
clarifier
decryer
aspire
attire
bemire
bonfire
conspire
defier
denier
desire
empire
entire
esquire
expire
grandsire
inspire
inquire
perspire
quagmire
relier
replier
retire
supplier
umpire
amplifier
crucifier
edifier
enquire
vire
classifier
exemplifier
eyer
lammergeier
mystifier
"skyer"
spyer
fortifier
mortifier
gratifier
glorifier
horrifier
justifier
magnifier
modifier
stupefier
verifier
indemnifier
indentifier
liquefier
occupier
"speechifier"
trior
fructifier
qualifier
multiplier
pacifier
petrifier
prophesier
purifier
putrefier
terrifier
villifier
intensifier
mystifier
revivifier
spryer
versifier
mollifier
ratifier
rectifier
sanctifier
satisfier
scarifier
simplifier
specifier
testifier
vivifier

IRGE, *see* ERGE

IRK, *see* ERK

IRL, *see* EARL

IRM, *see* ERM

IRP, *see* URP

IRST, ERST, URST

burst	durst	becursed (t)	abstersed
curst	erst	thirst	accurst
cursed (*and past of verbs in* ERCE)	first	versed	amerced
	hurst	worst	athirst

IRT, *see* ERT

IRTH, *see* EARTH

IS (*soft*), IZ

biz	viz	whiz	quiz
fizz	his	befrizz	friz
'tis	is	phiz	

Also plurals of nouns in Y (*short*), as possible rhymes. There are several thousand of these, but a working list will be found under Y.

IS, ISS, ICE (*hard*)

hiss	dehisce	dentifrice	*anabasis*
kiss	fortalice	edifice	analysis
miss	"siss"	emphasis	antithesis
spiss	y-wis	generis	aphæresis
this	"bis"	genesis	diæresis
wis	bliss	metastasis	hypostasis
abyss	*armistice*	necropolis	hypothesis
amiss	artifice	clematis	metathesis
dismiss	interstice	dialysis	paralysis
premiss	liquorice	nemesis	*apotheosis*
remiss	avarice	verdigris	abiogenesis
metabasis	benefice	orifice	cuisse
metropolis	chrysalis	precipice	diathesis
parenthesis	cicatrice	prejudice	*periphrasis*
metamorphosis	cockatrice	synthesis	vis
cropolis	cowardice		

ISE (*hard*), *see* ICE

ISE (*soft*) IZE

ayes	prize	comprise	excise
buys (*and add s to verbs and nouns in* Y (*long*))	rise	demise	incise
	size	despise	*likewise*
	wise	devise	mainprise
	advise	disguise	misprise
guize	allies	emprise	reprise

ISE (*soft*) IZE—*Cont.*)

revise
eulogize
surmise
surprise
unwise
uprise
advertise
agonize
catechize
cauterize
centralize
certifies
christianize
circumcise
civilize
clarifies
compromise
colonize
criticize
crystallize
dogmatize
egotize
emphasize
enterprise
equalize
exercise
exorcize
fertilize
formalize
fossilize
fraternize
apprise
apprize
arise
assize
avise
baptize
capsize
chastise
idolize
legalize
localize
manumise
merchandise
minimize
organize
otherwise
patronize
alkalize
anglicize
authorize
bastardize
brutalize
canonize
improvise
magnetize
memorize
mesmerize
mobilize
oxidize
pauperize
pluralize
galvanize
gluttonize
gormandize
harmonize
humanize
hypnotize
jeopardize
latinize
mercerize
methodize
modernize
moralize
neutralize
ostracize
penalize
pyetize
polarize
presurmise
pulverize
philosophize
realize
rebaptize
recognize
rhapsodize
satirize
scandalize
scrutinize
signalize
solemnize
specialize
sterilize
stigmatize
naturalize
popularize
sanctuarize
singularize
systematize
ventriloquize
anathematize
particularize
improvise
summarize
supervise
syllogize
symbolize
sympathize
nationalize
synchronize
tantalize
temporize
tranquillize
tyrannize
utilize
victimize
villanize
vocalize
vulcanize
vulgarize
weatherwise
allegorize
analogize
antagonize
anatomize
apologize
apostatize
astrologize
phlebotomize
secularize
solidifies
systematize
visualize
epigrammatize
revolutionize
astronomize
capitalize
characterize
contrariwise
demoralize
deodorize
desilverize
economize
epitomize
eternalize
evangelize
extermorize
familiarize
generalize
geologize
geometrize
idealize
idolatrize
immortalize
italicize
macadamize
materialize
monopolize
plagiarize
rationalize
sensualize
soliloquize
synonymize
volatilize
municipalize
spiritualize
internationalize

Ish

cuish
dish
fish
pish
wish
womanish
empoverish
swish
dowdyish
ogreish
unwish
anguish
cleverish
devilish
feverish
vaporish
forewish
babyish
kittenish
Quakerish
gibberish
heathenish
interwish
licorice
willowish
yellowish
slish
bitterish
mammonish
vizenish
squish

Isk

bisque
brisk
disc
odalisque
frisk
risk
whisk
tamarisk
fisc
asterisk
basilisk
obelisk
bisk
fisk

Ism, Ysm

chrism
prism
schism
altruism
atheism
anarchism
aneurism
Anglicism
aphorism
archaism
barbarism
Calvinism
cataclysm
catechism
criticism
Darwinism
despotism
egoism
egotism
euphemism
euphuism
exorcism
Gallicism
libertinism
patriotism
polytheism
radicalism
unionism
Armenianism
imperialism
Presbyterianism
absolutism
achromatism
agonism
alienism
Aromism
asterism
atomism
boobyism
centralism
communism
demoniacism
dogmatism
emotionalism
etherealism
exoticism
Hebraism
Hellenism
heroism
hibernism
hypnotism
mechanism
Ibsenism (etc)
Judaism
laconism
Latinism
magnetism
mesmerism
Methodism
modernism
monarchism
Mormonism
mysticism
occultism
optimism
organism
ostracism
paganism
pantheism
paroxysm
parallelism
plagiarism
Protestantism
ritualism
Wesleyanism
Malthusianism
Congregationalism
academism
actinism
agariarism
anatomism
asceticism
astigmatism
biblicism
brutalism
chloralism
cretinism
demonism
dualism
equestrianism
etherism
exquisitism
priapism
pyrrhonism
quietism
realism
rheumatism
syllogism
sabbatism
scepticism
socialism
solecism
stoicism
synchronism
tritheism
vandalism

ISM, YSM—(*Cont.*)

vulgarism
witticism
agnosticism
Catholicism
conservatism
empiricism
epicurism
evangelism
fanaticism
liberalism
paralogism
polyphonism
Puritanism
Shavianism
Americanism
colloquialism
Orientalism
abolitionism
accidentalism
æstheticism
alcoholism
antiquarianism
asteism
atavism
bogeyism
cabalism
classicism
cynicism
devilism
eclecticism
esotericism
euphonism
fanaticism
feticism
formalism
galvanism
individualism
journalism
loyalism
materialism
moralism
neologism
peanism
philosophism
platonism
proverbialism
religionism
puppyism
royalism
satanism
scoundrelism
somnolism
terrarism
unionism
verbalism
feudalism
fossilism
humanism
intellectualism
literalism
lyricism
metacism
mativism
nominalism
pedantism
physicism
pragmatism
provincialism
pythonism
revivalism
ruffianism
savagism
sensualism
subtilism
totemism
vampirism
vitalism
Yankeeism
fogeyism
frivolism
idiotism
italicism
localism
mannerism
monasticism
naturalism
pauperism
peonism
pietism
prelatism
pugilism
rationalism
romanticism
ruralism
sciolism
sentimentalism
syncretism
tribalism
ventriloquism
vocalism
zanyism

ISP

crisp
encrisp
whisp
lisp
wisp

IST, ISSED, YST

cist
cyst
fist
gist
grist
hissed (*and past of verbs in* IS *hard*)
hist
list
mist
twist
whist
wist
absist
dramatist
egoist
ecorcist
formalist
herbalist
idolist
entravist
glist
triste
accompanist
agamist
allopathist
apothist
apologist
agist
assist
consist
desist
exist
insist
persist
resist
subsist
untwist
alchemist
amethyst
amorist
anarchist
dualist

IST, ISSED, YST—(*Cont.*)

egotist
fabulist
Hebraist
humanist
atravist
enlist
schist
tryst
Æolist
agonist
animist
aphorist
arabalist
annalist
aorist
atheist
bicyclist
bigamist
botanist
cabalist
Calvinist
casuist
catechist
coexist
colonist
colorist
dogmatist
duelist
eucharist
fatalist
Hellenist
humorist
bemist
frist
sist
absolutist
aërologist
allegorist
antipathist
apiarist
balladist
biblicist
cabalist
circumlocu-
tionist
colonist
cremationist
despotist
equilibrist
eulogist
fictionist
fossilist
illusionist
journalist
lapidist
Latinist
loyalist
medalist
metalist
Methodist
millenist
moralist
motorist
novelist
oculist
optimist
organist
pessimist
pianist
pluralist
pre-exist
pugilist
realist
rhapsodist
satirist
schematist
entomologist
genealogist
materialist
nationalist
physiognomist
rationalist
biologist
canonist
classicist
communist
dactylist
destinist
essayist
euphirist
formalist
harmonist
intertwist
sciolist
suffragist
symmetrist
syncopist
theorist
vocalist
votarist
academist
acolothist
analogist
antomist
chirographist
chronologist
diplomatist
economist
emblematist
enigmatist
epitomist
eternalist
evangelist
externalist
geologist
idealist
metallurgist
epigrammatist
imperialist
martyrologist
mineralogist
physiologist
religionist
devotionalist
botanist
choralist
colloquist
contortionist
demonist
elegist
ethicist
feudalist
fossilist
hyperbolist
scientist
misogamist
misogynist
monogamist
monopolist
mythologist
naturalist
ontologist
philologist
phlebotomist
phrenologist
polygamist
ritualist
sensualist
separatist
sexualist
socialist
tautologist
theologist
theomachist
tobacconist
ventriloquist
anagrammatist
anti-socialist
etymologist
malthusianist
memorialist
opinionist
protectionist
spiritualist
meteorologist

It, Ite (*short*)

bit
bitt
chit
fitt
demit
fit
flit
grit
hit
kit
knit
lit
smit
spit
split
frit
permit
sprit
refit
twit
whit
wit
writ
acquit
outsit
cit
outwit
misfit
favorite
pewit
tit
remit
submit
titbit
tomtit
transmit
nit
pit
quit
sit
skit
slit
counterfeit
infinite
intromit
opposite
pretermit
admit
befit
bowsprit
commit
emit
omit
intermit
Jesuit
perquisite
recommit
indefinite
unfit
apposite
benefit
definite
exquisite
hypocrite
plebiscite
manumit
preterite
requisite
prerequisite

Itch, Ich

bitch
ditch
fitch
flitch
hitch
bewitch
enrich
itch
lych
niche
pitch
rich
hemstitch
chich
stitch
switch
twitch
which
witch
inditch
miche
quitch
scritch

Ite (*long*), **Ight**

bite
bight
blight
bright
cite
dight
fight
flight
fright
height
hight
kite
knight
light
mite
might
night
pight
plight
quite
right
rite
sight
site
sleight
slight
smite
spite
sprite
tight
trite
white
wight
wright
write
accite
affright
alight
aright
bedight
benight
contrite
delight
despite
downright
enlight
excite
foresight
ignite
incite
indict
indite
insight
invite
midnight
moonlight
outright
polite
recite
requite

ITE (*long*), IGHT—(*Cont.*)

sunlight
twilight
unite
upright
aconite
acolyte
anchorite
appetite
bedlamite
bipartite
Carmelite
chrysolite
cœnobite
disunite
dynamite
eremite
expedite
impolite
midshipmite
neophyte
overnight
oversight
parasite
proselyte
recondite
reunite
satellite
second-sight
stalactite
stalagmite
sybarite
troglodyte
underwrite
yesternight
archimandrite
cosmopolite
hermaphrodite
theodolite
actinodite
aërolite
aluminite
angelite
aright
anthracite
behight
beknight
blatherskite
copyright
crystallite
daylight
dolomite
ebonite
electrolyte
entomolite
enwrite
erudite
forthright
good-night
grapholite
ichnolite
mammonite
meteorite
overdight
plebiscite
sideralite
starlight
tonight
toxophilite
tripartite
undight
unright
unsight
malachite
vulcanite
zoölite
zoöphyte
unwrite

ITH, YTH

acrolith
aërolith
lith
monolith
palæolith
frith
kith
myth
pith
sith
smith
with
withe
forthwith
herewith
therewith
wherewith

ITHE

blithe
hithe
lithe
scythe
tithe
writhe
withe

IVE (*long*), YVE

dive
drive
five
gyve
hive
live
rive
shive
I've
shrive
strive
thrive
wive
alive
arrive
beehive
connive
contrive
deprive
derive
revive
survive
overdrive
devive
skive
undive

IVE (*short*)

give
live
sieve
forgive
misgive
outlive
ablative
causative

IVE (*short*)—(*Cont.*)

curative
formative
fugitive
genitive
lambative
laxative
lenitive
lucrative
narrative
negative
nutritive
positive
primitive
privative
punitive
purgative
putative
relative
sanative
semblative
sensitive
substantive
talkative
tentative
vocative
abdicative
accusative
acquisitive
affirmative
alterative
alternative
appellative
applicative
cogitative
comparative
copulative
consecutive
conservative
contemplative
contributive
correlative
declarative
definitive
demonstrative
deprecative
derivative
derogative
desiccative
diminutive
distributive
emanative
executive
explicative
figurative
generative
illustrative
imitative
imperative
inchoative
indicative
infinitive
inquisitive
intuitive
legislative
meditative
operative
palliative
preparative
prerogative
preservative
procreative
provocative
recitative
recreative
reparative
restorative
retributive
speculative
superlative
accumulative
administrative
argumentative
authoritative
commemora-
tive
communicative
co-operative
corroborative
deliberative
determinative
discriminative
eradicative
illuminative
imaginative
inoperative
insinuative
interrogative
justificative
remunerative
representative
significative
opinionative
ratiocinative
overlive
admonitive
amative
coercitive
combative
compellative
compensative
competitive
complimenta-
tive
compulsative
confirmative
dispensative
disputative
exclamative
expletive
impedetive
imputative
incarnative
incrossative
insensitive
intensative
laudative
nominative
premonitive
prohibitive
pulsative
quantitive
reformative
sedative
siccative
transitive
vibrative

IX, ICS, ICKS

bricks (*and add s to nouns and verbs in* IC)
fix
mix
nix
pyx
six
styx
admix
affix
matrix
prefix
prolix
transfix
unfix
cicatrix
commix
inheritrix
crucifix
intermix
sardonyx
executrix

O, Ow, Eau, Oe

beau
boh
bow
blow
co
crow
doe
dough
floe
flow
foe
fro
glow
go
grow
ho
hoe
know
lo
low
mow
no
oh
O
owe
pro
roe
row
sew
shew
show
sloe
slow
snow
so
sow
stow
strow
though
throe
throw
toe
tow
trow
woe
ago
although
arow
banjo
below
bestow
bureau
chapeau
château
cocoa
depot
forego
foreknow
foreshow
heigh-ho
hello
outgo
outgrow
plateau
rondeau
soho
allegro
apropos
buffalo
calico
cameo
comme il faut
domino
embryo
folio
furbelow
indigo
mistletoe
nuncio
oleo
overflow
overgrow
overthrow
portico
portmanteau
ratio
undergo
vertigo
adagio
imbroglio
incognito
intaglio
magnifico
malapropos
mustachio
papilio
pistachio
punctilio
seraglio
braggadocio
duodecimo
internuncio
generalissimo
in statu quo
quid pro quo
aglow
alow
archipelago
bateau
besnow
"bo"
bravissimo
bungalow
tremolo
cachalot
canivaux
de trop
do
eau
embow
escrow
fortissimo
haricot
impresario
indigo
trousseau
oboe
nobo
morceau
oratorio
outflow
overstrow
pianissimo
portfolio
rainbow
rondeau
sabot
studio
tableau
ultimo
undertow
upthrow

Obe

conglobe
disrobe
enrobe
globe
Job
lobe
probe
robe

OACH

broach
brooch
encroach
abroach
loach
poach
roach
approach
encroach
reproach

OAD, ODE, OWED

bode
code
goad
roed
strode
toad
toed
woad
abode
bestrode
commode
hoed
load
mode
rode
corrode
erode
explode
forebode
unload
à la mode
dominoed
node
ode
road
episode
folioed
incommode
overload
porticoed
portmanteau'd
mustachio'd
snowed (*and past of verbs in* OW)
antipode
arrode
discommode
lode
lycopode
pigeon-toed
unowed

OAF

loaf
oaf
sauf
goaf

OAK, OKE

bloke
broke
choke
cloak
coke
croak
folk
joke
moke
oak
poke
sloke
smoke
soak
spoke
stoke
stroke
toque
woke
yoke
yolk
awoke
bespoke
besmoke
convoke
invoke
provoke
revoke
unyoke
artichoke
equivoke
gentlefolk
masterstroke
asoak
cloke
coak
counterstroke
evoke
outbroke
poak
"toke"
unbroke

OAKS, OKES, OAX

hoax
coax
oaks (*and add s to nouns and verbs in* OAK, OKE)

OAL, OLE, OL, OLL, OUL, OWL

bole
bowl
coal
dole
droll
foal
goal
hole
jole
knoll
mole
pole
poll
role
roll
scroll
shoal
sole
soul
stole
stroll
thole
toll
troll

OAL, OLE, OL, OLL, OUL, OWL—(*Cont.*)

vole
whole
cajole
comptrol
condole
console
control
creole
enroll
parole
patrol
pistole
unroll
aureole
capriole
caracole
girandole
girasole
rantipole
bacarolle
bibliopole
boll
camisole
carambole
cole
enbowl
foliole
fumarole
furole
fusarole
ghole
gloriole
inscroll
koll
oriole
pinole
rigmarole
seghol
unwhole
uproll
virole

OAM, OME

clomb
comb
dome
foam
holme
home
loam
mome
roam
tome
aërodome
catacomb
currycomb
harvest-home
hippodrome
palindrome
afoam
aplome
befoam
brome
chrome
endome
gastronome
gloam
gnome
heliochrome
holm
metronome
monochrome
ohm
polychrome
"pome"
sloam
aërodrome
"no'm"

OAN, ONE

bone
blown
cone
crone
drone
flown
groan
grown
hone
known
moan
own
prone
roan
sewn
shewn
shown
sown
stone
tone
throne
thrown
zone
alone
atone
bemoan
depone
dethrone
disown
enthrone
intone
postpone
unknown
unsewn
unsown
unthrone
antepone
chaperone
cornerstone
grindlestone
gramophone
knucklebone
monotone
telephone
undertone
backbone
baritone
begroan
bestrown
cicerone
condone
dispone
eau-de-cologne
electrophone
enzone
flagstone
interpone
impone
lirocone
lodestone
microphone
millstone
mown
morone
overthrown
pone
propone
saxophone

OAP, *see* OPE

Oar, Ore, *see also* **Or**

blore
boar
bore
core
corps
door
floor
fore
four
gore
hoar
lore
more
nore
oar
o'er
ore
pore
pour
roar
score
shore
snore
soar
sore
splore
store
swore
tore
whore
wore
yore
adore
afore
ashore
before
claymore
deplore
encore
explore
forbore
forswore
ignore
implore
restore
abhor
battledore
blackamoor
commodore
evermore
furthermore
hellebore
heretofore
matadore
sycamore
troubadour
albacore
chore
crore
folklore
footsore
frore
galore
heartsore
outpour
outroar
outsoar
pinafore
sagamore
semaphore
sophomore
stevedore
Terpsichore

also possible rhymes in Ower (2-syllables)

Oard, Ored, Ord (*long*)

board
floored (*and past tense of verbs in* Oar)
fiord
gourd
hoard
horde
sword
toward
aboard
afford
untoward

Oarse, *see* **Orce**

Oast, Ost (*long*)

boast
coast
ghost
host
most
post
roast
toast
almost
hindermost
innermost
lowermost
nethermost
outermost
undermost
uppermost
uttermost
aftermost
riposte
dosed (*and past of verbs in* Ose *sharp*)

Oat, Ote

bloat
boat
coat
cote
dote
float
goat
gloat
groat
outvote
promote
remote
anecdote
antidote
asymptote
slote
lote
moat
mote
note
oat
quote
rote
smote

OAT, OTE—(*Cont.*)

stoat	troat	connote	overcoat
petticoat	throat	denote	scoat
table d'hôte	tote	devote	shote
afternote	vote	misquote	sloat
bedote	wrote	commote	underwrote
bequote	afloat	*footnote*	unsmote
capote			

OATH, OTH (*long*)

both	oath	quoth	*troth*
growth	loth	sloth	*betroth*
loath			

OATHE, OTHE

clothe	loathe	betrothe

OAX, *see* OAKS

OB

bob	cabob	nob	athrob
cob	job	quab	*hobnob*
fob	lob	rob	*nabob*
gob	knob	sob	thingumbob
hob	mob	snob	athrob
blob			

OBE

globe	probe	conglobe	enrobe
lobe	robe	disrobe	

OCK

block	lock	laughing-stock	drock
brock	lough	stumbling-	*forelock*
cock	mock	block	half-cock
clock	pock	weathercock	interlock
crock	rock	amok	laverock
dock	shock	baroque	lok
flock	smock	belock	ploc
frock	sock	bemock	roc
hock	stock	billicock	soc
hough	*padlock*	bock	unfrock
knock	*pibroch*	chock	unlock
loch	hollyhock	*deadlock*	

OCKS, *see* OX

Oct, Ocked

concoct	decoct	recoct	blocked (*and past of verbs in* Ock)

Od

cod	pod	tod	goldenrod
clod	prod	trod	lycopod
god	quad	wad	platypod (etc.)
hod	quod	untrod	slipshod
nod	rod	demigod	squad
odd	shod	begod	ungod
plod	sod	dry-shod	unshod

Ode, *see* Oad

Odge

hodge	unlodge	lodge	dislodge
hodge-podge	bodge	podge	*hodgepodge*
horologe	dodge		

Oe, *see* O *and* Ew

Off

cough	toph	shroff	trough
doff	off	"*soph*"	golf
cloff	scoff	toff	*philosophe*

Oft

coughed	scoffed	oft	sloft
croft	loft	soft	toft
doffed			

Og, Ogue (*short*)

bog	jog	epilog	"incog"
clog	log	monolog	mystagog
cog	prog	pedagog	nog
dog	shog	synagog	pettifog
flog	slog	"travelog"	philolog
fog	agog	analog	scrog
frog	catalog	apolog	"theolog"
gog	decalog	befog	trogue
grog	demagog	egg-nog	unclog
hog	dialog		

OGUE (*long*)

brogue
rogue
vogue
prorogue
apologue
astralogue
collogue
embogue
pirogue

OICE

choice
voice
invoice
rejoice

OID

buoyed
cloyed (*and past tense of verbs in* OY)
void
avoid
devoid
alkaloid
asteroid
unemployed
paraboloid
actinoid
albuminoid
aneroid
anthropoid
crystalloid
deltoid
dendroid
hyaloid
metalloid
negroid
ovoid
pyramidoid
tabloid
unalloyed
varioloid

OIL

assoyle
counterfoil
entoil
estoil
overtoil
roil
uncoil
upcoil
boil
broil
coil
foil
moil
oil
soil
spoil
toil
despoil
embroil
recoil
turmoil
disembroil

OIN

eloin
frankalmoigne
sejoin
tenderloin
coign
coin
foin
groin
join
loin
proin
quoin
adjoin
benzoin
conjoin
disjoin
enjoin
purloin
rejoin
sainfoin
sirloin
subjoin
interjoin

OINT

adjoint
coverpoint
deadpoint
dry-point
joint
oint
point
anoint
appoint
aroint
conjoint
disjoint
counterpoint
disappoint

OIR, *see* OR

OISE, OYS

avoirdupois
erminoise
froise
noise
poise
boys
enjoys (*and add s to nouns and verbs in* OY)
counterpoise
equipoise

OIST

foist, hoist, joist, moist, roist, *noised*, *poised*

OIT

coit, doit, quoit, adroit, dacoit, exploit, introit, droit, maladroit

OKE, *see* **OAK**

OL (*short*), **OLL**

doll, loll, "Poll", alcohol, *capitol*, *parasol*, protocol, vitriol, *atoll*, *consol*, entresol, kroal

OL (*long*), **OLE**, **OLL** (*long*), *see* **OAL**

OLD, **OULD**

bold, cold, coaled (*and past of verbs in* OAL), fold, gold, hold, mould, old, scold, sold, told, wold, behold, cuckold, enfold, foretold, *freehold*, retold, *threshold*, unfold, untold, uphold, withhold, copyhold, manifold, marigold, acold, ahold, *foothold*, *household*, interfold, mold, multifold, overbold, *stronghold*, twice-told, twofold

OLK, *see* **OAK**

OLT

bolt, colt, dolt, holt, jolt, moult, poult, volt, revolt, thunderbolt, lavolt, smolt, unbolt

OLVE

solve, absolve, convolve, devolve, dissolve, evolve, exsolve, involve, resolve, revolve, circumvolve, intervolve

OM

bomb, from, pompom, dom, *hecatomb*, rhomb, swom

OM (*as in* martyrdom), *see* **UM**

OMB, *see* OAM *and* OOM

OME, *see* OAM *and* UM

OMP

pomp
romp
swamp
tromp
"comp"

ON

con
don
gone
on
shone
swan
wan
yon
antiphon
echelon
encephalon
gonfalon
Helicon
irênicon
mastodon
agone
anon
begone
bonbon
hereon
thereon
whereon
pantechnicon
parthenon
prolegomenon
quarteron
Rubicon
stereopticon
dies non
sine qua non
bonne
cretonne
upon
automaton
Amazon

See also UN for words of three syllables and over ending in ON.

ONCE, ONSE

nonce
sconce
ensconce
response

ONCE (*as* wunce), *see* UNCE

OND, ONNED

bond
fond
pond
wand
yond
beyond
abscond
despond
conned
donned
respond
correspond
vagabond
blond
frond

ONE, *see* OAN

ONE, *see* UN

ONG

daylong
dugong
erelong
evensong
gong
headlong
headstrong
jong
lifelong
prong
singsong
scuppermong
wong
long
prong
song
strong
thong
throng
tong
wrong
along
belong
dingdong
diphthong
oblong
prolong
overlong

ONGUE, *see* UNG

ONS, *see* ONZE

Onse, *see* Once

Ont (*short*)

font	want	Hellespont

Ont (*long*)

don't	wont	won't

Onze

bronze	pons	swans (*and add s to nouns and verbs in* On)
bonze		

Oo (*as in* boo); *see note after* Ew

boo	true	drew	taboo
blue	undo	grew	ragoût
clue	accrue	shrew	début
coup	bamboo	cockatoo	woo
fou	who	Kangaroo	ado
untrue	accrue	who	bamboo
slew	bamboo	unglue	flue
through	do	shampoo	tattoo
two	"gout"	imbrue	billet-doux
zoo	shoo	chew	hitherto
woo	threw	loo	hullabulloo
ado	to	rue	entre nous
moo	*impromptu*	shrew	rendezvous
screw	yahoo	flew	halloo
crew	surtout	*Zulu*	cuckoo
glue	eschew	withdrew	pooh
shoe	blue	beshrew	pooh-pooh
strew	brew	bestrew	gnu
too	coo	canoe	

Add to these, as possible rhymes, all words in Ue

Oob

boob	"rube"

Add to these, as imperfect rhymes, other words in Ube

Ood (*as in* blood), *see* Ud

Ood (*as in* good)

could	firewood	withstood	misunderstood
good	stood	agood	unhood
hood	wood	understood	*wildwood*
should	would	underwood	

OOD (*as in* mood)

brood
food
crude
mood
prude
rood
rude
snood
conclude
cuckooed
detrude
exclude
extrude
include
intrude
obtrude
preclude
protrude
seclude
shrewd
brewed (*and past tense of verbs in* OO)

Add to these, as imperfect rhymes, all words in UDE

OOF

hoof
oof
proof
roof
spoof
woof
aloof
approof
behoof
disproof
reproof
loof
fire-proof

OOK; *see also* UKE *for imperfect rhymes*

spook
peruke
chibouque

OOK (*short*)

book
brook
cook
stook
crook
hook
look
nook
rook
shook
took
betook
forsook
mistook
overlook
Chinook
overtook
undertook
snook
outlook
partook
rukh

OOL; *see also* ULE *for imperfect rhymes*

cool
fool
pool
rule
school
spool
stool
tool
who'll
befool
misrule
overrule
drool
footstool
ghoul
lool

OOL, *as in* wool (*see* UL)

OOM; *see also* UME *for imperfect rhymes*

bloom
boom
broom
coomb
doom
flume
gloom
groom
loom
plume
rheum
room
tomb
whom
womb
beplume
deplume
entomb
dining-room
drawing-room
elbow room
addoom
anteroom
begloom
brume
combe
coom
disentomb
enbloom
foredoom
heirloom
jibboom
predoom
spoom
grume

OON; *see also* UNE *for imperfect rhymes*

boon	bassoon	poltroon	bridoon
chewn	batoon	pontroon	caissoon
coon	bestrewn	quadroon	forenoon
croon	buffoon	racoon	frigatoon
June	cartoon	shalloon	gambroon
loon	cocoon	simoon	gazon
moon	doubloon	typhoon	godroon
noon	dragoon	afternoon	fossoon
prune	eftsoon	honeymoon	maroon
rune	eschewn	macaroon	overstrewn
screwn	festoon	musketoon	patroon
shoon	galoon	octoroon	quateroon
soon	harpoon	oversoon	ratoon
spoon	jejeune	pantaloon	saloon
strewn	lagoon	picaroon	seroon
swoon	lampoon	rigadoon	spadroon
baboon	monsoon	aswoon	spittoon
balloon	platoon	barracoon	walloon

OOP, OUP

coop	poop	troop	roop
croup	scoop	whoop	scroup
droop	sloop	nincompoop	troupe
group	soup	aggroup	unhoop
hoop	stoop	drupe	*dupe*
houp	stoup	liripoop	"supe"
loop	swoop	recoup	

OOR; *see also* URE *for imperfect rhymes*

boor	truer	cocksure	paramour
bluer	wooer	conjure	reinsure
brewer	abjure	contour	altambour
doer	adjure	detour	blackamoor
fluor	amour	ensure	reassure
moor	*sewer*	insure	spoor
poor	assure	unsure	"who are"
sure	brochure	evildoer	"you are" (etc.)
tour			

OOR (*as in* floor), *see* OAR

OOSE (*sharp*), *see also* USE (*sharp*) *for imperfect rhymes*

goose	loose	noose	spruce
juice	moose	sluice	truce

OOSE (*sharp*)—(*Cont.*)

abstruse	recluse	vamose	calaboose
occluse	unloose	caboose	pappoose

OOSE (*flat*), OOZE; *see also* USE (*flat*) *for imperfect rhymes*

blues,	bruise	peruse	choose
brews (*and*	booze	ruse	whose
plurals	lose	snooze	who's
in OO)	ooze	cruise	

OOST; *see also past of verbs in* UCE *for imperfect rhymes*

boost	noosed	unloosed	spruced
juiced	roost	joust	vamoosed
loosed	sluiced		

OOT (*short*)

foot	put	afoot	soot

OOT (*long*); *see also* UTE *for imperfect rhymes*

baldicoot	en route	hoot	cheroot
cahoot	soot	jute	outroot
chute	upshoot	loot	recruit
enroot	bruit	moot	uproot
imbrute	brute	root	overshoot
marabout	coot	shoot	parachute
mahout	flute	adjute	waterchute

OOTH (*hard*) OUTH, UTH

ruth	truth	forsooth	insooth
sooth	booth	uncouth	sleuth
tooth	youth	untruth	

OOTH (*soft*)

smooth	besmooth	soothe	

OOVE, OVE

move	approve	improve	disapprove
groove	behoove	remove	amove
prove	disprove	reprove	ingroove
you've			

OOZE, *see* OOSE (*flat*)

OP

chop	crop	flop	hop
cop	drop	fop	lop

OP—(*Cont.*)

mop
plop
pop
prop
shop
slop
sop
stop
strop
top
atop
bedrop
co-op
aftercrop
overtop
underprop
eavesdrop
estop
forestop
knop
lollipop
snowdrop
swap
tiptop
unstop
whop
"wop"

OPE

afterhope
agrope
astroscope
dispope
electroscope
Ethiope
galvanoscope
gyroscope
hydroscope
polariscope
seismoscope
spectroscope
stethescope
stope
unpope
cope
dope
grope
hope
lope
mope
ope
pope
rope
scope
slope
soap
tope
trope
aslope
elope
antelope
antipope
baroscope
envelope
bioscope
horoscope
hygroscope
interlope
microscope
misanthrope
polyscope
telescope
thermoscope
anemoscope
helioscope
heliothrope
kaleidoscope
polemoscope

OR; *see also, for passable rhymes,* OAR

for
lor
nor
or
tor
war
abhor
lessor
señor
vendor
servitor
terpsichore
louis d'or
metaphor
seignior
minotaur
mortgagor
devoir
memoir
ancestor
auditor
bachelor
chancellor
conqueror
corridor
creditor
counselor
councilor
editor
emperor
escritoir
governor
meteor
orator
reservoir
senator
warrior
ambassador
anterior
apparitor
competitor
compositor
conspirator
contributor
excelsior
executor
expositor
exterior
inferior
inheritor
inquisitor
interior
posterior
progenitor
solicitor
superior
vice-chancellor

ORCE, OARSE, OURSE

coarse
course
force
hoarse
source
concourse
discourse
divorce

ORCE, OARSE, OURSE—(*Cont.*)

enforce	intercourse	horse	corse
perforce	reinforce	unhorse	gorse
recourse	retrorse	torse	endorse
resource	watercourse	morse	remorse

ORCH (*short*)

porch	scorch	torch

ORD (*long*), *see* **OARD**

ORD (*short*)

chord	ward	record	aboard
cord	warred	reward	board
ford	abhorred	clavichord	bord
horde	accord	harpsichord	gourd
lord	afford	monochord	hoard
ord	concord	pentachord	sword
sward	discord	perigord	

ORE, *see* **OAR**

ORGE

forge	disgorge	regorge	overgorge
gorge	engorge		

ORK

ork	fork	stork	York
New York	pork		

ORLD, *see* **URLED**

ORM

form	deform	chloroform	thunderstorm
storm	inform	cruciform	uniform
swarm	perform	cuneiform	vermiform
warm	reform	misinform	iodoform
conform	transform	multiform	

ORN, ORNE

born	scorn	worn	barley-corn
borne	shorn	adorn	capricorn
corn	sorn	forborne	heaven-born
horn	sworn	forsworn	overborne
lorn	thorn	forlorn	peppercorn
morn	torn	lovelorn	unicorn
norn	warn	suborn	foreswom

Orn, Orne—(*Cont.*)

mourn	bemourn	bourne	weatherworn
forewarn	betorn		

Orp

dorp	thorp	warp	"corp"

Orse, *see* Orce

Ort

fort	porte	exhort	decourt
mort	sport	deport	forte
short	comport	disport	*passport*
snort	assort	export (verb)	*seaport*
sort	cohort	import (verb)	report
tort	consort (verb)	rapport	support
wart	contort	extort	transport
court	distort	resort	misreport
port	escort (verb)	retort	disport

Orth

fourth	swarth	thenceforth	setter-forth
north	henceforth		

Os, *see* Oss

Ose (*sharp*)

close (adj.)	annulose	floccose	glubose
dose	engross	foliose	glucose
gross	jocose	verbose	grandiose
actuose	morose	bellicose	nodose
adipose	cellulose	comatose	otiose
albuminose	cose	gibbose	overdose
animose	diagnose		

Ose (*flat*), Oze, Ows

beaus (*and plurals in* O)	oppose	transpose	*depots*
	propose	unclose	disclose
chose	repose	discompose	dispose
close	suppose	indispose	enclose
clothes	nose	interpose	predispose
froze	pose	arose	presuppose
glose	prose	compose	recompose
hose	rose	depose	tuberose
foreclose	those	decompose	punctilios
impose	expose		

Oss

boss
cross
doss
dross
gloss
joss
loss
moss
toss
across
emboss
albatross
cerebos
setebos
bos
colosse
encephalos
floss
foss
fosse
lacrosse
rhinoceros

Ost (*long*), *see* Oast

Ost (*short*), **Ossed**

accost
geognost
unlost
bossed, (*and past of verbs in* Oss)
cost
frost
lost
wast
Pentecost
exhaust
holocaust

Ot, Otte

asquot
beauty-spot
besot
bott
cachalot
calotte
capot
forget-me-not
Huguenot
kumquot
love-knot
shallot
somewhat
underplot
unforgot
wat
witenagemot
blot
clot
cot
dot
got
grot
hot
jot
knot
lot
not
plot
pot
quot
rot
scot
shot
slot
sot
spot
squat
swot
tot
trot
what
wot
yacht
allot
begot
boycott
cocotte
forgot
garotte
gavotte
aliquot
apricot
bergamot
camelot
chariot
counterplot
eschalot
gallipot
heriot
idiot
misbegot
patriot
polyglot
unbegot
undershot
compatriot

Otch

blotch
botch
crotch
notch
potch
scotch
swatch
watch
hotch-potch
gotch
hotch
splotch
Scotch

Ote, *see* Oat

Oth (*long*), *see* Oath

OTH (*short*)

broth
cloth
froth
moth
betroth
wroth
Ashtaroth
Goth
saddlecloth
thoth
troth
visigoth

OTHE, *see* OATHE

OU, *see* EW *and* OW

OUCH

mouch
couch
crouch
ouch
pouch
slouch
grouch
vouch
avouch
disvouch
scaramouch

OUD, OWED

bowed (*and past of verbs in* OW)
cloud
crowd
loud
proud
shroud
aloud
enshroud
o'ercloud
o'ershroud
becloud
beshroud
encloud
overcrowd

OUGH, *see* OFF, UFF, OW, OCK, EW, O

OUGT, *see* AUGHT

OUL, *see* OLE, OWL

OULD, *see* OLD *and* OOD

OUNCE

bounce
flounce
frounce
ounce
pounce
trounce
announce
denounce
pronounce
renounce
enounce
rounce

OUND, OWNED

bound
crowned (*and past of verbs in* OWN)
found
ground
hound
mound
pound
round
sound
wound
abound
aground
around
astound
compound
confound
dumfound
expound
imbound
inbound
outbound
profound
propound
rebound
redound
renowned
resound
surround
unbound
unsound
underground
superabound
background
hell-bound (etc.)
hidebound
icebound
impound
merry-go-round
unground

Ount

count	amount	recount	paramount
fount	discount (verb)	remount	tantamount
mount	dismount	surmount	catamount
account	miscount		

Oup, *see* **Oop**

Our, *see also* **Oor**

bower	our	embower	imbower
cower	power	endower	lower
dour	scour	empower	horse-power
dower	shower	cauliflower	overtower
flour	sour	overpower	vower
flower	tower	besour	"kowtower"
glower	avower	allower	plower (etc.),
hour	deflower	enflower	(*see* Ow)
lour	devour		

Ourn; *see also* **Orn** *and* **Earn**

bourn	mourn

Ourse, *see* **Orce**

Ous, *see* **Us**

Ouse (*sharp*)

chouse	louse	souse	custom-house
dowse	mouse	charnel-house	chapterhouse
grouse	nous	counting-house	(etc.)
house			

Ouse (*flat*), **Owze**

bowse	bows (*and add s to nouns and verbs in* Ow)	house (verb)	carouse
drowse	browze	rouse	espouse
blouse		spouse	unhouse
blowze		touse	uprouse
boughs			

Out

bout	grout	shout	trout
clout	lout	snout	about
doubt	out	spout	devout
flout	pout	sprout	misdoubt
glout	rout	stout	redoubt
gout	scout	tout	throughout

OUT—(*Cont.*)

without	whereabout	drinking bout	out-and-out
roundabout	beshout	gadabout	roustabout
sauerkraut	bespout	hereabout	stirabout
thereabout	diner-out (etc.)	knout	drouth

OUTH (*short*); *see also* OOTH

drouth	mouth	south	bemouth

OVE (*as in* prove), *see* OOVE

dove	love	lady-love	turtledove
glove	shove	above	unglove
belove			

OVE (*long*)

clove	rove	wove	inwove
cove	stove	*alcove*	dove
drove	strove	behove	mauve
grove	throve	interwove	shrove
hove	trove	treasure-trove	

OW (*as* O), *see* O

OW (*diphthong*)

bough	row	bow-wow	anyhow
bow	slough	endow	disavow
brow	sow	enow	dhow
cow	thou	kowtow	mow
frau	trow	powwow	overbrow
how	vow	somehow	scrow
now	allow	disallow	scow
plough	avow	disendow	landau
prow			

OWL; *see also* OAL

cowl	growl	scowl	dowle
foul	howl	befoul	rowl
fowl	owl	afoul	water-fowl
ghoul	prowl	behowl	jowl

OWN; *see also* OAN

brown	drown	town	upside-down
clown	frown	adown	decrown
crown	gown	embrown	discrown
down	noun	renoun	eider-down

OWN; *see also* OAN—(*Cont.*)

godown	tumble-down	uptown	downtown
reach-me-down	ungown		

OWSE, *see* OUSE (*flat*)

OX, OCKS

box	cocks (*and add s to nouns and verbs in* OCK)	fox	equinox
cox		ox	orthodox
		phlox	paradox
		pox	heterodox

OY

ahoy	boy	alloy	envoy
corduroy	buoy	annoy	savoy
dalmahoy	cloy	convoy	sepoy
deploy	coy	decoy	misemploy
foy	joy	destroy	overjoy
paduasoy	toy	employ	pomeroy
soy	troy	enjoy	saveloy

OZE, *see* OSE (*flat*)

U, *see* UE

UB

blub	dub	slub	hubbub
bub	grub	snub	sillabub
chub	hub	stub	beelzebub
club	rub	sub	fub
cub	scrub	tub	nub
drub	shrub	rub-a-dub	

UBE; *see also* OOB *for imperfect rhymes* (*note, p.* 114)

cube	tube	jujube

UCE, USE; *see also* OOSE *for imperfect rhymes* (*note, p.* 114)

adduce	use (noun)	excuse	seduce
pertuse	abduce	induce	subduce
retuse	abuse	misuse	traduce
transluce	conduce	obduce	introduce
calaboose	deduce	obtuse	reproduce
cruse	diffuse	produce	hypotenuse
deuce	disuse (noun)	profuse	superinduce
puce	educe	reduce	

UCH, UTCH

clutch
crutch
hutch
much
mutch
such
slutch
touch
retouch
inasmuch
insomuch
overmuch
cutch
scutch
amutch

UCK

amuck
beduck ill-luck
misluck poverty-struck
shuck
stuck
buck
chuck
sluck
duck
luck
muck
pluck
puck
ruck
struck
suck
truck
tuck
thunderstruck

UCT

duct
abduct
conduct
deduct
induct
instruct
obstruct
aqueduct
misconduct (verb)
usufruct
viaduct
construct
eruct
misconstruct
reduct
subduct
substruct
bucked (*and past of verbs in* UCK)

UD

blood
bud
cud
flood
mud
rud
scud
spud
stud
thud
bestud
fud

UDE, UED, EUD, EWED; *see also* OOD *for imperfect rhymes* (*note p.* 114)

cued
dewed (*and past tense of all verbs in* UE)
dude
feud
lewd
nude
you'd
allude
collude
delude
denude
elude
exude
illude
prelude
transude
acritude
altitude
amplitude
aptitude
attitude
certitude
crassitude
finitude
fortitude
gratitude
habitude
interlude
lassitude
latitude
longitude
magnitude
multitude
parvitude
platitude
plenitude
promptitude
pulchritude
quietitude
rectitude
sanctitude
servitude
solitude
torpitude
turpitude
assuetude
beatitude
consuetude
decrepitude
desuetude
disquietude
exactitude
inaptitude
incertitude
ineptitude
infinitude
ingratitude
mansuetude
necessitude
serenitude
similitude
solicitude
vicissitude
inexactitude
dissimilitude
abatude
acerbitude
amaritude
claritude

UDE, UED, EUD, EWED—(*Cont.*)

inquietude	mallitude	subnude	vastitude
interclude	occlude	unpursued	verisimilitude
lenitude	retrude	unrenewed, etc.	abstrude
limitude	senectitude		

UDGE

budge	judge	trudge	prejudge
drudge	nudge	adjudge	rejudge
fudge	sludge	forejudge	begrudge
grudge	smudge	misjudge	

UE, EW, EU, U; *see also* OO *for imperfect rhymes* (*note, p.* 114)

cue	pew	bedew	detinue
dew	spue	bellevue	parvenu
due	stew	endue	avenue
ewe	sue	ensue	*impromptu*
few	thew	imbue	residue
hew	view	mildew	barbecue
hue	yew	purlieu	interview
knew	you	pursue	retinue
mew	adieu	renew	revenue
lieu	anew	review	*Jew*
new	askew	subdue	

UFF

bluff	slough	snuff	fluff
buff	blindman's buff	*sough*	powder-puff
chough	gruff	stuff	scuff
chuff	huff	counterbuff	tuff
clough	luff	bepuff	tough
cuff	muff	besnuff	enough
ruff	puff	duff	rebuff
scruff	rough		

UG

trug	jug	rug	sug
bug	lug	shrug	thug
drug	mug	slug	tug
dug	pug	smug	humbug
hug	plug	snug	

UICE, *see* UCE

UISE, *see* USE (*flat*)

Uit, *see* Ute

Uke; *see also* Ook *for imperfect rhymes* (*note*, *p.* 114)

duke
fluke
juke
puke
stuke
archduke
rebuke
beduke
pentateuch

Ul, Ull (*as in* bull)

tulle
bull
full
pull
wool
brimful (etc.)
beautiful
bountiful
dutiful
masterful
pitiful
thimbleful
weariful
fanciful
merciful
plentiful
powerful
sorrowful
wonderful
worshipful (etc.) (*Words ending in* FUL, *having accent on the antepenultimate, are possible rhymes*)

Ul, Ull (*as in* cull)

cull
dull
gull
hull
lull
mull
null
scull
skull
trull
annul
bulbul
numskull
disannul
shull
picul
strull
stull
barnacle
chronicle
kehul
miracle
monocle
obstacle
pinnacle
spectacle
vehicle
versicle (*adjectives with suffix* FUL *are imperfect rhymes*)

Ule, *see* Ool *for imperfect rhymes* (*note*, *p.* 114)

buhl
mule
pule
you'll
yule
reticule
ridicule
vermicule
vestibule
mewl

Ulge

bulge
divulge
emulge
indulge
promulge
effulge

Ulk

bulk
hulk
skulk
sulk

Ulp

gulp
pulp
sculp
sulp

Ulse

appulse
bulse
compulse
dulse
mulse
pulse
convulse
expulse
impulse
insulse
repulse

Ult

cult
adult
consult
incult
exult
insult
occult
indult
result
catapult
difficult
uncult

Um, Umb

chum
come
crumb
drum
dumb
from
glum
grum
gum
hum
mum
mumm
numb
plum
plumb
rum
scum
slum
some
fee-fo-fum
crum
humdrum
succumb
burdensome
cranium
platinum
quietsome
radium
rascaldom
rebeldom
cumbersome
frolicsome
humorsome
kettledrum
laudanum
mascimum
meddlesome
medium
mettlesome
venturesome
worrisome
wranglesome
quarrelsome
speculum
troublesome
tympanum
wearisome
adventuresome
compendium
delirium
effluvium
emporium
encomium
exordium
rhumb
"scrum"
stum
sugar-plum
tedium
gymnasium
millennium
crematorium
equilibrium
pandemonium
pericranium
sanatorium
epithalamium
ad libitum
adytum
aquarium
bumbledom
Christendom
chrysanthemum
curriculum
drearisome
flunkydom
geranium
heatherdom
pabulum
strum
sum
swum
thrum
thumb
tum
become
benumb
minimum
misbecome
modicum
odium
opium
overcome
pendulum
premium
opprobrium
palladium
petroleum
residuum
sensorium
solatium
symposium
auditorium
pelargonium
vacuum
viaticum

Ume; *see also* **Oom** *for imperfect rhymes* (*note*, *p.* 114)

fume
spume
assume
consume
exhume
illume
inhume
perfume
presume
relume
resume
reassume
infume
legume

Ump

bethump
sump
tump
bump
chump
clump
crump
dump
frump
hump
jump
lump

UMP—(*Cont.*)

mump	pump	slump	thump
plump	rump	stump	trump

UN

bun	spun	*cinnamon*	overdone
done	stun	*comparison*	overrun
dun	sun	everyone	euroclydon
fun	ton	fanfaron	*oblivion*
gun	tun	antiphon	*simpleton*
none	won	ganglion	*singleton*
nun	begun	*garrison*	*skeleton*
one	forerun	*halcyon*	*tarragon*
pun	outrun	*lexicon*	*ternion*
run	undone	*myrmidon*	*unison*
shun	anyone	*orison*	*venison*
son	*benison*	*orthogon*	*caparison*

(*See also words of three syllables and over, ending in* AN *and* EN *with accent on antepenultimate, for possible rhymes*)

UNCE

dunce	once	unce	stunts (*and add s to nouns and verbs in* UNT)

UNCH

brunch	hunch	munch	scrunch
bunch	lunch	punch	clunch
crunch			

UND

bund	punned (*and past of verbs in* UN, ON)	rotund	immund
fecund		rubicund	matafund
jocund		orotund	retund
obrotund	refund	verecund	

UNE; *see also* OON *for imperfect rhymes* (*note, p.* 114)

attune	lacune	stewn	subduen
commune	lune	suen	triune
dune	oppugn	tune	untune
excommune	picayune	viewn	importune
expugn	hewn	immune	opportune
impugn	lune	persuen	inopportune

Ung

bung	sprung	wrung	betongue
clung	underhung	young	high-strung
dung	strung	overhung	lung
flung	stung	unstrung	mother tongue
hung	sung	among	pung
rung	swung	unsung	unwrung
slung	tongue	behung	upsprung

Unge

allonge	emplunge	plunge	spunge
blunge	lunge	sponge	expunge
dispunge			

Unk

bunk	junk	skunk	sunk
chunk	monk	slunk	trunk
drunk	plunk	spunk	flunk
funk	punk	stunk	quidnunc
hunk	shrunk		

Unt

blunt	hunt	shunt	confront
bunt	lunt	sprunt	"won't"
brunt	punt	stunt	exeunt
front	runt	affront	forefront
grunt			

Up

cup	sup	up	crup
pup	tup	buttercup	

Upe; *see* **Oop** *for imperfect rhymes* (*note*, *p.* 114)

dupe	pupe	"supe"	"cupe"

Upt

cupped	abrupt	incorrupt	disrupt
pupped	corrupt	interrupt	erupt
supped			

Ur, *see* **Er**

Urb, *see* **Erb**

Urch, *see* **Earch**

Urd, *see* **Eard**

URE; *see also* OOR *for imperfect rhymes* (*note, p.* 114)

abature
abbreviature
amateur
aperture
breviature
candidature
caricature
colure
connoisseur
divestiture
enmure
expenditure
garmenture
geniture
liqueur
mature
perdure
perendure
quadrature
tablature
vestiture
cure
dure
ewer
fewer
hewer
lure
newer
pure
sewer
skewer
your
you're
allure
azure
demure
endure
immure
impure
inure
manure
obscure
ordure
procure
pursuer
renewer
reviewer
secure
subduer
voiture
armature
calenture
comfiture
coverture
curvature
cynosure
epicure
forfeiture
furniture
garniture
immature
insecure
ligature
overture
portraiture
premature
sepulture
signature
sinecure
discomfiture
entablature
investiture
literature
miniature
temperature
primogeniture

URF, *see* ERF

URGE, *see* ERGE

URK, *see* ERK

URL, *see* EARL

URLED, ORLD, IRLED, EARLED

curled (*and past of verbs in* EARL)
world
old-world
underworld

URN, *see* EARN

URP

chirp
discerp
extirp
usurp

URSE, *see* ERCE

URST, *see* IRST

URT, *see* ERT

URVE, *see* ERVE

Us, Uss, Ous

bus
fuss
plus
pus
thus
truss
us
discuss
nonplus
amorous
platypus
credulous
courteous
aqueous
arduous
arquebus
barbarous
beauteous
bibulous
blasphemous
blunderbuss
curious
crapulous
boisterous
bounteous
calculous
cautelous
cavernous
chivalrous
clamorous
congruous
copious
dangerous
devious
dexterous
dolorous
dubious
duteous
emulous
envious
exodus
fabulous
fatuous
frivolous
furious
garrulous
generous
globulous
glorious
glutinous
gluttonous
hazardous
hideous
humorous
igneous
impetus
impious
incubus
infamous
jeopardous
languorous
lecherous
libelous
ligneous
ludicrous
luminous
marvelous
membranous
mischievous
mountainous
murderous
mutinous
nauseous
nautilus
nebulous
nucleus
numerous
obvious
odious
odorous
ominous
omnibus
onerous
overplus
pendulous
perilous
pervious
phosphorus
phosphorous
piteous
plenteous
poisonous
polypus
ponderous
populous
posthumous
previous
prosperous
querulous
radius
rancorous
ravenous
resinous
rigorous
riotous
ruinous
scandalous
scrofulous
scrupulous
scrutinous
scurrilous
sedulous
sensuous
serious
sinuous
sirius
slanderous
sonorous
spurious
stimulus
strenuous
studious
succubus
sulphurous
sumptuous
syllabus
synchronous
tartarus
tedious
thunderous
timorous
tortuous
traitorous
treacherous
treasonous
tremulous
tyrannous
vacuous
valorous
various
venomous
vigorous
villainous
virtuous
abaculus
abacus
Angelus
animus
buss
caduceus
convolvulus
cumulus
"cuss"
denarius
excuss
incuss
minimus
muss
octopus
percuss
platypus
repercuss
rhus
tantalus
terminus
untruss
acclivitous
ecephalous

Us, Uss, Ous—(*Cont.*)

acidulous
albuminous
aliferous
aligerous
alimonious
alkalious
alluvious
aluminous
amatorius
anfractuous
angulous
anserous
antipathous
arborous
armigerous
augurous
balsamiferous
bicephalous
bigamous
bipetalous
bituminous
blusterous
burdenous
bulbiferous
burglarious
cancerous
cankcrous
circuitous
contrarious
covetous
criminous
doloriferous
dulciphluous
endogenous
eponymous
equilibrious
ethereous
fatuitous
flumious
fossiliferous
imaginous
immeritous
imposturous
incendious
incommodious
inconspicuous
indecorous
inebrious
infelicitous
inharmonious
inquisitorious
insensuous
meticulous
monogamous
monotonous
murmurous
nectareous
pendulous
periculous
perjurous
pesterous
petalous
platinous
polygamous
pseudonymous
quarrelous
rapturous
roysterous
sanguineous
savourous
scintillous
sibilous
slumberous
stentorious
stridulous
tautologous
tenebrous
tenuous
timidous
tintinnabulous
torturous
tuberculous
unchivalrous
undulous
unscrupulous
uproarious
vagarious
valetudinous
vaporous
vegetous
verdurous
verminous
vernaculous
vertiginous
viperous
vitreous
voraginous
vortiginous
vulturous
abstemious
acephalous
adventurous
adulterous
ambiguous
amphibious
analogous
androgynous
anomalous
anonymous
asparagus
assiduous
cadaverous
calamitous
calcareous
cantankerous
carnivorous
censorious
chrysoprasus
commodious
conspicuous
contemptuous
conterminous
contiguous
continuous
courageous
cretaceous
deciduous
delirious
diaphanous
discourteous
erroneous
exiguous
extraneous
fastidious
felicitous
felonious
ferruginous
fortuitous
fuliginous
gelatinous
gratuitous
gregarious
harmonious
herbaceous
hilarious
homologous
idolatrous
illustrious
impetuous
imperious
impervious
imponderous
incestuous
incongruous
incredulous
incurious
indigenous
indubious
industrious
ingenious
ingenuous
inglorious
iniquitous
injurious
innocuous
inodorous
insidious
invidious

Us, Uss, Ous—(*Cont.*)

laborious
lascivious
leguminous
Leviticus
libidinous
litigious
lugubrious
luxurious
magnanimous
mellifluous
melodious
miraculous
multivious
mysterious
necessitous
nefarious
notorious
oblivious
obsequious
obstreperous
œsophagus
omnivorous
opprobrious
outrageous
penurious
perfidious
perspicuous
pestiferous
precarious
precipitous
predaceous
preposterous
presumptuous
promiscuous
punctilious
ranunculus
rebellious
ridiculous
salacious
salubrious
sarcophagus
setaceous
solicitous
somniferous
spontaneous
sulphurous
superfluous
synonymous
tempestuous
tenebrious
tumultuous
ubiquitous
umbrageous
unanimous
ungenerous
usurious
uxurious
vainglorious
vicarious
victorious
vociferous
voluminous
voluptuous
acrimonious
advantageous
atrabilious
ceremonious
contumelious
deleterious
disingenuous
farinaceous
graminivorous
hippopotamus
homogeneous
hydrocephalus
ignis fatuus
ignominious
impecunious
instantaneous
meritorious
metalliferous
miscellaneous
mucilaginous
multifarious
multitudinous
odoriferous
oleaginous
pachyderma-
tous
parsimonious
pusillanimous
sanctimonious
saponaceous
simultaneous
subterraneous
supercilious
temerarious
contempora-
neous
disadvanta-
geous
extemporane-
ous
heterogeneous
zoöphagous

Use (*sharp*), *see* Uce

Use (*flat*); *see also* Oose *for imperfect rhymes* (*note, p.* 114)

affuse
fuze
guze
incuse
interfuse
cues
dews (*and add s to nouns and verbs in* Ue) (*and* Oo *for imperfect rhymes*)
fuse
muse
news
use (verb)
abuse
accuse
amuse
bemuse
confuse
contuse
diffuse
disuse
effuse
enthuse
excuse
infuse
intuse
misuse
perfuse
refuse
suffuse
transfuse
circumfuse
disabuse
impromptus
revenues

Ush (*as in* bush)

bush	push	*ambush*	"cush"

Ush (*as in* blush)

blush	hush	outrush	tush
brush	lush	rush	mush
crush	plush	slush	underbrush
flush	outblush	thrush	"shush"
gush			

Usk

busk	husk	rusk	adusk
dusk	lusk	subfusk	dehusk
fusc	musk	tusk	

Uss (*as in* fuss), *see* **Us**

Uss (*as in* puss)

puss	"à la Russe"	"au jus" (etc.)	

Ust

bust	thrust	entrust	dost
crust	trust	incrust	fust
dust	adjust	mistrust	bussed
gust	august (adj.)	nonplused	fussed
just	disgust	robust	trussed
lust	distrust	unjust	discussed
must	adjust	bedust	mussed
betrust	combust	angust	cussed
rust	coadjust	untoussed	unmussed

Ut, Utt

but	nut	outshut	englut
butt	putt	uncut	rebut
crut	rut	smut	cocoanut (etc.)
cut	scut	strut	halibut
glut	shut	stut	occiput
gut	slut	tut	waterbutt
hut	astrut	abut	clear-cut (etc.)
jut	besmut	catgut	

Ut (*as in* put), *see* **Oot**

Utch, *see* **Uch**

Ute, Uit; *see also* Oot *for imperfect rhymes* (*note, p.* 114)

astute
cornute
emeute
hirsute
immute
involute
meute
solute
subacute
suppute
versute
cute
lute
mute
newt
suit
acute
arbute
argute
commute
compute
confute
depute
dilute
dispute
impute
minute (adj.)
permute
pollute
pursuit
refute
repute
salute
transmute
volute
absolute
attribute
comminute
constitute
"beaut"
contribute
destitute
dissolute
disrepute
execute
institute
persecute
prosecute
prostitute
resolute
substitute
irresolute
Ute
Piute

Uth, *see* Ooth

Ux, Ucks

crux
dux
flux
lux
conflux
efflux
influx
reflux
superflux
afflux
bucks (*and add s to nouns and verbs in* Uck)

Y (*long*), **Igh**

aye (yes)
buy
by
cry
die
dry
dye
eye
fie
fry
guy
hie
high
lie
my
nigh
pie
ply
pry
rye
sky
sigh
sly
spy
sty
thigh
thy
tie
try
vie
why
wry
ally
apply
awry
belie
comply
decry
defy
deny
descry
espy
foreby
go-by
good-bye
hereby
imply
outcry
outfly
outvie
rely
reply
supply
thereby
untie
whereby
alkali
amplify
beautify
brutify
by-and-by
candify
certify
clarify
crucify
deify
dignify
dulcify
edify
falsify
fortify
frenchify
fructify
glorify
gratify
horrify

Y (*long*), Igh—(*Cont.*)

justify
labefy
lenify
liquefy
lullaby
magnify
modify
mollify
mortify
multiply
notify
nullify
occupy
ossify
pacify
petrify
prophesy (verb)
purify
putrefy
qualify
ramify
rarefy
ratify
rectify
rubefy
sanctify
satisfy
scarify
signify
simplify
specify
stupefy
tabefy
terrify
testify
typify
verify
versify
vilify
vivify
beatify
disqualify
diversify
exemplify
fecundify
harmonify
indemnify
intensify
personify
preoccupy
solidify
acidify
adry
alacrify
alibi
alkalify
angelify
anglify
assai
ay
bedye
bespye
butterfly
classify
codify
countrify
damnify
dandify
demy
dissatisfy
electrify
emulsify
ensky
eternify
firefly
fossilify
gasify
genii
gry
heigh
humanify
hushaby
identify
termini
incubi (etc.), *see nouns from the Latin, in* Us
lazuli
lignify
mystify
nye
passer-by
preachify
quantify
revivify
saccharify
scye
shy
sny
spry
stellify
stultify
torpify
torrefy
underlie
unify
verbify
vitrify
wye

Y (*short*)

(*NOTE.*—There are several thousand words ending in Y short, with the accent on the antepenultimate. As these are not good rhymes either to one another or to words with any other ending, only a partial list is given here. They are, however, freely used by all poets as rhymes to words ending in E *long*, Ea and Ee.)

academy
agony
amity
anarchy
apathy
artery
augury
battery
bigamy
bigotry
blasphemy
bribery
brevity
calumny
canopy
charity
clemency
colony
comedy
company
constancy
courtesy
cruelty
decency
destiny
dignity
drapery
drollery

Y (*short*)—(*Cont.*)

drudgery
ecstasy
embassy
enemy
energy
equity
eulogy
euphony
factory
family
fallacy
fecundity
flattery
foolery
gaiety
gallantry
gallery
galaxy
granary
history
idolatry
industry
injury
infamy
jollity
knavery
laxity
legacy
leprosy
lethargy
levity
liberty
livery
lottery
loyalty
lunacy
majesty
malady
melody
memory
misery
modesty
monarchy
mummery
mutiny
mystery
nicety
novelty
nunnery
nursery
penalty
penury
perfidy
perjury
pillory
piracy
pleurisy
policy
poverty
primary
privacy
prodigy
quality
quantity
raillery
rectory
remedy
ribaldry
rivalry
robbery
royalty
salary
sanctity
secrecy
slavery
sorcery
subsidy
surgery
symmetry
sympathy
symphony
tapestry
tragedy
treachery
treasury
trinity
trumpery
tyranny
unity
usury
vacancy
vanity
victory
villainy
votary
absurdity
activity
adversity
affinity
agility
ambiguity
anatomy
animosity
antiquity
anxiety
apostasy
apostrophe
aristocracy
austerity
authority
calamity
capacity
captivity
catastrophe
complexity
concavity
conformity
congruity
conspiracy
credulity
curiosity
declivity
deformity
democracy
discovery
dishonesty
dexterity
disparity
diversity
divinity
doxology
duplicity
emergency
enormity
eternity
etymology
extremity
familiarity
fatality
felicity
ferocity
fertility
fidelity
frivolity
frugality
genealogy
gratuity
hostility
hospitality
humanity
hypocrisy
idiosyncrasy
immortality
impetuosity
impiety
impossibility
importunity
impurity
inability
incapacity
incivility
inclemency
incongruity
inconsistency
inconstancy
indemnity
inequality
infidelity

Y (*short*)—(*Cont.*)

infinity
infirmary
instability
integrity
intensity
liberality
magnanimity
malignity
maturity
mediocrity
mendacity
minority
mortality
municipality
mutability
nationality
nativity
neutrality
nobility
nonconformity
obscurity
opportunity
partiality
perplexity
philosophy
pomposity
probability
prodigality
profanity
profundity
propensity
prosperity
rascality
reality
reciprocity
rotundity
satiety
security
seniority
sensibility
sensuality
severity
simplicity
sincerity
sobriety
society
solemnity
solidity
soliloquy
sovereignty
sublimity
supremacy
stupidity
temerity
theology
theosophy
timidity
tranquillity
transparency
unanimity
uncertainty
uniformity
university
vacuity
variety
veracity
verbosity
vicinity
virginity
visibility
vivacity
volubility

TWO-SYLLABLE RHYMES

ABARD, ABBARD, ABBERED

scabbard
tabard
jabbered
beslabbered

ABBER

blabber
drabber
jabber
slabber
stabber
beslabber
dabber
grabber
knabber
nabber

ABBET, ABBIT, ABIT

habit
rabbet
rabbit
cohabit
riding-habit (etc.)
"grab it" (etc.)
inhabit

ABBLE

babble
dabble
gabble
rabble
scrabble
bedabble
bedrabble
brabble
cabble
drabble
grabble
(ribble-rabble)
scabble

ABBLE (*as in* squabble, *see* OBBLE)

ABBLER, ABBLING, etc., *see* ABBLE

ABBOT

abbot
sabot

Abbey, Abby

abbey
cabby
crabby
flabby
scabby
shabby
slabby
tabby
"babby"
dabby
drabby
grabby
rabbi
rabi

Abies

rabies
scabies

Able, Abel

able
babel
cable
fable
gabel
label
sable
stable
table
disable
enable
unable
unstable
flabel
Abe'll (etc.)

Ablish, Abblish

babblish
rabblish
establish
disestablish
stablish

Abor, Abour, Abre

labor
neighbor
saber
tabor
belabor
caber

Aby

baby
gaby
maybe

Accy, *see* **Ackey**

Aceless, graceless (etc.) *see* **Ace**

Acely, *see* **Asely**

Acement, *see* **Asement**

Acent

adjacent
complacent
complaisant
subjacent
circumjacent
interjacent
jacent
naissant
renaissant
superjacent
"daycent"
"raycent"
(etc.)

Aceous, Aseous, Atious

caseous
gracious
spacious
audacious
bibacious
bulbaceous
capacious
cetaceous
cretaceous
edacious
fallacious
herbaceous
linguacious
loquacious
mendacious
minacious
mordacious
palacious
predaceous
procacious
pugnacious
rapacious
sagacious
salacious
sequacious
setaceous
tenacious
ungracious
veracious
vexatious
vivacious
voracious
contumacious
disputatious
efficacious
farinaceous

Aceous, Aseous, Atious—(*Cont.*)

incapacious	rampacious	crustaceous	orchidaceous
ostentatious	execratious	erinoceous	palmaceous
perspicacious	flirtatious	faboceous	pearlaceous
pertinacious	acanaceous	ferulaceous	perlaceous
pervicacious	acanthaceous	filaceous	pomoceous
saponaceous	alliaceous	folioceous	resinaceous
disgracious	amylaceous	fungaceous	rosaceous
feracious	arenaceous	gemmaceous	rutaceous
fugacious	cactaceous	lappaceous	sebaceous
fumacious	camphoraceous	lardaceous	setaceous
inefficacious	capillaceous	liliaceous	testaceous
malgracious	carbonaceous	marlaccous	tophaceous
meracious	corallaceous	micaceous	vinoceous
misgracious	coriaceous	olivaceous	violaceous

Acer

facer (etc.), *see* Ace

Acet, *see* Asset

Achment, Atchment

hatchment	attachment	catchment	ratchment
patchment	detachment	despatchment	

Acic, *see* Assic

Acid

acid	placid	flacid

Acious, *see* Aceous

Acis, Asis

basis	crasis	phasis	*spaces* (etc.), *see* Ace *for imperfect rhymes*
glacis	oasis	*faces*	
antanaclasis			

Acit, *see* Asset

Acken

blacken	bracken	slacken	cracken

Acker, Acquer

clacker	knacker	slacker (etc.), *see* Ack	"attack her" (etc.)
cracker	lacquer		
hijacker	packer		

ACKET

bracket	placket	flacket	tacket
jacket	racket	packet	"hic jacet"

ACKEY, ACKY, ACCY

"baccy"	lackey	tacky	knacky
blacky	"cracky"		

ACKISH

blackish	quackish	knackish	slackish
brackish			

ACKLE

cackle	quackle	tackle	"whack'll"
crackle	macle	ramshackle	(etc.)
hackle	shackle		

ACKLER, ACKLING (etc.), *see* **ACKLE**

ACKLESS

sackless (etc.), *see* **ACK**

ACKLY

blackly (etc.), *see* **ACK**

ACKNEY, ACNE

acne	hackney

ACKY, *see* **ACKEY**

ACNE, *see* **ACKNEY**

ACON, *see* **AKEN**

ACRE, *see* **AKER**

ACTER, ACTOR

abstracter	detractor	enacter	climacter
compacter	phylacter	exacter	extractor
distracter	refractor	transactor	protractor
infractor	retractor	actor	benefactor
olfactor	subtracter	factor	malefactor
contractor	tractor	attractor	

ACTIC

tactic	emphractic	lactic	stalactic
didactic	empractic	parallactic	syntactic
prophylactic	galactic	protactic	

ACTILE
tactile
tractile
attractile
contractile
protactile
retractile

ACTING
subtracting, (etc.), *see* ACT

ACTION
action
faction
fraction
paction
taction
traction
abstraction
attraction
coaction
contaction
contraction
detraction
distraction
exaction
extraction
inaction
infraction
protraction
reaction
refraction
retraction
subaction
subtraction
transaction
arefaction
benefaction
calefaction
liquefaction
malefaction
petrifaction
putrefaction
rarefaction
retroaction
satisfaction
stupefaction
dissatisfaction
assuefaction
compaction
counteraction
interaction
labefaction
lubrifaction
modifaction
patefaction
redaction
rubefaction
tabefaction
tepefaction
torrefaction
tremefaction
tumefaction

ACTISED, ACTIST, ACTEST
actest
exactist (etc.), *see* ACT
practised

ACTIVE
active
abstractive
attractive
inactive
protractive
refractive
calefactive
petrifactive
putrefactive
retroactive
stupefactive
coactive
contractive
counteractive
detractive
distractive
enactive
olfactive
retractive
satisfactive
subtractive
tractive

ACTLESS
tactless (etc.), *see* ACT

ACTLY
abstractly
compactly
tactly
matter-of-factly
exactly

ACTOR, *see* ACTER

ACTRESS
actress
contractress
benefactress
exactress
detractress
malefactress
factress

Acture
fracture compacture manufacture vitrifacture
facture

Acy
lacy racy spacy

Adam
madam Adam "had 'em" "bade 'em" (etc.)
macadam

Adden
"bad un" engladden madden sadden
gladden

Adder
adder gladder sadder "had her" (etc.)
bladder ladder padder
gadder madder step-ladder

Adding, Odding
wadding podding codding nodding
plodding prodding

Addle
addle spaddle astraddle raddle
faddle straddle daddle staddle
paddle skedaddle fiddle-faddle unsaddle
saddle "dad'll" (etc.)

Addler, Addling (etc.), *see* **Addle**

Addock
haddock paddock raddock shaddock

Addy
caddy faddy Finnan-haddie *cadi*
daddy laddy paddy waddy

Adence, Aidance
aidance cadence decadence

Adent, *see* **Aidant**

Ader, *see* **Adir**

Adger
badger padger spadger agger
cadger

Adiant, Adient

gradient	radiant

Ading

fading (etc.), *see* Ade

Adir

nadir	aider (etc.), *see* Ade

Adish, Addish

radish	baddish	caddish (etc.), *see* Ad

Adle

cradle	ladle	stadle	encradle

Adly, Addly

straddly	badly (etc.), *see* Ad

Adness

badness (etc.), *see* Ad

Ado (*pronounced either* ā *or* ä, *except* dado)

dado	stoccado	camisado	grenado
bravado	strappado	carbonado	imbrocado
crusado	tornado	desperado	muscovado
gambado	ambuscado	El Dorado	renegado
passado	barricado	fumado	travado
scalado	bastinado		

Adow

cadeau	foreshadow

Ady, Adi

cadi	belady	"fady" (etc.), *see* Ade	*landlady*
lady	braidy	glady	"played he," (etc.)
maidie	cascady	irade	
shady			

Aerie, *see* Airy

Afe, *see* Affy

Afer

safer	chafer	cockchafer	"strafer"
afer	wafer		

Affer, Affir

chaffer	graffer	laugher (etc.), *see* Aff	zaffre
gaffer	kaffir		

AFFIC, AFFICK, APHIC

graphic	cacographic	heterographic	monographic
maffick	calligraphic	hierographic	orthographic
traffic	cartographic	holographic	pantographic
seraphic	chirographic	hydrographic	paragraphic
phonographic	choregraphic	hyetographic	pasigraphic
photographic	clinographic	ichnographic	petrographic
pornographic	cosmographic	ideographic	polygraphic
telegraphic	cryptographic	stylographic	scenographic
cinemato-graphic	diagraphic	topographic	sciagraphic
autobiographic	epigraphic	idiographic	seismographic
autographic	epitaphic	lexicographic	stenographic
biographic	ethnographic	lexigraphic	stratigraphic
bibliographic	geographic	lithographic	xylographic
	heliographic	logographic	zoöagraphic

AFFLE

baffle	gaffle	kaffle	yaffle
raffle	haffle	scraffle	"calf'll" (etc.)
snaffle			

AFFLESS, *see* AFF

AFFLED, AFFOLD

raffled (etc.) *see* AFFLE	*scaffold*

AFFY

baffy	draffy	taffy	"daffy"
chaffy			

AFTER

after	draughter	rafter	thereafter
dafter	hafter	hereafter	"chaffed her" (etc.)
grafter	laughter	ingrafter	

AFTY

crafty	draughty	grafty

AGELESS

pageless (etc.), *see* AGE

AGELY

pagely	sagely	stagely

AGEMENT

engagement	encagement	gagement	presagement
assuagement	enragement	gaugement	suagement

AGEOUS, AGIOUS

contagious	umbrageous	disadvan-	oragious
courageous	advantageous	tageous	rampageous
outrageous		ambagious	

AGER, *see* AJOR

AGGARD, AGGERED

haggard	staggered	swaggered	staggard
laggard			

AGGER

bragger	swagger	carpet-bagger	nagger
dagger	wagger (etc.),	gagger	ragger
lagger	*see* AG	jagger	sagger
fagger	"three-bagger"	"magger"	tagger
stagger	"two-bagger"		

AGGISH

naggish	haggish	staggish	waggish

AGGLE

daggle	haggle	bedaggle	waggel
draggle	straggle	bedraggle	"hag'll" (etc.)
gaggle	waggle	raggle	

AGGOT

faggot	maggot

AGGY

baggy (etc.), *see* AG

AGIC

magic	archipelagic	hemorrhagic	pelagic
tragic	ellagic		

AGILE

agile	fragile

AGLESS

bagless (etc.), *see* AG

AGO

sago	farrago	lumbago	vorago
imago	plumbago	virago	"they go" etc.

AGON

dragon	flagon	snapdragon	wagon
pendragon			

Agrant

flagrant	infragrant	vagrant	fragrant

Aic

mosaic	archaic	Pharisaic	stanzaic
alcaic	algebraic	Paddusaic	tesseraic
alhambraic	deltaic	saic	trochaic
prosaic	laic	sodaic	voltaic
altaic	paradisaic	spondaic	

Aidant

aidant	cadent	abradant	decadent

Ailer, Aoler

gaoler	jailer (etc.), *see* Ail	whaler sailor	tailor

Ailiff, *see* Aliph

Ailing, Ayling

ailing (etc.), see Ail	grayling strayling

Ailment

ailment (etc.), *see* Ail

Aily, Ailly, *see* Aly

Aighten, *see* Atan

Aimant, Amant, Aiment, Ayment

claimant	payment	defrayment	displayment
clamant	raiment		

Aimless

shameless (etc.), *see* Aim

Ainder

attainder	remainder

Ainful, Aneful

baneful	painful	disdainful	complainful
gainful			

Aining

raining	entertaining (etc.), *see* Ain

AINLESS
painless (etc.), *see* AIN

AINLY, *see* ANELY

AINTER
fainter
tainter (etc.), *see* AINT

AINTING
painting (etc.), *see* AINT

AINTLESS
taintless (etc.), *see* AINT

AINTLING
faintling
saintling

AINTLY
faintly
quaintly
unsaintly

AINTY
dainty
fainty
feinty
"ain't he," etc.

AINY, *see* ANY (*long*)

AIRY, ARY
airy
chary
dairy
eyrie
fairy
hairy
snary
vary
wary
canary
ablutionary
accidentiary
accustomary
actuary
additionary
admincularly
adversary
ancillary
antiquary
apothecary
arbitrary
beneficiary
capillary
cautionary
centenary
commentary
commissary
confectionary
constabulary
contemporary
contrary
corollary
contributary
culinary
customary
depositary
dictionary
dietary
dignitary
dromedary
epistolary
estuary
extraordinary
evolutionary
fiduciary
formulary
fragmentary
functionary
hereditary
honorary
imaginary
incendiary
intermediary
Janissary
January
legendary
legionary
literary
luminary
mercenary
military
momentary
monetary
mortuary
necessary
obituary
ordinary
passionary
pecuniary
planetary
prairie
prebendary
proprietary
pulmonary
questuary
reliquary
residuary
salivary
salutary
sanctuary

AIRY, ARY—(*Cont.*)

sanguinary	seminary	tertiary	unwary
sanitary	solitary	titulary	vagary
scapulary	stationary	tributary	visionary
secondary	statuary	tumulary	vocabulary
voluntary	sublunary	tutelary	voluptuary
secretary	sumptuary	ubiquitary	vulnerary
sedentary	temporary	unchary	

AISANCE

complacence	*obeisance*	nascence	renascence
complaisance			

AISANT, *see* ACENT

AISER, *see* AZER

AISIN, *see* AZEN

AISY, *see* AZY

AITER, *see* ATOR

AITEN, *see* ATAN

AITHFUL

faithful	scathful

AITIFF, *see* ATIVE

AITRESS

creatress	waitress	imitatress	spectatress
traitress	dictatress		

AITY, *see* AIETY

AJOR, AGER

ager	major	sager	wager (etc.),
gauger	pager	stager	*see* AGE

ALER

squalor	paler (etc.),	"fail her"
	see AIL	(etc.)

ALLIC

fallic	Gallic	metallic	oxalic

ALMENT

instalment	appalment	disenthral-	epaulement
enthralment		ment	

ALMEST, ALMIST

calmest	palmist	psalmist (etc.), *see* ALM

ALMLESS

balmless	psalmless	palmless	qualmless (etc.), *see* ALM

ALMON, *see* AMMON

ALMY

balmy	palmy

ALOE, *see* ALLOW

ALON, ALLON

ballon	gallon	talon

ALOP, ALLOP

gallop	shallop	escalop	jalop
scallop			

ALOR, ALLOR

pallor	valor	caballer

ALSAM

balsam	brawlsome	"call some," etc.

ALTAR, ALTER, AULTER

altar	palter	assaulter	unalter
alter	psalter	defaulter	"halt her" (etc.)
falter	salter	drysalter	
halter	vaulter	exalter	

ALTRY

paltry	psaltery	drysaltery

ALTY, *see* AULTY

ALY, AILY, ALELY

bailie	maily	stalely	halely
baily	palely	taily	capercailie
daily	scaly	traily	pali
frailly	shaly	*vale*	rationale
gaily	snaily	waly	shillaly
greyly			

AMA

drama, diorama, neorama, rama
llama, georama, panorama, yama
lama, kaama, pyjama, cosmorama
melodrama, kama

AMANT, *see* AIMANT

AMBEAU, *see* AMBO

AMBER

amber, camber, clamber, tambour

AMBIT

ambit, gambit

AMBLE, AMBOL

amble, ramble, wamble, tramble
bramble, scamble, preamble, skimble-skamble
gamble, scramble, shamble
gambol

AMBLER, AMBLING, etc., *see* AMBLE

AMBO, AMBEAU

crambo, Sambo, ambo, Zambo
flambeau

AMBOL, *see* AMBLE

AMEFUL

blameful, shameful, flameful

AMEL, AMMEL

camel, enamel, hammel, mammal
trammel, entrammel

AMELESS

shameless (etc.), *see* AIM

AMELY

gamely, lamely, namely, tamely

AMENESS, *see* AIM

AMER, *see* AIM

AMFER, AMPHOR

camphor, chamfer

AMINE

famine	examine	reëxamine	"am in" (etc.)
gamin	cross-examine		

AMISH

famish	lambish	enfamish	rammish
hammish	affamish		

AMLET

camlet	hamlet	samlet	

AMMAR, AMMER, AMOR

clamor	hammer	enamour	slammer
crammer	rammer	ninnyhammer	sledge-hammer
gammer	shammer	yellowhammer	"damn her" (etc.)
glamour	stammer	dammer	
grammar	yammer		

AMMOCK

cammock	hammock	mammock	

AMMON, ALMON

gammon	salmon	*damon*	ammon
mammon	backgammon	Shamon	

AMMY

clammy	hammy	gammy	tammy
Sammy	mammy	shammy	chamois
drammie	ramie	tamis	"damme"

AMOR, *see* AMMAR

AMPAS, *see* AMPUS

AMPER

damper	scamper	stamper (etc.), *see* AMP	"vamp her" (etc.)
hamper	tamper		
pamper			

AMPHOR, *see* AMFER

AMPIAN, AMPION

campian	champion	grampian	

AMPING

camping (etc.), *see* AMP

AMPLE

ample	trample	ensample	example
sample			

AMPLER, AMPLING, *see* AMPLE

AMPLY

amply	damply	tramply

AMPUS, AMPAS

grampus	pampas	campus	"vamp us" (etc.)

AMUS, AMOUS

camus	squamous	biramous	"shame us"
famous	mandamus	hamous	(etc.)
ramous	ignoramus	Shamus	

AMY, *see* AIM

ANA, ANNA

banana	liana	bandanna	savannah
sultana	zenana	hosannah	tanna
befana	anna	ipecacuanha	Hannah
iguana	Anna	manna	Havana
kerana			

ANATE, ANET, ANITE

granite	pomegranate	tannate	"can it" (etc.)
planet	khanate		

ANCEL

chancel	handsel

ANCELESS

chanceless (etc.), *see* ANCE

ANCER, ANSWER

answer	geomancer	anser	glancer
cancer	chiromancer	merganser	prancer
dancer	necromancer	advancer	"advance her"
lancer	enhancer	chancer	(etc.)
romancer	entrancer		

ANCET, ANSIT

lancet	transit	"chance it" (etc.)

ANCHION, *see* ANSION

ANCHOR, *see* ANKER

ANCHORED, *see* ANKARD

ANCOR, *see* ANKER

Ancy

chancy
fancy
mischancy
acromancy
arithmancy
chiromancy
hesitancy
geomancy
lithomancy
necromancy
onomancy
rhabdomancy
termagancy
aldermancy
alectoromancy
alectryomancy
aleuromancy
alomancy
alphitomancy
anthropomancy
astragalomancy
austromancy
axinomancy
belomancy
bibliomancy
botanomancy
catoptromancy
ceromancy
chaomancy
cleromancy
consonancy
coscinomancy
crithomancy
crystallomancy
dactyliomancy
sideromancy
significancy
spodomancy
stichomancy
dancy
enoptomancy
exorbitancy
extravagancy
exuberancy
gastromancy
gyromancy
hieromancy
hydromancy
lecanomancy
mendicancy
meteoromancy
militancy
myomancy
occupancy
œnomancy
oneiromancy
ophiomancy
ornithomancy
pedomancy
pessomancy
petulancy
precipitancy
psychomancy
sciomancy
sibilancy
supplicancy
sycophancy
tephramancy
unchancy

Andal, *see* Andle

Andant, Andent

candent
commandant
demandant

Andate, Andit

bandit
mandate
"demand it," etc.

Andem, –om, –um

random
memorandum
avizandum
mandom
tandem
"hand 'em" (etc.)

Andent, *see* Andant

Ander, Andor

candor
dander
gander
grander (etc.), *see* And
pander
slander
bystander
"land her" (etc.)
commander
meander
philander
pomander
coriander
jerrymander
oleander
salamander
back-hander
dittander
glander

Anders

glanders
sanders
ganders (*and add s to nouns and verbs above*)

Andeur, *see* Andier

ANDID

bandied	candid	candied	uncandid
brandied	"man did," etc.		

ANDING

landing	notwithstanding	banding (etc.), *see* AND

ANDISH

blandish	standish	outlandish	grandish
brandish			

ANDIT, *see* ANDATE

ANDLE, ANDAL

candle	handle	scandal	vandal
dandle	sandal		

ANDLER

chandler	dandler	handler	tallow-chandler

ANDLING, *see* ANDLE

ANDOM, *see* ANDAM

ANDOUR, *see* ANDER

ANDSOME, *see* ANSOM

ANDUM, *see* ANDAM

ANDY

bandy	dandy	sandy	jackadandy
brandy	handy	unhandy	pandy
candy	randy	jaborandi	"Andy"

ANEFUL, *see* AINFUL

ANEL, ANIL, ANNEL

anil	flannel	empanel	stannel
cannel	panel	annal	trannel
channel	scrannel	pannel	unpannel

ANELY, AINLY

gainly	sanely	profanely	inanely
mainly	vainly	ungainly	insanely
plainly	humanely	mundanely	

ANEOUS (*pronounced two or three syllables*)

cutaneous	instantaneous	subterraneous	extemporaneous
extraneous	miscellaneous	contemporaneous	
spontaneous	simultaneous		

ANER, AINER

plainer
stainer (etc.), *see* AIN
chicaner
attainer

ANET, *see* ANATE

ANGAR, *see* ANGER (*hard* G)

ANGELY

changely
strangely

ANGER (*hard* G), **ANGAR, ANGOR, ANGUOR, ANGUER**

anger
languor
sangar
angor
hangar

ANGER (*silent* G)

banger
clangor
ganger
hanger
haranguer
paper-hanger (etc.)
whanger
"bang her" (etc.)

ANGER (*soft* G)

danger
manger
ranger
stranger
endanger
money-changer
arranger
bushranger
changer
deranger
disarranger
estranger
exchanger
granger
interchanger
"change her" (etc.)

ANGING

hanging (etc.), *see* ANG

ANGLE

angle
bangle
dangle
fangle
interjangle
mangle
spangle
strangle
intertangle
twangle
brangle
embrangle
phalangle
quackangle
wrangle
entangle
untangle
disentangle
bemangle
bespangle
triangle

ANGLED, ANGOLD

angled
new-fangled
mangold
dangled (etc.), *see* ANGLE

ANGLER, ANGLING, *see* ANGLE

ANGLESS

fangless (etc.), *see* ANG

ANGOLD, *see* ANGLED

ANGUOR, *see* ANGER (*hard* G)

ANGUISH

anguish languish

ANGOR, *see* ANGER (*hard* G)

ANGY

changy mangy rangy

ANIC, ANNIC

panic tannic Britannic botanic mechanic Alcoranic aldermanic Aristophanic Brahmanic charlatanic ferricyanic galvanic Germanic hydrocyanic tyrannic satanic diaphanic oceanic talismanic interoceanic lexiphanic Messianic organic Ossianic Puritanic quercitannic rhodanic stannic Sultanic tetanic tympanic valerianic volcanic vulcanic Espanic

ANICS, *see* ANNEX

ANIL, *see* ANEL

ANION, ANON

canyon companion banyan

ANISH, ANNISH

banish clannish mannish planish vanish evanish

ANITE, *see* ANATE

ANKARD, ANCHORED, ANKERED

anchored cankered rancored hankered tankard brancard "drank hard" (etc.)

ANKER, ANCOUR

blanker clanker danker (etc.), *see* ANK unanchor anchor canker hanker rancor ranker spanker "thank her" (etc.)

ANKLE

ankle rankle crankle hankle

ANKLY

ankly	crankly	rankly	lankly
blankly	frankly	dankly	

ANLESS

manless, planless (etc.), *see* AN

ANNA, *see* ANA

ANNALS

annals	channels (etc.), *see* ANEL

ANNER, ANOR

banner	manor	lanner	planner (etc.),
manner	tanner	"fan her," etc.	*see* AN

ANNEX, ANICS

annex	panics	mechanics	humanics

ANNY

branny	clanny	manny	uncanny
cranny	granny	canny	"can he," etc.

ANON, *see* ANION

ANOR, *see* ANNER

ANSION, ANCHION

panchion	stanchion	mansion	expansion
scansion			

ANSIT, *see* ANCET

ANSOM, ANDSOME

handsome	ransom	transom	unhandsome
hansom			

ANSWER, *see* ANCER

ANSY

pansy	tansy	*chimpanzee*

ANTAM, ANTOM, ANTUM

bantam	phantom	*quantum*	*tantum*

ANTE, ANTY

ante	janty	dilettante	"Santy"
anti	scanty	infante	"can't he"
chanty	shanty	pococurante	(etc.)
auntie	andante	zante	

ANTEL, *see* ANTLE

ANTER

descanter	recanter	chanter	enchanter
implanter	transplanter	grantor	almacanter
instanter	trochanter	planter	"plant her"
levanter	banter	ranter	(etc.)
panter	canter	decanter	

ANTHER

anther	panther

ANTI, *see* ANTE

ANTHIC

œnanthic	zanthic

ANTIC

antic	romantic	corybantic	necromantic
frantic	sycophantic	geomantic	onomantic
Atlantic	bullantic	hierophantic	pyromantic
gigantic	chiromantic	hydromantic	spodomantic
pedantic	consonantic	mantic	transatlantic

ANTINE

adamantine	chryselephan-	dragantine	*Levantine*
elephantine	tine	gigantine	*Byzantine*

ANTLE

cantle	mantel	dismantle	scantle
hantle	mantle	immantle	

ANTLER

antler	mantler	pantler	dismantler

ANTLESS

pantless (etc.), *see* ANT

ANTLING

bantling	mantling	scantling	dismantling

ANTLY

scantly	slantly	ignorantly (etc.), *see* ANT

ANTO, ANTEAU

canto	couranto	Esperanto	quo-warranto
panto	portmanteau	pro-tanto	

ANTOM, *see* ANTAM

ANTRESS

enchantress	supplantress	covenantress	chantress

ANTRY

chantry	gantry	pantry

ANTY, *see* ANTE

ANUAL, ANNUAL

annual	manual	Emmanuel

ANY (*short*), *see* ENNY

ANY (*long*), AINY

brainy	drainy	rainy	veiny
cany	grainy	trainy	zany

ANZA

stanza	bonanza	extravaganza	Sancho Panza

APAL, *see* APLE

APEL, *see* APPLE

APELESS

capeless (etc.), *see* APE

APEN, APON

capon	misshapen	unshapen	tapen

APER, APIR, APOUR

caper	taper	aper	sky-scraper
draper (etc.), *see* APE	tapir	sapor	"escape her" (etc.)
paper	vapour	chaper	

APHIC, *see* AFFIC

APID

rapid	sapid	vapid

APIR, *see* APER

APIST

papist	shapest (etc.), *see* APE	landscapist	redtapist

APLE, APAL

maple	papal	staple	caple

APLESS

capless
hapless (etc.), *see* AP

APLING, APPLING

chapelling
grappling
knappling
papling
sapling
scrapling
thrappling
dappling
lapling
tapling

APNEL

grapnel
shrapnel

APON, *see* APEN

APOUR, *see* APER

APPER

capper
entrapper (etc.), *see* AP
fly-sapper
wrapper
"yapper"
clapper
dapper
flapper
sapper
understrapper
whipper-snapper

APPET

lappet
tappet
"wrap it," etc.

APPIE, *see* APPY

APPING

strapping (etc.), *see* AP

APPLE, APEL

apple
chapel
grapple
knapple
love-apple
thrapple
dapple
rappel
scapple

APPY, APPIE

chappie
flappy
happy
mappy
nappy
pappy
sappy
unhappy
knappy
scrappy
snappy

APSION, *see* APTION

APTER, APTOR

apter
captor
chapter
adapter
rapter
recaptor
"slapped her"

APTION

caption
adaption
collapsion
contraption
recaption

APTIST, APTEST

aptest	adaptest	inaptest	raptest
baptist	anabaptist		

APTOR, *see* APTER

APTURE

capture	rapture	recapture	enrapture

ARAB

Arab	scarab

ARAGE, *see* ARRIAGE

ARASS, *see* ARRAS

ARBER, ARBOR

arbor	enharbor	harbor	unharbor
barber			

ARBLE, ARBEL

barbel	marble	garbel	enmarble
garble			

ARBLESS

barbless (etc.), *see* ARB

ARBOARD

larboard	starboard

ARBOIL

garboil	parboil

ARBOR, *see* ARBER

ARCEL, ARSEL

parcel	tarsel	sarcel

ARCHER

archer	starcher (etc.), *see* ARCH	clear-starcher	departure
marcher			

ARCHLESS, *see* ARCH

ARCHLY

archly	starchly

ARDEN, ARDON

garden	bear-garden	bombardon	gardon
harden	case-harden	enharden	Arden
pardon			

ARDER

harder (etc.), *see* ARD	larder	ardor	"guard her" (etc.)

ARDLESS, *see* ARD

ARDON, *see* ARDEN

ARDY

hardy	lardy	foolhardy	tardy

AREL, ARREL

barrel	apparel	*carol*

ARELESS, *see* AIR

ARELY, AIRLY

barely	rarely	warely	debonairly
fairly	squarely	yarely	unfairly

ARENT, *see* ARRANT

ARER

fairer (etc.), *see* AIR

ARET, ARAT, ARRET

arret	carat	claret	garret

ARFLESS

scarfless (etc.), *see* ARF

ARGENT, ERGEANT

argent	margent	sergeant	serjeant

ARGER

charger	larger (etc.), *see* ARGE

ARGLE, ARGOL

gargle	gargol	argle-bargle

ARGO

argot	embargo	supercargo	botargo
cargo	potargo	largo	"far go" (etc.)

ARIC

barbaric	pindaric	cinnabaric

ARID, ARRIED

arid	harried	married	parried
carried	intermarried	tarried	miscarried

ARING, AIRING

airing
bearing
daring
fairing (etc.), *see* AIR
hair-ring
seafaring
wayfaring (etc.)
chairing
charing
forswearing
outdaring
outstaring
outswearing
outwearing
overbearing
unbaring
unsparing
tale-bearing
upbearing
upstaring
uptearing

ARION, ARRION

clarion
carrion
"marry on," etc.

ARIOUS

various
bifarious
contrarious
gregarious
nefarious
ovarious
precarious
vicarious
multifarious
temerarious
"carry us" (etc.)

ARISH

barish
bearish
fairish
garish
rarish
sparish
squarish
debonairish

ARKEN

darken
hearken

ARKER

barker (etc.), *see* ARK

ARKISH

"clerkish"
darkish
larkish
sparkish

ARKLE

sparkle
monarchal
disembarkal
patriarchal
darkle

ARKLESS

sparkless (etc.), *see* ARK

ARKLING

darkling
sparkling

ARKLY

"clerkly"
darkly
parkly
sparkly
starkly

ARKY

barky
"clerky"
heark'ee
larky
parquet
parky
sharky
sparky (etc.), *see* ARK
hierarchy
matriarchy
darky
heterarchy
oligarchy
patriarchy
markee

Arler, Arlor

marler	parlor	snarler	gnarler

Arless

starless (etc.), *see* Ar

Arlet

scarlet	varlet	carlet	starlet

Arley, Arly

barley	parley	gnarly	particularly
marly	snarly		(etc.), *see* Ar

Arlic

garlic	harlech	pilgarlick	sarlik

Arling

darling	marling	sparling	starling
gnarling	snarling		

Arlor, *see* Arler

Arly, *see* Arley

Armer

armor	farmer (etc.),	baby-farmer	"harm her"
charmer	*see* Arm	snake-charmer	(etc.)

Arming

uncharming	farming	alarming (etc.),
		see Arm

Armless

harmless (etc.), *see* Arm

Armor, *see* Armer

Arnal, Arnel

carnel	uncharnel	carnal	charnel
darnel			

Arner

garner	yarner (etc.), *see* Arn

Arness

farness	harness

Arnish

garnish	tarnish	varnish

Aron, *see* Arren

ARPER
harper (etc.), *see* ARP

ARRACK

arrack	barrack	carrack

ARRANT, ARENT

arrant	apparent	transparent

ARRAS, ARRASS, ARASS

arras	harass	embarrass

ARREL, *see* AREL *and* ORAL (*short*)

ARREN, ARON

baron	barren	fanfaron	charon

ARRET, *see* ARET

ARROT

carrot	parrot

ARRIAGE, ARAGE

carriage	disparage	miscarriage	intermarriage
marriage			

ARRIER

barrier	harrier	parrier	charier
carrier	marrier	tarrier	warier
farrier			

ARRION, *see* ARION

ARRIOR, *see* ORRIER

ARROT, *see* ARET

ARROW

arrow	marrow	yarrow	*caballero*
barrow	narrow	rest-harrow	faro
farrow	sparrow	bolero	*sombrero*
harrow			

ARRY (*long*)

sparry	tarry	barry	charry
starry	aracari	carbonari	scarry

ARRY (*as in* marry)

harry	parry	intermarry	charivari
marry	miscarry	cassowary	harri-karri

ARRY (*as in* marry)—(*Cont.*)

ablutionary
accessary
accustomary
actuary
additionary
adversary
ancillary
antiquary
apothecary
arbitrary
beneficiary
canary
capillary
cautionary
centenary
chary
commentary
commissary
confectionary
constabulary
contemporary
contrary
contributary
corollary
carry
culinary
customary
dairy
dictionary;
see also ERRY *and* AIRY

ARSEL, *see* ARCEL

ARSELY, *see* ARSLEY

ARSHAL

marshal
martial
partial
impartial
immartial

ARSLEY

parsley
sparsely

ARSON

arson
parson
"Kit Carson"

ARTAN, ARTEN

hearten
marten
smarten
Spartan
tartan
dishearten
kindergarten
barton
carton
enhearten

ARTAR, ARTER, ARTYR

barter
carter (etc.), *see* ART
charter
garter
martyr
tartar
bemartyr
"darter"
protomartyr
upstarter
"start her" (etc.)

ARTEL, *see* ARTLE

ARTER, *see* ARTAR

ARTEST, *see* ARTIST

ARTFUL

artful
cartful
heartful

ARTIST

artist
smartest (etc.), *see* ART

Artle, Artel

cartel	startle	dartle

Artless

heartless (etc.), *see* Art

Artlet

martlet	partlet	tartlet	heartlet

Artly

smartly	partly	tartly

Artner

partner	heartener	smartener	disheartener

Artridge

cartridge	partridge

Arture, *see* Archer

Arty

hearty	smarty	tea-party	ex parte
party	astarte	(etc.)	

Arvel

carvel	marvel	*larval*

Arvest

carvest	harvest	starvest

Arving

carving	starving

Ary, *see* Airy

Asal, Asil, Azel

nasal	basil	jazel	witch-hazel
hazel	appraisal		

Ascal, Aschal

mascle	paschal	rascal

Ascar, *see* Asker

Ascent

nascent	adnascent	indurascent	"daycent"
depascent	connascent	violascent	complaisant
renascent	enascent	adjacent	subjacent
renaissant	jacent	complacent	circumjacent
naissant	interjacent	"raycent"	

Aschish
haschish flashish rashish

Aseless
baseless (etc.), *see* Ace

Asely
basely spacely common-placely

Asement
casement abasement debasement defacement effacement embracement basement begracement belacement displacement enlacement erasement interlacement misplacement retracement

Aseous, *see* Aceous

Ashen, Ashion, Assion, Ation (*short*)
ashen fashion passion ration compassion empassion dispassion impassion

Asher (*short*)
flasher (etc.), *see* Ash rasher haberdasher

Asher (*long*)
washer (etc.), *see* Osh

Ashes
ashes spatterdashes (etc.), *see* Ash

Ashion, *see* Ashen

Ashie, Ashy
ashy flashy mashie plashy sachet slashy splashy mashy trashy "hashy"

Ashless
hashless (etc.), *see* Ash

Asil, *see* Azzle, *also* Asal

Asin, *see* Asten

Asion
abrasion dissuasion evasion invasion occasion persuasion evasion *Caucasian* Asian pervasion suasion Eurasian

ASIS, *see* ACIS

ASIVE

suasive	dissuasive	invasive	pervasive
assuasive	evasive	persuasive	quasive

ASKER, ASCAR

lascar	basker (etc.), *see* ASK	"ask her" (etc.)

ASKET

basket	flasket	gasket	lasket
casket			

ASKLESS

taskless (etc.), *see* ASK

ASON, *see* ASTEN, *also* AZEN

ASPER

asper jasper (etc.), *see* ASP

ASPLESS

haspless (etc.), *see* ASP

ASSAL, *see* ASTLE

ASSAIL, *see* OSTLE

ASSES

asses molasses (etc.), *see* ASS

ASSET, ACET, ACIT

asset	facet	tacit	fascet
basset	placet	brasset	

ASSIC, ACIC

classic	quaiacic	liassic	sebacic
boracic	jurassic	potassic	triassic
thoracic			

ASSING

passing surpassing (etc.), *see* ASS

ASSION, *see* ASHEN

ASSIVE

massive	passive	impassive

ASSLESS

gasless (etc.), *see* ASS

ASSOCK

bassock	cassock	hassock	

ASSY, ACE, ASSIE, ASSE

brassie	glassy	classy	brassy
chassé	grassy	massy	gassy
glacé	lassie	passé	morassy

ASTARD, ASTERED

bastard	castored	beplastered	plastered(etc.),
dastard	mastered		*see* ASTER

ASTEFUL

wasteful	distasteful	tasteful	

ASTEN, ASIN, ASON

basin	hasten	enchasten	caisson
chasten	mason		

ASTER (*long*)

baster	haster	foretaster	"chased her"
chaster	paster	waster	(etc.)

ASTER (*short*)

aster	disaster	band-master	interpilaster
caster	emplaster	beplaster	latinitaster
castor	piastre	blaster	medicaster
master	alabaster	cadaster	oleaster
pastor	burgomaster	sticking-plaster	overmaster
plaster	poetaster	criticaster	schoolmaster
vaster (etc.),	quartermaster	"flabbergaster"	taskmaster
see AST	balastre	goniaster	

ASTIC

drastic	chiliastic	bombastic	docimastic
mastic	clastic	ceroplastic	dynastic
plastic	ecclesiastic	dentoplastic	emplastic
elastic	enthusiastic	dichastic	encomiastic
fantastic	amphiblastic	onomastic	esemplastic
gymnastic	anaclastic	orgiastic	galvanoplastic
monastic	antiphrastic	paraphrastic	gelastic
sarcastic	antonomastic	paronomastic	iconoclastic
scholastic	bioplastic	peirastic	inelastic

ASTIC—(*Cont.*)

metaphrastic	periphiastic	proplastic	scholiastic
neoplastic	plagioclastic	protoplastic	spastic
pepastic	pleonastic		

ASTEING

hasteing (etc.), *see* AST

ASTING

lasting	everlasting (etc.), *see* AST

ASTLE, ASSAL, ASSEL

castle	entassel	wrastle	*wassail*
tassel	anvassal		

ASTLESS

castless (etc.), *see* AST

ASTLING

castling (etc.), *see* ASTLE

ASTLY

ghastly	lastly	vastly

ASTOR, *see* ASTER

ASTY (*long*)

hasty	pasty	tasty

ASTY (*short*)

nasty	vasty	epinasty	masty
pasty	blasty	genioplasty	

ASURE, AZURE, AZIER

azure	glazier	erasure	embrasure
brazier	grazier		

ATA (*English* A)

strata	errata	postulata	ultimata
albata	data	imbrocata	invertebrata
batata	dentata	serenata	pro rata

ATA (*continental* A) *Any of above, also*

sonata	inamorata	reata	regatta
cantata	matamata		

ATAL

datal	natal	ante-natal	statal
fatal	"fate 'll" (etc.)	post-natal	

Atan, Aighten, Aiten

Satan	straighten	straiten	

Atant, Atent

blatant	latent	natant	patent

Atcher, *see* Ature (*short*)

Atchet

hatchet	latchet	ratchet	"catch it" (etc.)

Atchless

matchless (etc.), *see* Atch

Atchman, Otchman

Scotchman	watchman		

Ateless, *see* Ait

Ately, Aitly

greatly accurately (etc.), *see* Ait *long and* Ate *short*

Aten, *see* Atten

Atent, *see* Atant

Ater (*as in* later), *see* Ator

Ater (*as in* water), *see* Aughter

Ather (*long*)

father	rather	*bother*	*pother*

Ather (*short*)

blather	foregather	upgather	lather

Athing, *see* Aything

Athless

pathless (etc.), *see* Ath

Atheless

scatheless (etc.), *see* Athe

Atial, Acial

glacial	craniofacial	palatial	spatial
abatial	racial	prelatial	unifacial

Atic, Attic

attic	dogmatic	erratic	pragmatic
static	dramatic	fanatic	prismatic
asthmatic	ecstatic	phlegmatic	quadratic
chromatic	emphatic	pneumatic	rheumatic

ATIC, ATTIC—(*Cont.*)

schismatic
stigmatic
aërostatic
emblematic
hydrostatic
mathematic
muriatic
pancreatic
symptomatic
systematic
epigrammatic
idiomatic
pathematic
phosphatic
piratic
plutocratic
poematic
vatic
viatic
achromatic
acousmatic
acroamatic
acroatic
acrobatic
adiabatic
agnatic
anagrammatic
anastatic
aphorismatic
aplanatic
aquatic
aristocratic
arithmocratic
aromatic
astatic
autocratic
automatic
axiomatic
bureaucratic
caryatic
clematic
commatic
dalmatic
democratic
dichromatic
dilemmatic
diplomatic
problematic
protatic
rhematic
sabbatic
schematic
sciatic
villatic
ecbatic
eleatic
endermatic
enigmatic
fluviatic
geostatic
grammatic
hepatic
hieratic
hyperbatic
hypostatic
idiocratic
idiosyncratic
isodiabatic
pinematic
lavatic
lymphatic
megastatic
melodramatic
miasmatic
mobocratic
morganatic
noematic
numismatic
ochlocratic
operatic
palatic
pancratic
sulphatic
sylvatic
thematic
timocratic
traumatic
truismatic

ATID

hydatid
caryatid
fatted
matted, etc.

ATIN

Latin
matin
patin
satin
platin

ATING

skating (etc.), *see* AIT

ATION, ATIAN

nation
ration
station
ablation
climation
efflation
flotation
fluxation
friation
frication
gunation
lallation
laudation
monstration
palpation
pausation
phonation
predation
quartation
quassation
reptation
tralation
afflation
agnation
Alsatian
aration
cantation
carnation
cassation
castration
causation
cessation
citation
cognation
collation
creation

Ation, Atian—(*Cont.*)

conflation
cremation
cubation
cunctation
curtation
curvation
dalmatian
damnation
deflation
delation
dictation
dilation
donation
dotation
duration
elation
equation
falcation
filtration
fixation
flagration
flammation
flirtation
formation
foundation
gestation
gradation
gustation
gyration
hortation
illation
inflation
lactation
lavation
legation
libation
libration
ligation
location
luctation
lunation
lustration
mactation
mandation
migration
mutation
narration
natation
negation
nodation
notation
novation
nudation
nugation
oblation
oration
orbation
ovation
perflation
piscation
plantation
plication
potation
prelation
privation
probation
prolation
prostration
pulsation
purgation
quotation
relation
rigation
rogation
rotation
saltation
salvation
scrutation
sensation
serration
siccation
signation
stagnation
stellation
sudation
taxation
temptation
tentation
translation
vacation
venation
vexation
vibration
vocation
abdication
aberration
abjuration
abnegation
abrogation
acceptation
acclamation
accubation
accusation
adaptation
admiration
adoration
adulation
adumbration
advocation
aëration
affectation
affidation
affirmation
agitation
aggravation
aggregation
allegation
allocation
alteration
altercation
alternation
amputation
anhelation
animation
annexation
annotation
ablactation
absentation
acceptation
acervation
actitation
actuation
adequation
adhortation
adjuration
adornation
adversation
aërostation
ambulation
ampliation
angulation
angentation
arrestation
assentation
attrectation
auscultation
blusteration
bombilation
botheration
cameration
cantillation
castellation
coaxation
colligation
compellation
concertation
crenellation
crimination
cupellation
debarkation
decantation
decollation
decoration
decubation
decussation
deflagration
defraudation
dehortation

ATION, ATIAN—(*Cont.*)

denization
denotation
dentilation
deplication
deploration
deputation
depuration
deterration
disculpation
disputation
divulgation
ejulation
equitation
ereptation
eructation
evolation
exculpation
exhumation
exploitation
expugnation
exsiccation
exsufflation
fasciation
federation
feneration
fenestration
fibrination
filiation
fissipation
flagitation
floccillation
flucteration
faliation
fraternation
frequentation
gemination
glandulation
glomeration
gloriation
gratulation
gravidation
hebetation
hibernation
ideation
impugnation
induration
inchoation
incremation
inculpation
incurbation
infestation
infiltration
inhalation
innervation
innovation
instauration
insufflation
insultation
intensation
intrication
irritation
isolation
jubilation
lamination
lancination
laniation
levitation
liberation
lubrication
malformation
malleation
marmoration
maturation
matuation
obscuration
obstination
obviation
oneration
orchestration
otiation
panellation
pestination
perfectation
pestillation
presensation
profligation
propination
radication
reclamation
recusation
regelation
remanation
remonstration
ruination
rustication
salination
segmentation
sibilation
sideration
sinuation
suspensation
syncopation
temeration
tremulation
ultimation
vaccination
vellication
appellation
application
approbation
arbitration
arrogation
aspiration
assignation
attestation
augmentation
auguration
aviation
avocation
balneation
bifurcation
cachinnation
calcination
calculation
cancellation
capitation
captivation
castigation
celebration
circulation
cogitation
collocation
coloration
combination
commendation
commination
commutation
compensation
compilation
complication
compurgation
computation
concentration
condemnation
condensation
condonation
confirmation
confiscation
conflagration
conformation
confrontation
confutation
congelation
conglobation
congregation
conjugation
conjuration
connotation
consecration
conservation
consolation
constellation
consternation
consultation
consummation
contemplation
conversation
convocation

Ation, Atian—(*Cont.*)

copulation
coronation
corporation
correlation
corrugation
coruscation
crepitation
culmination
cultivation
cumulation
decimation
declamation
declaration
declination
dedication
defalcation
defamation
defecation
defloration
defœdation
deformation
degradation
degustation
delectation
delegation
dementation
demonstration
denudation
depilation
deportation
depravation
deprecation
depredation
deprivation
derivation
derogation
desecration
desiccation
designation
desolation
desperation
destination
detestation
detonation
detruncation
devastation
deviation
digitation
dilatation
dislocation
dispensation
disportation
dissertation
dissipation
distillation
divagation
divination
domination
dubitation
duplication
education
elevation
elongation
emanation
embarkation
embrocation
emendation
emigration
emulation
enervation
estimation
estivation
evagation
evocation
exaltation
excavation
excitation
exclamation
execration
exhalation
exhortation
expectation
expiation
expiration
explanation
explication
exploration
exportation
expurgation
extirpation
extrication
exudation
exultation
exundation
fabrication
fascination
fecundation
festination
fermentation
figuration
flagellation
fluctuation
fomentation
fornication
fulmination
fumigation
generation
germination
glaciation
graduation
granulation
gravitation
gubernation
habitation
hesitation
illustration
imitation
implantation
implication
importation
imprecation
impregnation
imputation
incantation
incarnation
incitation
inclination
incrustation
incubation
inculcation
indentation
indication
indignation
induration
infeudation
inflammation
information
inspiration
installation
instigation
instillation
intimation
intonation
inundation
invitation
invocation
irrigation
jactitation
jaculation
judication
laceration
lamentation
lapidation
laureation
legislation
levigation
supplication
suppuration
suspiration
sustentation
limitation
lineation
litigation
lucubration
maceration
machination
maculation
malversation

ATION, ATIAN—(*Cont.*)

manducation
mastication
mediation
medication
meditation
mensuration
ministration
misrelation
mitigation
moderation
modulation
molestation
mordication
mutilation
navigation
nidulation
numeration
obduration
obfuscation
objurgation
obligation
observation
occultation
occupation
operation
ordination
oscillation
osculation
pabulation
palliation
palpitation
peculation
penetration
percolation
perduration
perforation
permeation
permutation
peroration
perpetration
personation
perspiration
perturbation
population
postulation
predication
preparation
termination
titillation
toleration
presentation
preservation
proclamation
procreation
procuration
profanation
prolongation
propagation
prorogation
prosternation
protestation
provocation
publication
punctuation
radiation
recantation
recitation
recreation
recubation
reformation
refutation
registration
regulation
relaxation
relagation
renovation
reparation
replication
reprobation
reputation
reservation
resignation
respiration
restoration
retardation
retractation
revelation
revocation
rumination
salutation
scintillation
segregation
semination
separation
sequestration
simulation
situation
speculation
spoliation
sternutation
stimulation
stipulation
subornation
sublimation
suffocation
transformation
transmutation
transplantation
transportation
trepidation
tribulation
triplication
niceration
usurpation
vacillation
valuation
variegation
variation
vegetation
veneration
ventilation
vesication
vindication
violation
visitation
vitiation
abbreviation
abomination
acceleration
abbacination
adjudication
acclimatation
accreditation
accrimination
agglutination
aggrandization
alimentation
alineation
analyzation
anglification
annunciation
antilibration
appreciation
asphyxiation
averruncation
basification
brutalization
calcification
calumniation
caprification
carbonization
castramatation
catechization
codification
columniation
commiseration
contravallation
cornification
deconsecration
decrepitation
delimitation
deltafication
deoppilation
deosculation
depositation
depreciation
devirgination
diffarreation

ATION, ATIAN—(*Cont.*)

dimidiation
discoloration
disintegration
disseveration
dissociation
documentation
domestication
edulcoration
effectuation
effemination
effoliation
electrization
emaciation
endenization
enucleation
equalization
equilibration
eradication
eternization
evacuation
eventuation
evisceration
exacervation
excogitation
excruciation
exercitation
exfoliation
expatiation
expoliation
expropriation
exsuscitation
extravasation
facilitation
ferrumination
fertilization
feudalization
florification
flossification
foreordination
fortification
fossilization
galvanization
gasification
gelatination
geniculation
habilitation
habituation
harcolation
harmonization
Hellenization
horrification
hypothecation
illoquation
inanimation
infeodation
intoleration
jollification
legalization
licentiation
lignification
manipulation
modernization
moralization
mystification
nasalization
necessitation
predomination
protuberation
quantification
realization
recalcitration
recuperation
rejuvenation
reticulation
vaticination
vivification
accentuation
accommodation
accumulation
adjudication
administration
adulteration
affiliation
alienation
alleviation
alliteration
amalgamation
amplification
annihilation
anticipation
appropriation
approximation
argumentation
articulation
assassination
asseveration
assimilation
association
attenuation
authorization
canonization
capitulation
circumvallation
clarification
coagulation
cohabitation
coindication
commemora-
tion
commensura-
tion
communication
concatenation
conciliation
confabulation
confederation
configuration
conglomeration
congratulation
consideration
consolidation
contamination
continuation
co-operation
co-ordination
corroboration
crystallization
debilitation
decortication
degeneration
deification
deliberation
delineation
denomination
denunciation
depopulation
despoliation
deterioration
determination
dignification
dilapidation
disapprobation
discrimination
disfiguration
disinclination
disobligation
dissemination
dissimulation
divarication
dulcification
edification
ejaculation
elaboration
elicitation
elimination
elucidation
emancipation
emasculation
enumeration
enunciation
equivocation
evaporation
exacerbation
exaggeration
examination
exasperation
excoriation
exhilaration

ATION, ATIAN—(*Cont.*)

exoneration
expectoration
expostulation
extenuation
extermination
falsification
felicitation
fortification
gesticulation
glorification
gratification
hallucination
humiliation
illumination
imagination
immaculation
immoderation
impropriation
inapplication
inauguration
incarceration
incineration
incorporation
incrimination
inebriation
infatuation
ingemination
initiation
inoculation
insemination
insinuation
intercalation
interpolation
interpretation
interrogation
intoxication
investigation
irradiation
justification
legitimation
ludification
manifestation
matriculation
melioration
mellification
misinformation
modification
mollification
mortification
multiplication
negotiation
nidification
notification
obliteration
organization
origination
ossification
pacification
participation
perambulation
peregrination
perpetuation
precipitation
predestination
prefiguration
prejudication
premeditation
preoccupation
preponderation
prevarication
procrastination
prognostication
prolification
pronunciation
propitiation
purification
qualification
ramification
ratification
recommendation
recrimination
rectification
reciprocation
redintegration
reduplication
refrigeration
regeneration
regurgitation
reiteration
remuneration
renunciation
representation
repudiation
resuscitation
retaliation
reverberation
sanctification
scarification
signification
solemnization
sophistication
specification
subordination
subtilization
symbolization
tergiversation
testification
thurification
versification
vitrification
vituperation
vociferation
beatification
circumnavigation
contraindication
cross-examination
discontinuation
disqualification
diversification
excommunication
inconsideration
indemnification
indetermination
individuation
interlineation
lapidification
maladministration
misrepresentation
naturalization
personification
predetermination
ratiocination
recapitulation
reconciliation
seminification
spiritualization
superannuation
supererogation
transubstantiation
undervaluation
volatilization
abalienation
allegorization
amelioration
demonetization
deterioration
differentiation
domiciliation
economization
electrification
exemplification
experimentation
extemporization

Ation, Atian—(*Cont.*)

externalization	identification	sensualization	specialization
idealization			

Atish

latish	slatish	straightish	sedatish

Atist, *see* Attest

Ative, Aitiff

caitiff	dilative	vegetative	designative
dative	emulative	legislative	suffocative
native	estimative	meditative	violative (*and*
creative	generative	operative	*the suffix* tive
procreative	hesitative	quantitative	*in place of*
cogitative	imitative	sative	tion *on other*
continuative	innovative	stative	*words under*
cumulative	terminative	speculative	Ation)

Atless

hatless (etc.), *see* At

Atling, Attling

gatling	battling (etc.), *see* Attle	fatling

Atly, Attly

flatly	patly	rattly (etc.), *see* Attle

Ato (*English* A)

plato	potato	tomato	literato

Ato (*continental* A)

staccato	obligato	"got to"	"ought not to" (etc.)
tomato			

Ator, Ater, Aiter, Aitor

cater	collaborator	creator	testator
crater	(etc.), *and*	cunctator	agitator
gaiter	*verbs in* Ate	curator	alligator
mater	later (etc.), *see*	dictator	commentator
pater	Ait	equator	alma mater
greater	traitor	scrutator	satyr
hater	waiter	spectator	conservator

ATRIX

cicatrix	matrix	impropriatrix	administratrix
generatrix	testatrix	mediatrix	spectatrix

imitatrix (*and the suffix* atrix *may be arbitrarily substituted for* ATOR *in most cases*)

ATRON

matron	natron	patron

ATTEN, ATON, ATEN

baton	fatten	paten	platen
batten	flatten	patten	ratten

ATTER

batter	latter	smatter	bepatter
blatter	matter	spatter	bescatter
chatter	patter	tatter	blatter
clatter	platter	bespatter	ratter
fatter	scatter	attar	*satyr*
flatter	shatter	beflatter	splatter
hatter	"at her" (etc.)		

ATTERN, ATURN

pattern	lattern	Saturn	slattern

ATTEST, ATIST, ATTICED

bratticed	statist (etc.), *see* AT	flattest (etc.), *see* AT	latticed

ATTLE

battle	prattle	battel	rattle
tittle-tattle	cattle	tattle	chattel
embattle			

ATTLER, ATTLING, etc., *see* ATTLE

ATTO, ATEAU

plateau	chateâu	mulatto	annatto

ATTRESS

mulattress	mattress	flatteress

ATTY

batty	chatty	natty	catty
patty	matty	gnatty	ratty
fatty			

ATUM

datum	substratum	erratum	pomatum
desideratum	stratum	ultimatum	postulatum

ATURE (*long*)

nature	legislature	unnature	nomenclature
plicature			

ATURE (*short*), ATCHER

stature	patcher	hatcher	despatcher
thatcher	scratcher	snatcher	matcher
detacher	catcher	"detach her" (etc.)	

ATURN, *see* ATTERN

ATUS

literatus	afflatus	hiatus	"berate us" (etc.)
apparatus	saleratus	senatus	
stratus	status		

ATY, EIGHTY, ATEY

eighty	praty	weighty	platy
matey	slaty		

AUBLESS
daubless (etc.), *see* AUB

AUCHION, *see* AUTION

AUCTION, *see* OCTION

AUDAL, AUDLE, AWDLE

caudal	bicaudal	caudle	dawdle

AUDIT

audit	plaudit

AUDLIN

maudlin	"dawdlin'"

AUDY, AWDY

bawdy	gaudy	dawdy

AUGHLESS
laughless (etc.), *see* AFF

AUGHTER, ATER, AUTER (*for rhymes to* laughter *see* AFTER)

daughter	slaughter	firewater	"taught her" (etc.)
manslaughter	backwater	"hadn't oughter" (etc.)	
water	tauter		

AUGHTY, OUGHTY

doughty	haughty	naughty	

AUKLESS

chalkless (etc.), *see* ALK

AULIC

aulic	interaulic	hydraulic	*Gallic*

AULING, *see* ALLING

AULTER, *see* ALTAR

AULTY, ALTY

faulty	malty	walty	salty
vaulty			

AUNCHLESS, *see* AUNCH

AUNDER

launder	maunder		

AUNDRY

laundry	maundry		

AUNLESS

dawnless (etc.), AWN

AUNTER

haunter	vaunter (etc.), *see* AUNT	saunter	taunter

AUNTLESS, *see* AUNT

AUPER, *see* ORPOR

AUREL, *see* ORAL, (*short*)

AUSELESS

causeless (etc.), *see* AUSE

AUSEOUS, AUTIOUS

precautious	cautious	nauseous	"wash us" (etc.)

AUSTIC, *see* OSTIC

AUSTLESS

exhaustless (etc.), *see* AUST

AUSTRAL

austral	claustral		

AUTION, AUCHION
caution incaution fauchion precaution

AUTIOUS, *see* AUSEOUS

AVA
brava lava guava Nava
cassava

AVAGE
ravage savage scavage

AVEL (*short*), AVIL
cavil travel gavel travail
unravel gravel cavil ravel

AVELESS
naveless (etc.), *see* AVE

AVELIN
javelin ravelin "travelin'" (etc.)

AVELING
knaveling shaveling waveling

AVELY
bravely gravely suavely knavely
slavely

AVEMENT
depravement lavement pavement enslavement
engravement

AVEN
craven haven raven shaven
engraven graven

AVER
cadaver claver "have her" (etc.)

AVER (*as in* quaver, *see* AVOR)

AVERN
cavern tavern

AVID
avid impavid gravid pavid

AVIER, *see* AVIOR

AVIL, *see* AVEL

AVIOR

pavior, savior, havier, wavier, misbehavior, behavior, clavier, "save yer" (etc.)

AVISH (*long*)

bravish, knavish, slavish

AVISH (*short*)

lavish, enravish, MacTavish

AVIT

cessavit, indicavit, affidavit, "save it" (etc.), davit

AVO

bravo, octavo

AVOR, AVER

claver, craver, enslaver, graver (etc.), *see* AVE, papaver, waiver, favor, flavor, haver, quaver, savor, shaver, slaver, disfavor, engraver, semiquaver

AVY

gravy, wavy, navy, cavy, slavey, peccavi

AWDRY

bawdry, tawdry

AWDY, *see* AUDY

AWER

drawer (etc.), *see* OR *and* AW

AWFUL

awful, lawful, unlawful, "jawfull" (etc.)

AWKER, *see* ALKER

AWLER

trawler (etc.), *see* ALL

AWLESS

lawless (etc.), *see* AW

AWLING, *see* ALLING

AWNING

awning	spawning	yawning (etc.) *see* AUN

AWNLESS

dawnless (etc.), *see* AWN

AWNY

brawny	lawny	scrawny	mulligatawny
fawny	tawny	yawny	

AWY

flawy	pawy	strawy	thawy
jawy	*See also* OY—*one syllable*		

AWYER

lawyer	sawyer	topsawyer

AXEN, AXON

flaxen	Saxon	waxen	klaxon

AXLESS, *see* AX

AXY

flaxy	taxi	ataraxy	waxy

AYDAY, EYDAY

heyday	pay-day	May-day	play-day
layday			

AYER, EYOR (*for rhymes to* prayer *see* AIR)

purveyor	payer	layer	surveyor (etc), *see* AY

AYEY, EYEY

clayey	sprayey	wheyey

AYFISH, AFISH

crayfish	safish

AYFUL

playful	dismayful	"gayful" (etc.)	"tray full" (etc.)

AYING

saying (etc.), *see* AY

AYLING, *see* AILING

AYLESS
dayless (etc.), *see* AY

AYMAN

layman	"matinée man"	drayman	bay-man
highwayman			

AYMENT, *see* AIMANT

AYORESS, *see* EIRESS

AYTHING

plaything — scathing (etc.), *see* ATHE

AZARD

hazard	mazard	haphazard

AZEL, *see* ASAL

AZELESS
praiseless (etc.), *see* AISE

AZEN, AZON, ASON, AISIN

blazon	gazon	diapason	glazen
brazen	raisin	emblazon	"gazin'"
scazon			

AZEMENT

amazement — erasement — *casement* (etc.) *see* ASEMENT

AZER, AISER, AZOR

blazer	phaser	stargazer (etc.), *see* AISE	"amaze her" (etc.)
razor			

AZIER, *see* ASURE

AZZLE, ASIL

basil	razzle-dazzle	frazzle	bedazzle
dazzle	drazel	razzle	

AZY, AISY

crazy	lackadaisy	lazy	jasey
daisy	hazy	sleazy	mazy

EA

Althæa	dahabieh	spiræa	panacea
cavalleria	(dyspnœa)	zea	ratafia
cypræa	obeah	idea	onomatopœia

Eaceless
peaceless (etc.), *see* Eace

Eacher, Eature

breacher	creature	preacher	impeacher
breecher	defeature	reacher	entreature
screecher	feature	teacher	"beat yer"
beacher	peacher	beseecher	(etc.)
bleacher			

Eachless
peachless (etc.), *see* Each

Eachment

peachment	beseechment	impeachment	preachment

Eachy, *see* Eechy

Eacon, *see* Eaken

Eaden, (*short*)

deaden	threaden	leaden	redden

Eader
leader (etc.), *see* Ead

Eadle, Eedle

needle	*pedal*	beadle	tweedle

Ealment

concealment	revealment	congealment	repealment

Ealmless
helmless (etc.), *see* Ealm

Ealot

helot	zealot

Ealous

jealous	procellous	entellus	Marcellus
zealous	apellous	vitellus	

Ealy, Eely, Ely

chely	peely	squealy	wheely
freely	seely	steely	genteely
mealy			

Eamon, Æmon, Eeman, Eman, Emon

beeman	demon	leman	gleeman
dæmon	freeman	teaman	seaman

EAMER, EEMER, EMER, EMIR, EMUR

emir
femur
steamer
streamer
redeemer (etc.), *see* EAM

EAMISH

beamish
squeamish

EAMLESS

steamless (etc.), *see* EAM

EAMSTER, *see* EEMSTER

EAMY

seamy (etc.), *see* EAM

EAN, EIAN, IEN

lien
pæan
plebian
pygmean
empyrean
European
hymenean
tartarean
epicurean
adamantean
amœbean
amorean
amphigean
anomean
antipodean
apogean
astrean
didrochean
epistolean
gigantean
lethean
lyncean
mausolean
mymphean
pampean
perigean
phalangean
plumbean
protean
terpischorean
zoilean

EANER, *see* EANOR

EANING, ENING

gleaning
meaning
damascening (etc.), *see* EAN—*one syllable*

EANLESS

queenless (etc.), *see* EAN—*one syllable*

EANLING, EENLING

queenling
weanling
yeanling

EANLY, *see* ENELY

EANOR, EENER, ENER

cleaner
greener
demeanor
misdemeanor (etc.), *see* EAN—*one syllable*

EAPEN, EEPEN

cheapen
deepen
steepen

EAPER, EEPER

deeper
leaper (etc.), *see* EAP

Eaply

cheaply	deeply	steeply	

Eapy, *see* **Eap**

Earance, Erence

clearance	reappearance	perseverance	disappearance
adherence	coherence	interference	inherence
appearance	incoherence	arrearance	

Earcher, *see* **Ercher**

Earest, *see* **Erist**

Earful, Eerful

uncheerful	unfearful	tearful	sneerful
cheerful	earful		

Earier, *see* **Eerier**

Earing, Eering

cheering	ear-ring	hearing (etc.), *see* **Ear**	

Earless

cheerless (etc.), *see* **Ear**

Earlless

pearl-less (etc.), *see* **Earl**

Earling, *see* **Erling**

Early, Irly, Urly

churly	curly	pearly	whirly
knurly	early	surly	hurly-burly
burly	girly	twirly	

Earner, Ourner, Urner

adjourner	sojourner		
burner	(etc.), *see* **Earn**		

Earnest

earnest	furnaced	learnest (etc.), *see* **Earn**	

Earning, Urning, Erning

burning (etc.), *see* **Earn**	book-learning	undiscerning	

Earsal, Ersal

controversal	ursal	rehearsal	transversal
tercel	versal	reversal	universal

Earseless
purseless (etc.), *see* Erce

Earten, *see* Artan

Eartless
artless (etc.), *see* Art

Eary, Eery, Ery

beery	peri	aweary	jeery
cheery	query	*miserere*	leary
dearie	smeary	aërie	quære
dreary	sneery	bleary	sphery
eerie	weary	foreweary	veery

Easan, *see* Esen

Easand

reasoned	unseasoned	treasoned	weasand
seasoned			

Easant, Esent

displeasant	pheasant	present	omnipresent
peasant	pleasant	unpleasant	

Easel

easel	weasel	teasel	Lady Teazle

Easeless
ceaseless (etc.), *see* Eace

Easier, *see* Easy

Easing

unpleasing	sneezing (etc.), *see* Ease

Easles

easels	measles	weasels

Eason

reason	season	treason	"pleasin'"
unreason	unseason		(etc.)

Easoned, *see* Easand

Easoning

reasoning	seasoning

Easter

Easter	feaster	southeaster	"down-easter"
northeaster			

Easting

beasting	bee-sting	unpriesting	feasting
easting			

Eastless

feastless (etc.), *see* East

Eastly

beastly	priestly

Easure, Eisure

admeasure	leisure	pleasure	displeasure
entreasure	measure	treasure	outmeasure

Easy, Eesy, Eezy

breezy	queasy	wheezy	greasy
cheesy	sleazy	freezy	uneasy
easy	sneezy		

Eaten

overeaten	beaten	sweeten	worm-eaten
storm-beaten	heaten	wheaten	weather-beaten
unbeaten	seton	eaten	

Eater, *see* Etor

Eather (*long*), **Eether, Either**

bequeather	wreather	either	seether (etc.),
enwreather	breather	neither	*see* Eathe
sheather			

Eather (*short*), **Ether**

aweather	blether	nether	whether
patent-leather	feather	tether	belwether
pinfeather	heather	weather	together
whitleather	leather	wether	altogether

Eathing, Eething

breathing	seething, (etc.), *see* eathe	"wee thing"	"tea-thing"

Eathy

heathy	lethy	Lethe	wreathy
sheathy			

EATEST, *see* ETIST

EATHLESS
deathless (etc.), *see* EATH

EATING, EETING
greeting (etc.), *see* EAT

EATLESS
meatless (etc.), *see* EAT

EATLY (*see* EETLY, ATELY)

EATMENT

treatment	completement	entreatment	maltreatment

EATURE, *see* EACHER

EATY

meaty	sweety	entreaty	*spermaceti*
sleety	treaty	peaty	

EAVER

enfever	reaver	fever	unbeliever
beaver	reiver	lever	achiever
keever	weever	weaver	believer (etc.),
liever	beaver	coalheaver	*see* EAVE
livre	cleaver		

EAVEN

heaven	leaven	seven	eleven

EAVOUR, *see* EVER

EAVY, *see* EVY

EBBLE, EBEL, EBLE

pebble	rebel	treble	djebel

EBBLY, EBLY

pebbly	trebly

EBBLESS, EBLESS
webless (etc.), *see* EB

EBTOR, *see* ETTER

ECANT, *see* IQUANT

ECENT

decent	puissant	recent	indecent

Echer, Etcher

fletcher	lecher	stretcher	sketcher
etcher	fetcher	retcher	Fletcher

Echo

echo	Necco	secco

Ecian, *see* Etion, (*long*)

Ecious (*long*)

specious	facetious

Ecious (*short*)

precious	"refresh us" (etc.)

Ecker, Equer

checker	exchequer	wrecker (etc.),	"peck her"
chequer	woodpecker	*see* Eck	(etc.)

Ecklace, *see* Eckless

Eckle, Ekel

befreckel	keckle	bespeckle	deckle
heckle	shekel	speckle	seckel

Eckless, Ecklace

feckless	reckless	speckless	fleckless
necklace			

Eckling

heckling (etc.), *see* Eckle

Eckon

beckon	reckon

Eckoned, Econd

beckoned	unreckoned	second	*fecund*
reckoned			

Eckoning

beckoning	reckoning	unreckoning

Econd, *see* Eckoned

Ectant, Ectent

expectant	reflectent	disinfectant (etc.), *see* Ect

Ectar, *see* Ector

Ectent, *see* Ectant

ECTFUL
neglectful
respectful
disrespectful

ECTIC
actalectic
analectic
brachycatalectic
cachectic
electic
hectic
pectic
dialectic
ecectic
apoplectic
catalectic

ECTILE
insectile
projectile
sectile

ECTION, EXION
flexion
lection
section
vection
abjection
adjection
affection
aspection
bisection
collection
complexion
confection
convection
disinfection
effection
evection
implexion
incorrection
irreflection
misdirection
prospection
provection
rection
vivisection
connection
correction
deflection
defection
dejection
detection
dilection
direction
dissection
ejection
election
erection
infection
inflexion
injection
inspection
neglection
objection
perfection
prelection
profection
projection
protection
reflection
rejection
selection
subjection
subsection
trajection
trisection
by-election
circumspection
circumvection
coninsection
disaffection
genuflexion
imperfection
indirection
insurrection
intellection
interjection
intersection
introspection
predilection
recollection
re-election
resurrection
retrospection
venesection
incircumspection
superinjection

ECTIVE
deflective
erective
humective
introspective
neglective
recollective
refective
rejective
sective
selective
affective
collective
corrective
defective
detective
directive
effective
elective
infective
inflective
invective
objective
perfective
perspective
prospective
protective
reflective
respective
subjective
circumspective
ineffective
irrespective
retrospective

Ectly
correctly incorrectly indirectly circumspectly
directly

Ector, Ectre, Ectar
hector sector vector director (etc.),
nectar flector specter *see* Ect
rector lector

Ecture
lecture projecture belecture "expect yer"
conjecture architecture confecture (etc.)
prefecture

Edal, *see* Eddle

Edden, *see* Eaden

Edding
bedding redding wedding (etc.), *see* Ed

Eddle, Edal
medal peddle treadle heddle
meddle reddle intermeddle tripedal
pedal

Eddling
shredling meddling (etc.), *see* Eddle

Eddy, *see* Eady

Edeless
needless (etc.), *see* Ead

Edence
credence precedence antecedence intercedence

Edent
credent needn't precedent retrocedent
intercedent decedent antecedent sedent

Edgless
hedgeless (etc.), *see* Edge

Edger
ledger dredger (etc.), *see* Edge

Edging
dredging edging (etc.), *see* Edge

EDIAN

encyclopedian	median	comedian	tragedian

EDIENCE

expedience	obedience	disobedience	inexpedience

EDIENT

expedient	obedient	disobedient	inexpedient
ingredient			

EDING (*long*)
preceding (etc.), *see* EAD

EDIT

credit	discredit	sub-edit	accredit
edit	miscredit	"fed it" (etc.)	

EDIUM

medium	tedium

EDLAR

medlar	meddler	pedlar	treadler
medaler	pedaler	peddler	intermeddler

EDLEY, EADLY

deadly	medley	redly

EDNESS, EADNESS
redness (etc.), *see* ED

EDO

credo	toledo	stampedo	teredo
torpedo			

EECELESS
fleeceless (etc.), *see* EACE

EECHES, *see* ICHES

EECHLESS
speechless (etc.), *see* EACH

EECHY

beachy	preachy	speechy	bleachy
beechy	queachy	Campeachy	breachy
peachy	screechy	*Medici*	reechy

EECY

fleecy	greasy	creasy, *see also* EASY

EEDER
feeder (etc.), *see* EAD "treed her" (etc.)

EEDFUL
unheedful deedful speedful needful
unneedful meedful heedful

EEDLE, *see* EADLE

EEDLESS
heedless (etc.), *see* EAD

EEDLING
feedling seedling tweedling reedling
needling sweedling wheedling

EEDOM
freedom sedom "heed 'em" (etc.)

EEDY, EADY
deedy beady reedy speedy
"encyclopedy" greedy "indeedy" weedy
heedy needy seedy unheedy
predy

EEFLESS
beefless (etc.), *see* EEF

EEFY
beefy (etc.), *see* EAFY

EEKLESS
cheekless (etc.), *see* EAK

EEKLY
freakly weakly obliquely treacly
meekly weekly bleakly uniquely
sleekly

EELER, *see* EALER

EELING, *see* EALING

EELLESS
heelless (etc.), *see* EAL

EEMLY, *see* EMELY

EEMSTER, EAMSTER
deemster dreamster teamster seamster

EENISH, EANISH

cleanish	leanish	keenish	meanish
greenish	spleenish		

EENLESS

spleenless (etc.), *see* EAN

EENLY, *see* ENELY

EENY

fantoccini	greeny	sheeny	teeny
genie	queenie	tweeny	weeny
visne			

EEPEN, *see* EAPEN

EEPER, *see* EAPER

EEPIER

creepier	sleepier

EEPLE, EOPLE

people	steeple	empeople	unpeople

EEPLY, *see* EAPLY

EEPY

sleepy (etc.), *see* EAP

EERAGE

peerage	arrearage	clearage	pierage
steerage			

EERESS, *see* EAR

EERLESS

peerless (etc.), *see* EAR

EERLY, *see* ERELY

EERY, *see* EARY

EESELESS

cheeseless (etc.), *see* EASE

EESTONE

freestone	keystone

EETEN, *see* EATEN

EETLE

beetle	betel	decretal	fœtal

EETLESS, *see* **EATLESS** *and* **EAT**

EETLY, *see* **ETELY**

EETY, *see* **EATY**

EEVISH, IEVISH

peevish	thievish

EEZELESS, *see* **EASELESS** *and* **EASE**

EEZER

friezer	leaser	teaser	tweezer
easer	pleaser	freezer	wheezer (etc.),
greaser	sneezer	squeezer	*see* **EASE**
"geezer"			

EYSER, *see* **ISER**

EFACED, *see* **EAFEST**

EFTLESS

deftless (etc.), *see* **EFT**

EFTY

clefty	hefty	wefty

EGAL, *see* **EAGLE**

EGGY

dreggy	eggy	leggy	peggy

EGGLESS, EGLESS

legless (etc.), *see* **EG**

EGIAN, EGION

legion	collegian	glaswegian	Norwegian
region			

EGNANT

regnant	pregnant	impregnant

EGRESS

egress	negress	regress

EIAN, *see* **EAN**—*two syllables*

EIFER, EAFER

deafer	heifer	feoffor	zephyr

EIGHBOR, *see* **ABER**

EIGHTY, *see* ATY

EILING, *see* EALING

EING, *see* EA—*one syllable*

EIRESS

heiress	mayoress

EIST

deist	seest	theist (etc.), *see* EA—*one syllable*

EIZURE

seizure	*easier* (etc.), *see* EASY *for doubtful rhymes*

EKEL, *see* ECKLE

ELATE

prelate	appellate	debellate	interpellate
stellate	constellate	flabellate	ocellate

ELCHER, ELSHER

belcher	welsher	squelcher

ELDAM, ELDOM

beldam	seldom	"swelldom"

ELDER

elder	gelder	welder

ELDEST

eldest	heldest (etc.), *see* ELD

ELDING

gelding	welding

ELDOM, *see* ELDAM

ELEON, *see* ELIAN

ELFISH

elfish	pelfish	shell-fish	unselfish
selfish			

ELFLESS

selfless (etc.), *see* ELF

ELIAN, ELEON, ELION

pelion	chameleon	perihelion	carnelian
aphelion	cornelian	anthelion	

Elic

relic	evangelic	nickelic	pimelic
angelic	imbellic	parhelic	telic
bellic	melic	pentelic	

Eline

bee-line	feline	sea-line

Elion, *see* **Elian**

Elish, Ellish

hellish	disrelish	embellish	"swellish"
relish			

Ellar, Eller

cellar	dweller (etc.), *see* Ell	stellar	saltcellar
		teller	interstellar

Ellest, Ellised

quellest	trellised (etc.), *see* Ell

Elli, Elly

cancelli	smelly	felly	shelly
helly	belly	jelly	vermicelli
rakehelly	Donatelli	Kelly	

Elling

cloud-compelling (etc.), *see* **Ell**

Ellised

see **Ellest**

Ello, Elloe, Ellow

brocatello	bellow	mellow	prunello
good-fellow	cello	*hello*	punchinello
niello	felloe	yellow	"well O"
saltarello	fellow	duello	violoncello
scrivello			

Ellum

skellum	vellum	cerebellum	flabellum

Elly, *see* **Elli**

Elmless

helmless (etc.), *see* **Ealm**

Elon

felon	melon	enfelon	watermelon (etc.)

ELOP, ELOPE

develop	envelope (verb)

ELOT, EALOT

helot	zealot

ELPER

helper (etc.), *see* ELP

ELPLESS, *see* ELP

ELTER

melter	felter	smelter	helter-skelter
pelter	inshelter	spelter	"pelt her"
belter (etc.),	kelter	swelter	(etc.)
see ELT	shelter	welter	

ELTING

belting	felting	melting (etc.), *see* ELT

ELTLESS

beltless (etc.), *see* ELT

ELVING

delving	helving	shelving

EMBER

ember	December	November	September
member	dismember	remember	disremember

EMBLE

semble	assemble	dissemble	resemble
tremble			

EMBLER

dissembler (etc.), *see* EMBLE	temblor

EMBLY

trembly	assembly

EMELESS

schemeless (etc.), *see* EAM

EMELY, EEMLY

seemly	supremely	unseemly	extremely

EMER, *see* EAMER

Emic

chemic, epidemic, pandemic, systemic, endemic, alchemic, platychemic, theoremic, polemic, *anaemic*, strategemic, totemic, academic

Emish

blemish, clemmish, flemish

Emist, Emmest

chemist, stemmest (etc.), *see* Em

Emless

hemless (etc.), *see* Em

Emmer, Emner, *see* Emor

Emon (*long*), *see* Eaman

Emon (*short*)

gemman, lemon

Emor, Emmer, Emner

clemmer, tremor, condemner, contemner (etc.), *see* Em

Emplar

templar, exemplar

Emstress

dempstress, sempstress

Empter

tempter, exempter, unkempter, pre-empter, attempter

Emption

emption, coemption, pre-emption, diremption, ademption, exemption, redemption

Emur, *see* Eamer

Ena, Ina

arena, gena, scena, subpœna, catena, maizena, semolina, Tsarina, cavatina, philopena, verbena, concertina, farina, scarlatina, hyena, signorina, galena

ENACE, ENNIS

menace	Dennis	tennis	Venice
tenace			

ENAL

penal	venal	plenal	weanel
renal	machinal		

ENANT, ENNANT

pennant	tenant	lieutenant

ENATE, *see* ENNET

ENCELESS
defenceless (etc.), *see* ENCE

ENCER, ENSER, ENSOR

censer	condenser	commencer	intenser
censor	dispenser	denser	prehensor
fencer	extensor	incensor	tensor
Spencer	"contents her" (etc.)		

ENCEFORTH

henceforth	thenceforth

ENCHER, ENSURE

bencher	clencher	trencher	blencher (etc.),
censure	quencher	wencher	*see* ENCH

ENCHES, *see* ENSIOUS

ENCHLESS
benchless (etc.), *see* ENCH

ENCIL, *see* ENSAL

ENDAM, *see* ENDUM

ENDANCE, ENDENCE

attendance	condescendence	impendence	pendence
dependence	independence	interdepend-	tendance
resplendence	ascendance	ence	tendence
transcendence			

ENDANT, ENDENT

pendant	splendent	dependent	transcendent
pendent	appendant	descendant	independent
dependant	ascendant	descendent	interdepend-
equipendent	attendant	impendent	ent
interscendent	contendent	intendant	superintendent
transplendent	defendant	resplendent	

ENDER, ENDOR

fender	slender	surrender	perpender
gender	splendor	vendor	reprehender
lender	tender	amender	tail-ender (etc.)
render	engender	offender (etc.),	week-ender
sender	pretender	*see* END	

ENDING

pending pretending (etc.), *see* END

ENDLESS, *see* END

ENDLY

friendly *reverendly* unfriendly

ENDOR, *see* ENDER

ENDOUS

stupendous tremendous

ENDUM, ENDAM

addendum	commendam	referendum	"mend 'em"
agendum	corrigendum	credendum	(etc.)

ENELY, EANLY, EENLY

greenly	leanly	queenly	serenely
keenly	meanly	obscenely	cleanly

ENEOUS, *see* ENIUS

ENER, *see* EANOR

ENET, *see* ENNET

ENGLISH, INGLISH

English jinglish tinglish

ENGTHEN

lengthen strengthen

ENIAL

genial (etc.), *see three-syllable rhymes*

ENIC

scenic	arsenic (adj.)	mandarinic	phenic
splenic			

ENISH

plenish rhenish replenish wennish

ENIST, EENEST (etc.)
gleanest plenist magazinist routinist (etc.),
greenist machinist
see EAN

ENLESS, *see* EN

ENNA
senna gehenna henna antenna
duenna

ENNANT, *see* ENANT

ENNEL, ENOL
antennal pennal gennel phenol
fennel unkennel kennel

ENNER
penner tenner tenor tenour

ENNET
gennet rennet senate tenet
jennet

ENNIS, *see* ENACE

ENNIUM
millennium quinquennium (etc.)

ENNON, ENON
pennon tenon

ENNY, ANY
any many wenny tenney
fenny penny

ENSAL, ENCIL, ENSIL, ENSILE
mensal pensile stencil utensil
pencil extensile pensil tensile
prehensile Hensel

ENSELY
densely immensely intensely

ENSER, *see* ENCER

ENSIL, *see* ENSAL

ENSILE, *see* ENSAL

ENSION, *see* ENTIAN

ENSIOUS, ENTIOUS

pestilentious	contentious	sententious	silentious
pretentious	dissentious	conscientious	licentious

ENSIVE

pensive	ostensive	incomprehen- sive	inexpensive
ascensive	apprehensive	unapprehensive	influencive
defensive	comprehensive	descensive	protensive
expensive	condescensive	distensive	recompensive
extensive	inoffensive	incensive	suspensive
intensive	reprehensive	indefensive	tensive
offensive			

ENSOR, *see* ENCER

ENSURE, *see* ENCHER

ENTAIL

entail	ventail	entrail

ENTAL, *see* ENTLE

ENTANCE, ENTENCE

sentence	repentance	unrepentance	representance

ENTAUR, ENTOR

bucentaur	succentor	centaur	mentor, *see also* ENTRE
stentor			

ENTE, ENTY

plenty	scenty	"fermenty"	"tormenty," *see* ENT
twenty	"went he" (etc)		

ENTER, *see* ENTRE

ENTEST, *see* ENTIST

ENTFUL

contentful	relentful	repentful	resentful
eventful			

ENTIAL

agential	eminential	inconsequential	obediential
bigential	expediential	indulgential	omnipresential
conferential	evidential	inferential	precedential
confidential	experiential	intelligential	preferential
deferential	exponential	jurisprudential	presidential

ENTIAL—(*Cont.*)

provencial
querulential
referential
reminiscential
residential
sapiential
sciential
sentential
sequential
superessential
tangential
torrential
credential
essential
potential
prudential
consequential
differential
influential
penitential
pestilential
providential
quintessential
reverential
unessential

ENTIAN, ENTION, ENSION

deprehension
descension
inapprehension
incension
incomprehension
inextension
ostension
prehension
presention
propension
recension
subvention
thermo-tension
gentian
mention
pension
tension
abstention
accension
ascension
attention
contention
convention
declension
detention
dimension
dissension
distension
extension
intension
intention
invention
obvention
obtension
perpension
portension
pretension
prevention
retention
suspension
apprehension
circumvention
coextension
comprehension
condescension
contravention
inattention
intervention
reprehension
subtervention
misapprehension
preapprehension

ENTIC

authentic
identic

ENTICE, ENTIS

appentis
prentice
pentice
apprentice

ENTICED, *see* ENTIST

ENTILE

gentile
pentile
dentile

ENTING

unrelenting
fomenting (etc.), *see* ENT

ENTION, *see* ENTIAN

ENTIST, ENTEST, ENTICED

dentist
penticed
prenticed
sentest
apprenticed
preventist (etc.), *see* ENT

Entive

attentive
incentive
retentive
irretentive
assentive
presentive,
see Ent

Entle, Ental, Entil

dental
gentle
lentil
mental
rental
trental
parental
ungentle
accidental
detrimental
elemental
firmamental
fundamental
incidental
instrumental
monumental
Occidental
Oriental
ornamental
regimental
rudimental
sacramental
supplemental
transcendental
experimental
temperamental
alimental
antecedental
argental
argumental
atramental
bidental
cental
coincidental
complemental
complimental
continental
departmental
developmental
documental
fragmental
governmental
impedimental
intercontinental
kentle
labiodental
ligamental
linguadental
medicamental
nutrimental
parliamental
pedimental
pigmental
placental
predicamental
recremental
sagmental
tenemental
testamental
tridental

Entless

centless (etc.), *see* Ent

Ently

gently
intently
evidently (etc.), *see* Entle *and* Ent

Entment

contentment
presentment
resentment
discontentment
relentment
representment

Entor, *see* Entaur *and* Entre

Entous

immomentous
ligamentous
pedentous
pigmentous
sarmentous
unguentous
momentous
portentous

Entre, Enter, Entor

centre
enter
mentor
lentor
tenter
dissenter
inventor
denter
precentor
tormentor
(etc.), *see*
Ent

Entric

eccentric
enteric
acentric
anthropocentric
barrycentric
centric
concentric
geocentric
heliocentric
paracentric
selenocentric

ENTRY

entry	gentry	sentry

ENTURE

venture	debenture	misadventure	tenture
adventure	indenture	peradventure	

ENTY, *see* ENTE

ENU, ENUE

menu	venue	"detain you" or "seen you" (etc.)

ENUS (*short*), *see* ENACE

ENZA

cadenza	faenza	influenza

EOPARD, EPHERD, EPPERED

jeopard	leopard	peppered	shepherd

EOPLE, *see* EEPLE

EPER, *see* EPPER

EPHERD, *see* EOPARD

EPPER, EPER

leper	pepper	high-stepper	hepper

EPSY

apepsy	enpepsy	paralepsy	epilepsy
catalepsy	metalepsy	"dyspepsy"	

ERELY, EARLY, EERLY

cheerly	merely	sheerly	yearly
clearly	nearly	severely	austerely
dearly	peerly	sincerely	insincerely
drearly	queerly	cavalierly	

ERENCE, *see* EARANCE

ERENT, *see* ERRANT

ERFLESS, *see* ERF

ERGENCE

convergence	emergence	resurgence	submergence
divergence	deturgence		

Ergent, Urgent

assurgent	vergent	abstergent	divergent
insurgent	turgent	convergent	emergent
resurgent	urgent	detergent	

Ergeon, *see* **Urgeon**

Erger, Erjure, Erdure, Urger

merger	urger	converger	submerger
perjure	verdure	diverger	"urge her"
purger	verger	emerger	(etc.)
scourger			

Erging (etc.)

urging	converging	diverging (etc.), *see* **Erge**

Ergy, Urgy

clergy	scourgy	surgy	metallurgy
dirgy	sergy	liturgy	periergy
thaumaturgy	dramaturgy		

Eric, Erric, Errick

derrick	neoteric	endexoteric	myrrhic
ferric	aceric	enteric	numeric
spheric	alexiteric	ephemeric	peripheric
generic	amphoteric	helispheric	phylacteric
hysteric	anisomeric	homeric	piperic
climacteric	atmospheric	icteric	planspheric
esoteric	chimeric	isomeric	suberic
exoteric	chromospheric	masseteric	valeric
hemispheric	cleric	mesmeric	

Eries

series	forewearies	queries	wearies
dearies			

Eril, Erile, Eryl

beryl	peril	sterile

Erish

cherish	perish

Erist, Earest

dearest	querist	*theorist* (etc.), *see* **Ear**

Erit

merit	inherit	disinherit	ferret
demerit			

ERJURE, *see* ERGER

ERKER, *see* IRKER

ERKIN, IRKIN

firkin	jerkin	merkin	"lurkin'"
gherkin			(etc.)

ERKLESS, *see* ERK

ERKY, *see* URKEY

ERLING, EARLING, IRLING, URLING

curling	furling (etc.),	merling	herling
uncurling	*see* EARL	sterling	

ERMAN, ERMON

German	sermon	firman	merman

ERMENT

affirmant	deferment	referment	preferment
ferment	determent	averment	disinterment

ERMER, *see* IRMER

ERMIN, ERMINE

ermine	determine	predetermine	"squirmin'"
vermin			(etc.)

ERMLESS, *see* ERM

ERMLY, *see* IRMLY

ERMON, *see* ERMAN

ERNAL, ERNEL, OLONEL, OURNAL, URNAL

colonel	diurnal	internal	quartisternal
journal	external	maternal	supernal
kernel	eternal	nocturnal	hodiernal
vernal	infernal	paternal	sempiternal
cavernal	fraternal	lucernal	sternal
coeternal	hesternal	paraphernal	urnal
dinternal	hibernal		

ERNATE

alternate	cathurnate	ternate

ERNEL, *see* ERNAL

ERNION, *see* URNIAN

Ernless
sternless (etc.), *see* Earn

Ernly, Earnly
dearnly
sternly (etc.), *see* Earn

Ernness, *see* Urnace

Erny, *see* Ourney

Ero (*long*)
hero
zero
Nero

Ero (*short*)
pierrot
campero
cavalero
montero
dishero
paterero
sombrero
pederero
primero

Erple, *see* Urple

Errand, Erund
errand
gerund

Errant, Erent
errant
gerent
knight-errant
vicegerent

Erret, *see* Erit

Erric, Errick, *see* Eric

Errier
burier
terrier
merrier (etc.), *see* Erry

Erring
derring
herring
erring
deterring
preferring (etc.), *see* Er

Error
error
terror

Errule, *see* Erule

Erry
beriberi
cemetery
berry
bury
cherry
derry
ferry
lerry
merry
perry
serry
sherry
very
wherry
lamasery
millinery
monastery
presbytery
skerry
stationery; *see also* Arry

Erseless
verseless (etc.), *see* Erce

Ersey, Urzy

furzy	jersey	kersey

Ersial, *see* Ercial

Ersian, Ersion, Ertion, Ursion, Ercion

mersion	contravertion	eversion	nastertion
Persian	coercion	extersion	obversion
tertian	conversion	emersion	recursion
version	demersion	excursion	perversion
abstersion	desertion	exertion	reversion
aspersion	detersion	immersion	subversion
assertion	dispersion	incursion	intersertion
apertion	diversion	insertion	interspersion
aversion	contraversion	inversion	animadversion
circumversion	disconcertion	inspersion	retroversion
concertion	discursion	introversion	submersion

Ersive, *see* Ercive

Erson, Orsen

person	worsen

Ertain, Urtain

certain	encurtain	incurtain	uncertain

Erter

asserter	converter (etc.), *see* Ert

Ertest, *see* Ertist

Ertful, *see* Urtful

Erthless, *see* Earth

Ertian, *see* Ersian

Erting
diverting (etc.), *see* Ert

Ertion, *see* Ersian

Ertist (etc.)

controvertist	hurtest (etc.), *see* Ert

Ertive

assertive divertive enertive furtive
revertive

Ertly, Urtly

curtly apertly inertly malapertly
pertly inexpertly overtly alertly

Erule, Errule

ferule ferrule spherule perule

Ervant, Ervent

fervent servant eye-servant unobservant
conservant recurvant curvant

Erveless

nerveless (etc.), *see* Erve

Erver, *see* Ervor

Ervid

fervid scurvied perfervid

Erving

time-serving (etc.), *see* Erve

Ervish

dervish nervish

Ervor, Erver

fervor unnerver (etc.), *see* Erve preserver nerver
server time-server

Ervy, Urvy

nervy scurvy swervy topsy-turvy

Ery, *see* Eary *and* Erry

Eryl, *see* Eril

Esage, Essage

message presage expressage pesage

Escence, Essence

accrescence contabescence erubescence fremescence
aborescence defervescence feminescence frondescence
calescence deliquescence florescence frutescence
candescence delitescence fluorescence glaucescence
concrescence emollescence essence hyalescence

Escence, Essence—(*Cont.*)

incalescence	phosphorescence	tumescence	senescence
incandescence	ramollescence	virvidescence	turgescence
iridescence	recrudescence	virilescence	acquiescence
juvenescence	revalescence	vitrescence	adolescence
lactescence	reveriscence	excrescence	coalescence
lapidescence	rubescence	pubescence	convalescence
latescence	spumescence	putrescence	effervescence
opalescence	supercrescence	quiescence	efflorescence
petrescence	torpescence	quintessence	absolescence

Escience

nescience prescience

Eseless

breezeless (etc.), *see* Ease

Esence, Easance

pleasance presence omnipresence

Esent, *see* Easant

Esher, *see* Essure

Eshless

fleshless (etc.), *see* Esh

Eshly

fleshly freshly

Eshy

fleshy meshy

Esion

lesion	adhesion	Ephesian	Silesian
inadhesion	cohesion	inhesion	trapezian

Esis

thesis	synteresis	ochlesis	catachresis
anæthesis	exegesis	tmesis	diegesis
deesis	anamnesis	aposiopesis	mathesis
diesis	diaporesis	anthesis	schesis
mimesis	erotesis		

Esom

besom "threesome" "gleesome" "see some" (etc.)

Essant, Escent

crescent
decrescent
excrescent
incessant
cessant
cremescent
liquescent
nigrescent
putrescent
quiescent
convalescent
deliquescent
effervescent
efflorescent
evanescent
obsolescent
recrudescent
ignescent
jessant
papescent
senescent

Essel, *see* **Estle**

Esser, Essor

dresser
lesser
lessor
aggressor
assessor
confessor
depressor
oppressor
possessor
professor
successor
transgressor (etc.), *see* Ess
antecessor
intercessor
predecessor
"address her" (etc.)

Essful

distressful
successful
unsuccessful

Essing

blessing
dressing
pressing (etc.), *see* Ess

Ession, Etion

cession
freshen
ingression
incession
introcession
lococession
session
pression
repossession
supersession
suppression
intercession
retrocession
accession
aggression
compression
concession
confession
depression
digression
discretion
exgression
expression
transgression
introgression
retrogression
impression
obsession
oppression
possession
precession
procession
profession
progression
recession
succession
indiscretion
prepossession

Essive

accessive
compressive
concessive
concrescive
cressive
depressive
regressive
transgressive
aggressive
congressive
digressive
excessive
expressive
impressive
oppressive
retrogressive
possessive
progressive
recessive
redressive
repressive
successive
suppressive

Essless

guessless (etc.), *see* Ess

ESSOR, *see* **ESSER**

ESSURE, ESHER

pressure	tressure	fresher	refresher (etc.), *see* ESH
thresher			

ESTAL, ESTLE

pestle	vestal	festal

ESTER

fester	pester	vester	protester (etc.), *see* EST
jester	tester	mid-semester	"pressed her" (etc.)
nester	semester	wrester	
trimester	sequester	digester	

ESTIAL

bestial	celestial

ESTIC

agrestic	aposiopestic	gestic	domestic
anamnestic	asbestic	telestic	majestic
anapestic	catachrestic	telestich	

ESTINE

destine	clandestine	intestine	"rest in" (etc.)
predestine			

ESTIVE

attestive	estive	restive	suggestive
congestive	festive	digestive	tempestive
infestive			

ESTLE (T *sounded*), *see* **ESTAL**

ESTLE (*silent* T), **ESSEL**

nestle	trestle	vessel	unnestle
chessel	redressal	pestle	Cecil

ESTLER

wrestler	nestler

ESTLESS

restless (etc.), *see* EST

ESTO

presto	manifesto	"west O!" (etc.)

ESTRAL, ESTREL

ancestral	*kestrel*	campestral	trimestral
fenestral	orchestral		

ESTRY

vestry	festery	"semestery"	"sequestery"

ESTURE

gesture	revesture	divesture	"lest your" (etc.)
investure			

ESTY

breasty	resty	yesty	cresty
chesty	testy		

ETAIL

detail	sweet-ale	retail	sea-tale

ETAL, *see* **ETTLE**

ETCHLESS

stretchless (etc.), *see* ETCH

ETCHY

sketchy	"tetchy"	stretchy	fetchy
vetchy			

ETELY, EATLY, EETLY

featly	obsoletely	completely	discreetly
fleetly	neatly	concretely	indiscreetly
meetly	sweetly		

ETEMENT, *see* **EATMENT**

ETEOR, *see* **EATURE**

ETFUL

fretful	netful	forgetful	unforgetful
regretful			

ETHER (*short*), *see* **EATHER**

ETI, *see* **ETTY**

ETIC

æsthetic	emetic	poetic	arithmetic (adj.)
ascetic	magnetic	prophetic	dietetic
athletic	pathetic	synthetic	energetic
cosmetic	phrenetic		

ETIC—(*Cont.*)

hypothetic	antithetic	eugenetic	nosopoetic
plethoretic	apathetic	exegetic	ochletic
sympathetic	auletic	frenetic	pangenetic
theoretic	baphometic	gangetic	parathetic
apologetic	biogenetic	genetic	parenthetic
peripatetic	caechetic	geodetic	paretic
abietic	colletic	hermetic	philetic
allopathetic	cometic	homiletic	phonetic
aloetic	diamagnetic	idiopathetic	quercetic
alphabetic	diaphoretic	inergetic	splenetic
amuletic	docetic	kinetic	syncretic
anæsthetic	emporetic	masoretic	tabetic
anchoretic	epigenetic	mimetic	threnetic
anetic	epithetic	mythopoetic	puretic
antipathetic	erotetic	noetic	zetetic

ETION, ECIAN

Grecian	impletion	repletion	concretion
accretion	depletion	interecion	deletion
completion	excretion	secretion	

ETION (*short*), *see* ESSION

ETIOUS (*short*), *see* ECIOUS

ETISH, *see* ETTISH

ETIST, EATEST, EETEST

eatest	sweetest	defeatist	decretist (etc.), *see* EAT

ETIVE

expletive	secretive	accretive

ETLESS, *see* ET

ETOR, ETRE, ETER

eater	litre	prætor	beefeater
heater	meter	centimeter (etc.)	saltpetre
sweeter (etc.), *see* EAT	metre		

ETSAM, ETSOME

jetsam	fretsome	"wet some" (etc.)

Etten

threaten, wetten, fretten

Etter, Ettor, Ebtor

better, getter, whetter, enfetter
bettor, letter, abettor, forgetter
debtor, setter, begetter (etc.), unfetter
fetter, wetter, *see* Et

Etti, *see* **Etty**

Ettish, Etish

fetish, pettish, coquettish, Lettish
frettish, wettish

Ettle, Etal

abettal, kettle, nettle, settle
foresettle, metal, petal, unsettle
fettle, mettle

Ettling

settling (etc.), *see* **Ettle**

Etto

petto, amadetto, amoretto, terzetto
corvetto, lazaretto, ghetto, zuchetto
palmetto, allegretto, libretto, "met, O" (etc.)
stiletto

Ettor, *see* **Etter**

Etty, Eti, Etti

Betty, petty, confetti, petit
fretty, sweaty, spermaceti, netty
jetty

Eudal, *see* **Oodle**

Eudless, feudless (etc.), *see* **Ood**

Eum

museum, mausoleum, amœbæum, prytaneum
Te Deum, peritoneum, athenæum, "see 'em" etc.
bronteum, colosseum, lyceum

Eval, Evil (*long* E)

evil, primeval, jongeval, shrieval
weevil, medieval, retrieval, upheaval
co-eval

EVAL (*short* E)

beval	level	bedevil	kevel
devil	revel	dishevel	

EVELESS, *see* EVE

EVEN (*short*), *see* EAVEN

EVER (*long*), *see* EAVER

EVER (*short*), EAVOR

clever	endeavor	whoever	whensoever
ever	however	whatsoever	wheresoever
never	whatever	howsoever	whichever
sever	whenever	unsever	whomsoever
assever	wherever	whencesoever	whosoever
dissever			

EVIL, *see* EVAL

EVIOUS

devious	previous

EVY, EAVY

bevy	clevy	top-heavy	levy
chevy	levee	heavy	

EWAGE, *see* UAGE

EWAL, *see* UAL

EWARD, EWERED

leeward	sewered	*cured* (etc.), *see past of verbs in*
steward	skewered	OOR—*for imperfect rhymes*

EWDLY, UDELY

crudely	lewdly	rudely	shrewdly

EWER, *see* OOR—*one syllable*

EWESS, *see* EWIS

EWISH, UEISH

blueish	Jewish	shrewish	truish

EWIS

brewis	Jewess

EWLESS

pewless, (etc.), *see* EW

EWLY, *see* ULY

EWRY, *see* URY

EWTER, *see* OOTER

EWY, *see* UEY

EXER, *see* EXOR

EXILE
exile flexile

EXION, *see* ECTION

EXLESS
sexless (etc.), *see* EX

EXOR, EXER
flexor annexer convexer perplexer
yexer complexer

EXTANT
extant sextant

EXTILE
sextile textile bissextile

EXY
hecksy "prexy" sexy apoplexy
hemiplexy "genuflexy" kyriolexy pyrexy

EYANCE
seance conveyance purveyance

EYDAY, *see* AYDAY

EYELESS
skyless (etc.), *see* Y

EYLESS
keyless (etc.), *see* E *and* AY

EYSER, *see* EEZER

IAL, YAL
basihyal supplial trial decrial
espial dial vial denial
gayal phial viol retrial
rial (*see also* ILE, *one syllable, for imperfect rhymes*)

IANCE, IENCE

science	appliance	defiance	misalliance
affiance	compliance	reliance	suppliance
alliance	incompliance		

IANT, IENT

client	compliant	self-reliant	calorifient
giant	defiant	affiant	scient
pliant	reliant	alliant	

IAR, *see* IRE—*one syllable*

IAS, IOUS

bias	lias	ananias	eyas
pious	nisi prius		

IAT, IATE, IET, IOT, YOT

diet	quiet	*ryot*	disquiet
fiat	*riot*	striate	

IBAL, *see* IBLE

IBALD (*long*)

piebald	ribald

IBALD, IBBLED (*short*)

dibbled	nibbled	ribald	cribbled
dribbled	quibbled	scribbled	

IBBER

bibber	gibber	dibber	nibber
cribber	glibber	jibber	squibber
fibber	winebibber		

IBBET, IBIT

gibbet	exhibit	prohibit	adhibit
cohibit	inhibit	zibet	

IBBLE

cribble	fribble	scribble	sibyl
dibble	nibble	gribble	thribble
dribble	quibble	kibble	

IBBLER

scribbler (etc.), *see* IBBLE

IBEL, *see* IBLE

IBELESS
jibeless (*etc.*), *see* IBE

IBER, *see* IBRE

IBIT, *see* IBBET

IBLE, IBAL, IBEL
Bible libel tribal

IBLESS
bibless (etc.), *see* IB

IBLET
driblet giblet triblet

IBLY, IBBLY
dribbly glibly quibbly tribbly
fribbly nibbly scribbly

IBRE, IBER
briber tiber giber subscriber
fibre liber imbiber (etc.), *see* IBE

ICAR, ICKER, IQUOR
dicker slicker liquor wicker
knicker bicker snicker sicker (etc.),
licker flicker vicar *see* ICK

ICELESS
diceless (etc.), *see* ICE

ICELY, ISELY
nicely pricely concisely precisely

ICHEN, *see* IKEN

ICHES, EECHES, ITCHES
breeches riches witches (etc.), *see* ICH

ICHLESS
ditchless (etc.), *see* ITCH

ICHLY, ITCHLY
richly witchly

ICIAL, ITIAL
initial official beneficial superficial
judicial artificial prejudicial accrementitial

ICIAL, ITIAL—(*Cont.*)

comitial
edificial
exitial
extrajudicial
futuritial
getilitial
interstitial
natalitial
policial
recrementitial
rusticial
sacrificial
solstitial
tribunitial
veneficial

ICIAN, ITION, ISSION

abannition
abliguition
accrementition
acoustician
adhibition
affinition
aglutition
apician
atomician
bipartition
delinition
demission
departition
deperdition
dialectician
dismission
dissilition
electrician
epenicion
evanition
extradition
fission
futurition
hydrostatician
illinition
imbibition
immission
inition
magnetician
metrician
mnemonician
neoplatonician
nolition
obdormition
obstetrician
perquisition
practician
punition
rebullition
redition
resilition
reunition
rubrician
simplician
sortition
sublition
statistician
submonition
superaddition
tactician
proposition
readmission
requisition
supposition
predisposition
tradition
tralatition
tribunician
tripartition
vendition
vomition
mission
addition
adition
admission
ambition
attrition
audition
cognition
coition
commission
condition
contrition
dentition
edition
emission
fruition
ignition
insition
logician
magician
monition
munition
musician
arithmetician
contraposition
decomposition
geometrician
nutrition
omission
optician
partition
patrician
perdition
permission
petition
physician
position
prodition
reddition
remission
rendition
sedition
submission
recognition
repetition
rhetorician
transposition
presupposition
suspicion
transition
transmission
tuition
volition
abolition
acquisition
admonition
indisposition
interposition
juxtaposition
mathematician
metaphysician
ammunition
apparition
apposition
circuition
coalition
composition
competition
definition
demolition
deposition
disposition
disquisition
ebullition
emolition
erudition
exhibition
expedition
exposition
imposition
inanition
inhibition
inquisition

ICIAN, ITION, ISSION—(*Cont.*)

intermission
intromission
intuition
manumission
mechanician
opposition
parturition
politician
precognition
premonition
premunition
preposition
preterition
pretermission
prohibition
repetition
reposition
superstition
academician
recomposition

ICIENT

deficient
efficient
omniscient
proficient
sufficient
all-sufficient
coefficient
insufficient
beneficent
calorificient
inefficient
malificient
objicient
perficient
volitient

ICION, *see* ICIAN

ICIOUS, ITIOUS

vicious
ambitious
auspicious
capricious
cilicious
delicious
factitious
fictitious
flagitious
judicious
malicious
nutritious
officious
pernicious
propitious
seditious
suspicious
adventitious
avaricious
inauspicious
injudicious
insuspicious
meretricious
suppositious
superstitious
surreptitious
supposititious
addititious
adjectitious
adscititious
advectitious
arreptitious
ascititious
ascriptitious
deglutitious
deletitious
exitious
expeditious
gentilitious
impropitious
inofficious
lateritious
multiplicious
natalitious
obreptitious
obstetricious
piceous
profectitious
pumiceous
puniceous
satellitious
secretitious
sericeous
silicious
stillatitious
tractitious
tralatitious
veneficious
vermicious

ICKEN

quicken
sicken
stricken
thicken
chicken
wicken

ICKENING (*two syllables*)

quickening
sickening
thickening
strychnine

ICKER, *see* ICAR

ICKET

clicket
cricket
pricket
smicket
thicket
ticket
wicket
picket
piquet
snicket
"stick it"

ICKETS

rickets — tickets (etc.), *see* ICKET

ICKING

licking — ticking (etc.), *see* IC — "viking" (British)

ICKLE

fickle	prickle	strickle	trickle
mickle	sickle	tickle	nickel
pickle	stickle		

ICKLER

tickler (etc.), *see* ICKLE

ICKLING

chickling	pickling	prickling	trickling,
tickling			*see* ICKLE

ICKLY

fickly	quickly	slickly	thickly
prickly	sickly	stickly	trickly

ICKSET

quickset — thickset

ICKSHAW

kickshaw — rickshaw

ICKSY

dixie	pixie	tricksy	nixie
kicksy			

ICKY

bricky	kicky	thicky	dicky
chicky	sticky	tricky	

ICON, *see* IKEN

ICTER, ICTOR

lictor	inflicter	afflicter	fictor
victor	predicter	conflicter	pictor
constricter	boa-constrictor	contradicter	stricter

ICTION, IXION

confliction	suffixion	fiction	adstriction
depiction	transfixion	friction	afflixion
reliction	diction	addiction	affriction

ICTION, IXION--(*Cont.*)

astriction	infliction	contradiction	malediction
commixion	obstriction	crucifixion	valediction
constriction	prediction	dereliction	affliction
conviction	reviction	interdiction	prefixion
eviction	benediction	jurisdiction	restriction
indiction			

ICTIVE

afflictive	jurisdictive	benedictive	fictive
astrictive	inflictive	predictive	indictive
constrictive	restrictive	conflictive	interdictive
convictive	vindictive	contradictive	

ICTLESS, *see* ICT

ICTMENT, *see* ITEMENT

ICTUAL, *see* ITTLE

ICTURE

picture	depicture	impicture	"inflict yer" (etc.)
stricture			

ICY

icy	spicy

IDAL, *see* IDLE

IDAY, *see* IDY

IDDEN

bidden	midden	priest-ridden (etc.)	forbidden
chidden	ridden		slidden
hidden	hag-ridden	unbidden	stridden

IDDING

bidding — ridding (etc.), *see* ID

IDDLE

diddle	riddle	griddle	twiddle
fiddle	tiddle	kiddle	idyll
middle	taradiddle	quiddle	

IDDLER

fiddler (etc.), *see* IDDLE

IDDY

giddy	niddy	biddy	stiddy
kiddy	"chickabiddy"	middy	

IDELESS

tideless (etc.), *see* IDE

IDELY, *see* IDLY

IDEN, IDON

guidon	widen	"chidin'"	"abidin'" (etc.)

IDENT, IDANT

guidant	strident	dividant	bident
rident	trident		

IDER

cider	spider	provider	glider (etc.),
guider	backslider	lider	*see* IDE

IDGELESS

bridgeless (etc.), *see* IDGE

IDGEON, *see* YGIAN

IDGET

fidget	midget	digit

IDGY

midgy	ridgy

IDING

siding (etc.), *see* IDE

IDINGS

tidings	ridings (etc.), *see* IDE

IDLE, IDAL, IDOL, IDYL

bridal	idol	fratricidal	suicidal
bridle	idyl	homicidal	regicidal
idle	sidle	parricidal	tyrannicidal

IDLER, *see* IDLE

IDLESS

skidless (etc.), *see* ID

IDLING (*long*), *see* IDLE

IDLING (*short*), IDDLING
fiddling middling tiddling twiddling
kidling riddling

IDLY
idly widely

IDOW
widow lever-de-rideau "amid, O!" (etc.)

IDY, IDAY
Friday tidy vide bona fide
sidy

IEFLESS, *see* EEF

IEFLY
briefly chiefly

IELESS
eyeless (etc.), *see* Y

IENDLESS
friendless (etc.), *see* END

IENT, *see* IANT

IER, *see* IRE—*one syllable*

IERLESS
fearless (etc.), *see* EAR

IERS
pliers (etc.), *see* IRE—*one syllable*

IERY, *see* IRY

IESTLY, *see* EASTLY

IET, *see* IAT

IEVELESS
sleeveless (etc.), *see* EAVE

IFELESS
lifeless (etc.), *see* IFE

IFELY
rifely wifely

IFER, see IPHER

IFFIN

griffin	tiffin	biffin

IFFLE

piffle	whiffle	riffle

IFFLESS

cliffless (etc.), *see* IF

IFFLY

piffly	stiffly	whiffly

IFIC, YPHIC

horrific	soporific	finific	mirific
pacific	acidific	glyphic	morbific
prolific	pulsific	grandific	mercific
rubific	algific	honorific	somnific
specific	anaglyphic	humorific	vivific
beatific	aurific	sacrific	omnific
terrific	classific	lactific	ossific
calorific	damnific	lapidific	pontific
hieroglyphic	deific	lucific	salvific
scientific	dolorific	magnific	sensific

IFLE

rifle	stifle	trifle

IFLING

rifling	stifling	trifling	wifeling

IFTER

shifter	swifter	sifter	"lift her"
drifter	shoplifter	uplifter	(etc.)

IFTLESS

shiftless thriftless (etc.), *see* IFT

IFTY

fifty	shifty	clifty	drifty
rifty	thrifty		

IGATE, IGOT

vigot	*frigate*	gigot	spigot

IGEST

digest (noun)	obligest

IGEON, *see* YGIAN

Iggard, Igured, Iggered

"figured" (British)	jiggered	niggard	triggered (etc.) *see* Igger

Igger, Igour, Igure

ligger	bigger	rigor	vigor
digger (etc.), *see* Ig	sprigger	trigger	"configure"
snigger	"figure" (British)	outrigger	"disfigure"
swigger	jigger	market-rigger	"prefigure"
twigger	nigger	rigger	"transfigure"

Iggin

biggin	piggin

Igging

rigging	wigging (etc.), *see* Ig

Iggle

giggle	wiggle	jiggle	riggle
higgle	wriggle	niggle	squiggle
sniggle			

Iggly, *see* **Igly**

Igher

higher (etc.), *see* Ire—*one syllable*

Ighland, Island

highland	island	"dry land," etc.

Ighless

sighless, eyeless (etc.), *see* Y

Ighly, *see* **Ily**

Ighness, Iness

highness (etc.), *see* Y, *long*

Ighten, Iten

brighten	lighten	frighten	whiten
heighten	tighten	Titan	enlighten

Ighter, Itre

lighter	backbiter	inditer	writer (etc.), *see* Ite
mitre	prize-fighter	triter	
nitre	underwriter		

IGHTLESS
sightless (etc.), *see* ITE

IGHTLY, *see* ITELY

IGHTNING

brightening	whitening	frightening	tightening
lightning			(etc.), *see* ITE

IGHTY

blighty	mitey	whitey	highty-tighty
flighty	nightie	almighty	Aphrodite
mighty			

IGIL

strigil	sigil	vigil

IGION, *see* YGIAN

IGIOUS

litigious	irreligious	sacrilegious	prodigious
religious			

IGLESS
pigless (etc.), *see* IG

IGLY, IGGLY

bigly	higgly	sniggly	wriggly
giggly	niggly	"piggly-wiggly"	

IGMA

stigma	enigma	sigma

IGMENT

figment	pigment	strigment

IGNANT

benignant	indignant	malignant

IGNEOUS

igneous	ligneous

IGNING, *see* INING

IGNLESS
signless (etc.), *see* INE

IGNLY, *see* INELY

IGNMENT, INEMENT

alignment	consignment	designment	inclinement
assignment	refinement	entwinement	resignment
confinement			

IGOT, *see* IGATE

IGOUR, *see* IGGER

IGUER, *see* EAGER

IGUOUS

ambiguous	contiguous	exiguous	irriguous

IGURE, *see* IGGER

IKELESS

spikeless, *see* IKE

IKEN, ICON, ICHEN

icon	"lichen"	liken

IKING

biking	piking	striking	disliking
diking	spiking	viking	misliking
liking			

ILAX, ILACS

lilacs	smilax	"eye lacks" (etc.)

ILDER

rebuilder	guilder	wilder	"killed her" (etc.)
begilder	bewilder		

ILDING

rebuilding	unbuilding	gilding

ILDISH

childish	mildish	wildish

ILDLY

mildly	wildly	childly

ILDREN, *see* ILDERING

ILELESS

guileless (etc.), *see* ILE

ILER

smiler (etc.), *see* ILE

Illful

skillful	willful	unskillful	"fill full" (etc.)

Ilian, Illion, Ilion, Illon

billion	carillon	pavilion	vermilion
million	civilian	postillion	mandilion
pillion	cotillon	reptilian	stillion
Manilian	"villian"		

Ilient, *see* **Illiant**

Iling

filing (etc.), *see* **Ile**

Ilion, *see* **Ilian**

Ilious

bilious	punctilious	atrabilious	supercilious

Ilken

milken	silken

Ilkless

milkless (etc.), *see* **Ilk**

Ilky

milky	silky

Illa

villa	armilla	cedilla	guerrilla
vanilla	barilla	chinchilla	mantilla
sarsaparilla	camarilla	flotilla	sabadilla
anilla	cascarilla	gorilla	seguidilla

Illage

pillage	tillage	village	grillage
stillage			

Illar, Iller

chiller	miller	pillar	filler (etc.),
caterpillar	maxillar	griller	*see* **Ill**

Illet

billet	millet	rillet	gillet
fillet	quillet	skillet	willet

Illiant

brilliant	resilient	dissilient	transilient

ILLIARD
billiard milliard mill-yard

ILLING
shilling willing unwilling (etc.), *see* ILL

ILLION, *see* ILIAN

ILL-LESS
hill-less (etc.), *see* IL

ILLO
billow pillow willow armadillo peccadillo embillow grenadillo killow *kilo* negrillo pulvillo "will, O!" (etc.)

ILLON, *see* ILIAN

ILLY, ILY (*short*)
grilly illy piccalilli skilly billy chilly filly frilly gillie hilly lily shrilly silly stilly willy-nilly Piccadilly daffy-down-dilly "will he" (etc.)

ILOM, *see* YLUM

ILTER, ILTRE
infilter jilter milter philtre quilter tilter wilter kilter

ILTLESS
guiltless (etc.), *see* ILT

ILY (*long*), ILELY
drily highly nighly shily slily tily vilely wily *servilely* ancile cubile wryly

ILY (*short*), *see* ILLY

IMAGE
image scrimmage

IMATE
climate primate acclimate

Imber

limber	timber	timbre	unlimber
imber			

Imble, Ymbal, Ymbol

cymbal	nimble	thimble	wimble
gimble	symbol	tymbal	fimble

Imbo

limbo	akimbo	kimbo

Imeless

timeless (etc.), *see* Ime

Imely

primely	timely	sublimely	untimely

Imer (*short*), *see* Immar

Imer, Ymer, *see* Ime

Imic, Ymic

alchymic	etymic	metronymic	chymic
cacochymic	homonymic	pantomimic	mimic
cherubimic	leipothymic	synonymic	patronymic
eponymic	metonymic	zymic	

Imid

timid	jimmied

Iming, Yming

priming	rhyming	chiming	climbing, *see* Ime

Imless, *see* Im

Imly

dimly	trimly	primly	slimly
grimly			

Immer, Imer

brimmer	nimmer	skimmer (etc.), *see* Im	shimmer
dimmer	primer		gimmer
glimmer	simmer		

Imming

brimming	swimming	trimming (etc.), *see* Im

Imper

gimper	shrimper	whimper	scrimper (etc.),
limper	simper	crimper	*see* Imp

Imple

crimple	pimple	simple	bewimple
dimple	rimple		

Impless, *see* Imp

Impling

crimpling	impling	rimpling	shrimpling
dimpling	pimpling		

Imply

crimply	limply	pimply	simply
dimply			

Imsy

flimsy	whimsy	brimsey	slimsy

Imy

"blimey"	rimy	grimy	thymy
limy	slimy	stymie	

Inal

acclinal	crinal	officinal	trinal
anticlinal	declinal	piscinal	final
binal	equinal	shinal	spinal
caninal	matutinal		

Inborn

inborn	twinborn

Inceless

princeless (etc.), *see* Ince

Incers

pincers	convincers	wincers (etc.), *see* Ince

Incest

incest	wincest (etc.), *see* Ince

Incher

clincher	flincher	pincher	lyncher (etc.),
			see Inch

Inchless, *see* Inch

Income, Inkum

crinkum	income	"sink 'em" (etc.)	

Inctly

distinctly	succintly	indistinctly	

Incture

cincture	tincture	vincture	lincture
distincture	encincture		

Inder (*long*)

finder (etc.), *see* Ind

Inder

cinder	flinder	rescinder	"pinned her"
hinder	pinder	"winder"	(etc.)
tinder			

Inding

finding (etc.), *see* Ind

Indle

brindle	spindle	rekindle	"wind 'll"
dwindle	windle	enkindle	(etc.)
kindle			

Indless

mindless (etc.), *see* Ind

Indly

blindly	kindly	unkindly	

Indness

blindness (etc.), *see* Ind

Indy

findy	shindy	windy	Lindy

Inear, Innier

finnier	linear	skinnier	whinnier

Ineless

spineless (etc.), *see* Ine

Inely, Ignly

caninely	divinely (etc.), *see* Ine		*masculinely*

Iner, Igner

diner	liner	minor	assigner (etc.), *see* Ine
finer	miner		

Inet, Innet, Inute

ginnet	minute	spinet	pinet
linnet	"in it," etc.		

Inew, Inue

unsinew	continue	discontinue	"spin you" (etc.)

Ineyard

vineyard winyard

Inful

sinful skinful

Ingeless

hingeless (etc.), *see* Inge

Ingent

constringent	refringent	stringent	contingent
fingent	ringent	tingent	pertingent
impingent	restringent	astringent	

Inger (*hard* G)

finger mallinger

Inger (*silent* G)

singer (etc.), *see* Ing

Inger (*soft* G), **Injure**

cringer	twinger	ginger	infringer (etc.), *see* Inge
fringer	singer	injure	
hinger			

Inging

ringing (etc.), *see* Ing

Ingle

cingle	mingle	swingle	intermingle
cringle	shingle	tingle	gingle
dingle	single	commingle	jingal
jingle	springle	surcingle	tringle

Ingless

wingless (etc.), *see* Ing

INGLING
kingling singling wingling (etc.), *see* INGLE

INGLY (*hard* G)
jingly shingly singly tingly (etc.), *see* INGLE
mingly

INGLY (*silent* G)
kingly (etc.), *see* ING

INGO
lingo eringo flamingo jingo
stingo dingo

INGY (*hard* G)
clingy stringy wingy stingy
springy swingy

INGY (*soft* G)
cringy stingy twingy dingy
fringy swingy

INIAN, *see* INION

INIC
aclinic finic platinic rabbinic
actinic fulminic polygynic clinic
delphinic narcotinic quinic cynic

INING, IGNING
lining designing undesigning dining (etc.), *see* INE

INION, INIAN
minion dominion opinion *Virginian*
pinion

INISH (*short*), INNISH
finish thinnish diminish tinnish
minish

INISH (*long*)
brinish swinish

INJURE, *see* INGER

INKER
drinker thinker tinker (etc.), *see* INK

Inking
thinking (etc.), *see* Ink

Inkle
crinkle, twinkle, wrinkle, periwinkle
sprinkle, winkle, besprinkle, inkle
tinkle

Inkless
blinkless (etc.), *see* Ink

Inkling
inkling, sprinkling, twinkling (etc.), *see* Inkle

Inkum, *see* Income

Inky
chinky, inky, blinky, zinky
dinky, pinky, kinky

Inless
sinless (etc.), *see* In

Inly
inly, thinly, McKinley

Inner
dinner, sinner, winner, grinner (etc.), *see* In
inner, spinner, finner
pinner, tinner

Innet, *see* Inet

Inney, *see* Inny

Inning
beginning (etc.), *see* In

Innings
innings (etc.), *see* In

Innow
minnow, winnow, "begin, O!" (etc.)

Inny, Inney
finny, squinny, whinny, pickaninny
hinny, pinny, tinny, skinney
jinny, skinny, ignominy, vinny
ninny, spinney, guinea

INO

lino	rhino	albino	"fine, O!" (etc.)

INOR, *see* INER

INSTER

minster	spinster

INTAL, INTEL

lintel	quintal	pintle

INTER

dinter	printer	sprinter	squinter
hinter	splinter	winter	stinter
minter			

INTLESS

printless (etc.), *see* INT

INTRY

splintery	vintry	wintry

INTY

dinty	linty	squinty	shinty
flinty	minty	glinty	

INUE, *see* INEW

INUS, INOUS

binous	lupinus	minus	vinous
declinous	pinus	sinus	echinus
linous	salinous	spinous	

INUTE, *see* INET

INY

miny	viny	liny	tiny
piney	whiney	shiny	twiny
sunshiny	briny	spiny	winy

ION

lion	Orion	ion	"lie on" (etc.)
scion	dandelion		

IORESS, *see* IRIS

IOT, *see* IAT

IOUS, *see* IAS

Iped

biped	parallelopiped	stripèd	"wipèd" (etc.) *see* Ipe

Ipeless, *see* Ipe

Ipend, Ipened

ripened	stipend

Iper, Yper

piper	striper	viper	griper
riper	typer	wiper	swiper
sniper			

Ipher, Ifer

cipher	rifer	decipher	fifer
lifer			

Iphon, *see* Yphen

Iping

piping (etc.), *see* Ipe

Iple (*long*), **Ypal**

disciple	archetypal	ectypal

Iple (*short*), **Ipple**

cripple	stipple	triple	sipple
nipple	tipple	grippal	swiple
ripple			

Ipless

lipless (etc.), *see* Ip

Ipling, Ippling

crippling	stripling	stipling	tippling
rippling			

Ipper

clipper	shipper	skipper	slipper (etc.), *see* Ip
dipper			

Ippet

sippet	tippet	whippet	snippet
skippet			

Ipping

chipping	dripping	shipping	tripping (etc.), *see* Ip

IPPLE, *see* IPLE

IPPY
chippy
drippy
nippy
slippy
snippy
strippy
trippy
whippy
lippy
shippy

IPSTAFF
tipstaff
whipstaff

IPSY
gipsy
tipsy
ipse

IPTIC, YPTIC
cryptic
styptic
ecliptic
elliptic
anaglyptic
apocalyptic
diptych
glyptic
holocryptic
eatroliptic
triptych

IQUANT, ECANT
precant
piquant
secant
cosecant
intersecant

IQUELY, *see* EEKLY

IQUOR, *see* ICAR

IRANT, IRENT, YRANT
expirant
girant
gyrant
spirant
tyrant
virent
aspirant
conspirant

IRATE, YRATE
gyrate
circumgyrate
dextrogyrate
pirate
irate
lyrate

IRCHEN, URCHIN
birchen
urchin
"searchin'" (etc.)

IRCHLESS, *see* EARCH

IRCLING, URKLING
circling
turkling

IRDAR, IRDER, URDER
girder
herder
murder
thirder
sirdar
absurder (etc.), *see* EARD

IRDLE, URDLE
curdle
begirdle
hurdle

IRDLESS
birdless (etc.), *see* EARD

IRDLY, URDLY
birdly hurdly thirdly absurdly
curdly

IRELING
hireling squireling

IRELY
direly squirely entirely

IREN, IRON
siren lepidosiren palaeosiren "admirin'" (etc.)
environ

IRENT, *see* IRANT

IRER, *see* IRE

IRGELESS
dirgeless (etc.), *see* ERGE

IRIC, YRIC (*short*)
lyric panegyric satiric satyric
empiric (adj.) butyric

IRILE, IRREL
squirrel virile

IRIS
iris Osiris "admiress"

IRKER, ERKER, ORKER, URKER
jerker shirker burker smirker
lurker worker jerquer

IRKLESS
smirkless (etc.), *see* ERK "work less" (etc.)

IRKSOME, URKSOME
irksome murksome

IRLESS
firless (etc.), *see* ER

IRLING, *see* ERLING

IRLISH, URLISH

churlish	girlish		

IRLLESS

girlless (etc.), *see* EARL

IRLY, *see* EARLY

IRMER, ERMER, URMUR

firmer	affirmer	infirmer	squirmer
termer	confirmer	bemurmur	termor
murmur			

IRMISH

firmish	squirmish	wormish	infirmish
skirmish			

IRMLESS

squirmless (etc.), *see* ERM

IRMLY

firmly	termly	wormly	

IRMY

squirmy	wormy	gurmy	taxidermy

IRON, *see* IREN

IROUS, *see* IRUS

IRPER, ERPER, URPER

chirper (etc.), *see* URP

IRRAH

sirrah	tirra-lirra	*Lyra*	

IRRUP, YRUP

stirrup	syrup	chirrup	

IRTHLESS

mirthless (etc.), *see* EARTH

IRTLE, YRTLE, URTLE

hurtle	myrtle	turtle	whortle
kirtle	spirtle	fertile	

IRTLESS

skirtless (etc.), *see* ERT

Irty, Urty

dirty	spurty	thirty	"curt he"
flirty	squirty	cherty	(etc.)
shirty			

Irus

apyrous	papyrus	virus	desirous

Iry, Iary, Iery, Iory

briery	miry	wiry	eyrie
diary	*priory*	enquiry	squiry
fiery	spiry	acquiry	*friary*

Isal

reprisal	surprisal	comprisal	paradisal
revisal			

Iscount

discount	miscount

Iscous, *see* **Iscus**

Iscuit, *see* **Isket**

Iscus

abaciscus	lemniscus	meniscus	discus
discous	lentiscus	trochiscus	viscous
hibiscus			

Isel, *see* **Izzle**

Isely, *see* **Icely**

Iser, Isor, Izar

miser	divisor	erisor	"try, sir"
sizar	incisor	geyser	(etc.)
visor	supervisor	guiser (etc.),	"surprise her"
adviser	Kaiser	*see* **Ise**	(etc.)

Isher, Issure

disher	wisher	kingfisher	"wish her"
fisher	well-wisher	swisher	(etc.)
fissure			

Ishful

dishful	wishful

Ishless

fishless (etc.), *see* **Ish**

Ishy

dishy	fishy	swishy	

Isian, *see* **Ision**

Isic

phthisic	physic	metaphysic	paradisic

Ising

sunrising	surprising (etc.), *see* **Ise**		

Ision, Isian, Ysian, Ission

precision	vision	elision	prevision
allision	scission	Elysian	provision
concision	abscission	excision	recision
illision	collision	incision	rescission
invision	decision	misprision	revision
irrision	derision	Parisian	circumcision
supervision	division	precision	subdivision

Isis

crisis	isis	phthisis	

Isive

decisive	incisive	cicatrisive	divisive
derisive	undecisive	collisive	precisive

Isker

brisker	frisker (etc.), *see* **Isk**		whisker

Isket, Iscuit

biscuit	wisket	"whisk it" (etc.)	trisket
brisket			

Iskey, *see* **Isky**

Iskless

diskless (etc.), *see* **Isk**

Iskly

briskly	*fiscally*		

Isky, Iskey

frisky	risky	whiskey	

Isly, Izzly

drizzly	grisly	chisley	sizzly
frizzly	grizzly		

Ismal, Ysmal

dismal	aneurismal	chrismal	paroxysmal
abysmal	cataclysmal	embolismal	rheumatismal
baptismal	catechismal		

Ison, *see* **Izzen** *and* **Izen**

Isor, *see* **Iser**

Isper

crisper	lisper	whisper

Issal, *see* **Istle**

Issant, *see* **Ecent**

Issile, *see* **Istle**

Ission, *see* **Ician** *and* **Ision**

Issless

blissless (etc.), *see* Is

Issor, Izzer

scissor	whizzer

Issored, *see* **Izzard**

Issue

issue	tissue

Issure, *see* **Isher**

Istance, Istence

distance	insistence	inconsistence	desistance
assistance	resistance	non-existence	equidistance
consistence	subsistence	non-resistance	inexistence
existence	coexistence	pre-existence	persistence

Istant, Istent

distant	existent	coexistent	non-resistant
distent	insistent	equidistant	pre-existent
assistant	resistant	inconsistent	persistent
consistent	subsistent	non-existent	

Isten

christen	glisten	listen

ISTER
agister
bistre
magister
blister
glister
mister
sister
twister
"kissed her" (etc.)
persister
resister (etc.) see IST

ISTENCE, *see* ISTANCE

ISTENING
listening (etc.), *see* ISTEN

ISTENT, *see* ISTANT

ISTHMUS, *see* ISTMAS

ISTIC, YSTIC
cystic
fistic
mystic
hemistic
anarchistic
atheistic
cabalistic
communistic
pantheistic
socialistic
syllogistic
tritheistic
characteristic
polytheistic
absolutistic
agonistic
altruistic
anachronistic
animistic
annalistic
aoristic
artistic
bibliopolistic
cameralistic
canonistic
casuistic
catechistic
deistic
egoistic
egotistic
eristic
euphuistic
fatalistic
humanistic
humoristic
idealistic
illuministic
individualistic
intermistic
journalistic
juristic
linguistic
logistic
materialistic
nihilistic
optimistic
pessimistic
pietistic
pugilistic
puristic
quietistic
rationalistic
realistic
ritualistic
sensualistic
simplistic
solecistic
simplistic
sophistic
stylistic
theistic
touristic

ISTINE, YSTINE
pristine
amethystine
Christine

ISTING
listing (etc.), *see* IST

ISTLE, ISSAL, ISSILE, ISSEL
bristle
gristle
missal
abyssal
missel
missile
thistle
scissel
whistle
dismissal
epistle
sissile

ISTLESS
listless
resistless (etc.), *see* IST

ISTLY

bristly	whistly	gristly	thistly

ISTMAS, ISTHMUS

Christmas	isthmus

ISTOL, *see* YSTAL

ISTY

christy	misty	twisty

ISY, *see* IZY

ITCHER, ICHER

ditcher	pitcher	richer (etc.),	"ditch her"
hitcher	itcher	*see* ICH	(etc.)

ITCHLESS

witchless (etc.), *see* ITCH

ITCHY

hitchy	twitchy	pitchy	switchy
itchy	nichy	stitchy	

ITEFUL, IGHTFUL

frightful	spiteful	despiteful	sprightful
rightful	delightful	mightful	

ITELESS

miteless (etc.), *see* ITE

ITELY, IGHTLY

brightly	knightly (etc.),	sprightly	unsightly
	see ITE	unknightly	

ITEM, ITUM

item	*ad infinitum*	"bite 'em" (etc.)

ITEMENT, ICTMENT

excitement	indictment	affrightment	"frightment"
incitement	invitement		

ITEN, *see* IGHTEN

ITEY, *see* IGHTY

ITHELY

blithely	lithely

ITHER (*long*)

blither	scyther	mither	neither
either	lither	writher	tither

ITHER (*short*)

blither	whither	slither	swither
dither	hither	wither	thither

ITHING (*long*), YTHING

scything	writhing (etc.), *see* ITHE	nithing	trithing
tithing			

ITHLESS

mithless (etc.), *see* ITH

ITHESOME

blithesome	lithesome

ITHY

smithy	stithy	withy	pithy

ITIAL, *see* ICIAL

ITIC

critic	cenobitic	granitic	selenitic
aconitic	conchitic	hematitic	stalactitic
adamitic	dendritic	lignitic	syenitic
aërolitic	diacritic	mephitic	tonsilitic
anthracitic	dialytic	volitic	zeolitic
biolytic	dolomitic	pleuritic	arthritic
carolytic	enclitic	proclitic	hypocritic
catalytic	eremitic	rachitic	paralytic

ITID, ITIED

nitid	pitied (etc.), *see* ITTY

ITING

biting	whiting	writing (etc.), *see* ITE	handwriting

ITION, *see* ICIAN

ITIOUS, *see* ICIOUS

ITISH (*long*), IGHTISH

eremitish	lightish	whitish	tightish
anchoritish			

ITLE, ITAL

title	entitle	detrital	requital
vital	marital	recital	parasital
cital			

ITLESS

fitless (etc.), *see* ITLE

ITLING, ITTLING

witling	whittling	belittling

ITNESS

fitness	witness

ITRE, ITER

biter	mitre	nitre (etc.), *see* ITE	"bite her" (etc.)

ITTAL, *see* **ITTLE**

ITTANCE

pittance	admittance	remittance	permittance
quittance	acquittance	omittance	transmittance

ITTEE, *see* **ITTY**

ITTEN, ITAN

bitten	mitten	witan	written
kitten	smitten		

ITTER

bitter	glitter	litter	twitter
fitter	hitter	pitter	*zither*
fritter	knitter (etc.), *see* IT	quitter	committer
flitter		titter	embitter

ITTI, *see* **ITTY**

ITTING

fitting	flitting	sitting	befitting (etc.), *see* IT

ITTISH, ITISH

British	fittish	skittish

ITTLE, ITAL, ITTAL, ITTOL, ICTUAL

brittle	spital	victual	transmittal
knittle	spittle	whittle	committal
little	tittle	wittol	remittal
acquittal	belittle		

Itty, Ity, Itti, Ittee

bitty	gritty	pretty	committee
chitty	nitty	witty	flitty
city	pity	banditti	kitty
ditty			

Itum, *see* **Item**

Ity, *see* **Itty**

Ius, *see* **Ias**

Ival

rival	outrival	imperatival	conjunctival
adjectival	arrival	salival	nominatival
estival	archival	revival	survival

Ivance

connivance	survivance	contrivance	arrivance

Iven

driven	riven	scriven	thriven
forgiven	given	shriven	

Ivel, Ivil

civil	rivel	snivel	uncivil
drivel	shrivel	swivel	

Ively

lively	wively

Iver (*long*)

cliver	fiver	shriver	reviver
diver	hiver	conniver	surviver (etc.),
driver	liver	deriver	*see* **Ive**

Iver (*short*)

giver	river	deliver	freeliver
liver	shiver	cantaliver	misgiver
quiver	sliver	forgiver	outliver

Ivers (*long*)
divers (etc.), *see* **Iver** (*long*)

Ivet

civet	trivet	privet	unrivet
rivet	grivet		

Ivid

livid	vivid		

Ivil, *see* **Ivel**

Iving (*short*)

thanksgiving	unforgiving (etc.), *see* Ive (*short*)		

Ivot

divot	pivot		

Ivy (*short*), **Ivi**

chivy	privy	tivy	tantivy
divi			

Ixie, *see* **Icksy**

Ixer, Ixir

fixer	mixer (etc.), *see* Ix		elixir

Ixture

fixture	admixture	intermixture	afficture
mixture	commixture	immixture	

Izar, *see* **Iser**

Izard, Izzard, Issored

blizzard	lizard	vizard	bizard
gizzard	scissored	wizard	visored
izzard			

Izeless

sizeless (etc.), *see* **Ize**

Izen, Izon (*long*)

bison	horizon	ptison	"pizen"
bedizen			

Izier, *see* **Izzier**

Izy

misy	nizy	sizy	

Izzer, *see* **Issor**

Izzen, Ison, Izen (*short*)

mizzen	wizen	arisen	mizzen
prison	imprison	bedizen	

IZZIER, IZIER, USIER

busier	dizzier	vizier

IZZLE, ISEL

chisel	grizzle	crizzle	mizzle
drizzle	swizzle	fizzle	sizzle
frizzle			

IZZER, *see* IZZLE

IZZY, USY

busy	mizzy	tizzy	frizzy
dizzy	"is he" (etc.)		

OACHER

roacher (etc.), *see* OACH

OACHFUL

coachful	reproachful

OACHLESS

roachless (etc.), *see* OACH

OADLESS

toadless (etc.), *see* OAD

OAFLESS

loafless (etc.), *see* OAF

OAFY, OPHE, OPHI, OPHY

loafy	sophi	strophe	trophy
oafy			

OAKER, *see* OCHRE

OAKLESS

soakless (etc.), *see* OAK

OAKUM, OCUM

locum	oakum

OALLESS

foalless (etc.), *see* OAL

OALY, OLY, OLELY, OLLY (*long*), OWLY

coaly	lowly	solely	moly
drolly	shoaly	*wholly*	rolly
holy	slowly	roly-poly	

OAMER, *see* OMER

Oamless
roamless (etc.), *see* Oam

Oamy
loamy (etc.), *see* Oam

Oanless
moanless (etc.), *see* Oan

Oapless
soapless (etc.), *see* Oap

Oardless
boardless (etc.), *see* Oard

Oarish, Oorish
boarish *boorish* moorish whorish

Oarless
boarless (etc.), *see* Oar

Oarsely
coarsely hoarsely

Oary, Ory, Oory
dory moory story allegory
glory oary tory flory
gory pory more (Latin) promissory
hoary storey con amore shory
lory

Oastal, *see* Ostal (*long*)

Oaster, Oster
boaster poster toaster throwster
coaster roaster bill-poster

Oasting
coasting ghosting (etc.), *see* Oast

Oastless
toastless (etc.), *see* Oast

Oate
inchoate poet "know it" (etc.)

Oaten, *see* Otan

Oater, *see* Oter

Oathing, *see* **Othing**

Oathless

oathless	slothless	growthless

Obber

cobber	swobber	jobber	swabber
knobber	throbber	robber	"rob her"
snobber	blobber	slobber	(etc.)
sobber	clobber		

Obbet

gobbet	post-obit

Obbin, Obin

bobbin	robin	dobbin	robbin

Obble

cobble	hobble	squabble	coble
gobble	nobble	wobble	

Obbler

cobbler — squabbler (etc.), *see* **Obble**

Obby

bobby	lobby	pobby	snobby
hobby	mobby	cobby	squabby
knobby	nobby	scobby	

Obeless

noblesse — lobeless (etc.), *see* **Obe**

Ober

disrober	prober	October	"robe her"
enrober	sober		(etc.)

Obin, *see* **Obbin**

Obit, *see* **Obbet**

Obless

jobless (etc.), *see* **Ob**

Oblesse, *see* **Obeless**

Ocal

focal	strocal	phocal	vocal
bocal	local	yokel	socle

Ocean, *see* **Otion**

OCER, OSER, OSSER

closer	jocoser	moroser	grosser
grocer	engrosser	verboser	

OCHEE, OKEE, OKY

chokee	joky	roky	choky
hoky	moky	oaky	soaky
smoky	trochee	poky	yoky
croaky			

OCHRE, OAKER, OKER

broker	mediocre	evoker	stoker
choker	joker	stroker	cloaker
croaker	ochre	soaker	invoker
provoker	poker	smoker	yoker
convoker	revoker		

OCIOUS

atrocious	ferocious	precocious	nepotious

OCKER

blocker	shocker (etc.), *see* OCK	soccer	"sock 'er"
cocker		mocker	"frock her" (etc.)
knocker	locker	rocker	

OCKET

brocket	locket	rocket	cocket
docket	pocket	socket	crocket
sprocket	pickpocket		

OCKEY, OCKY

blocky	hockey	stocky (etc.), *see* OCK	flocky
cocky	jockey		locky
crocky	rocky		

OCKING

shocking	stocking (etc.), *see* OCK

OCKLE

cockle	hockle

OCKLESS

hockless (etc.), *see* OCK

OCKSY, *see* OXY

Oco, Ocoa, Oko

boko	cocoa	"locofoco"	coco
rococo	baroco	toko	troco

Octer, *see* **Octor**

Oction

auction	concoction	decoction

Octor, Octer

doctor	proctor	concocter	"knocked her" (etc.)

Octus

crocus	hocus	locus	hocus-pocus
focus			

Ocust, Ocussed

crocussed	focussed	hocussed	locust

Odden

sodden	trodden	untrodden	hodden

Odder

dodder	nodder	codder	prodder
fodder	odder	plodder	podder

Oddess, Odice

bodice	goddess

Oddle, Odel

coddle	noddle	remodel	waddle
model	swaddle	toddle	twaddle

Oddler, *see* **Oddle**

Oddling, *see* **Odling**

Oddly, Odly

godly	oddly	coddly (etc.), *see* **Oddle**

Oddy, Ody

body	noddy	embody	toddy
cloddy	shoddy	busybody	waddy
hoddy	odsbody	roddy	*wadi*
soddy	squaddy		

Odel (*Short*), *see* **Oddle**

Odeless

roadless (etc.), *see* **Oad**

ODER, OADER, ODOUR

loader exploder foreboder (etc.), *see* OAD
odour

ODEST (*short*), **ODICED**

bodiced noddest oddest (etc.), *see* OD immodest
modest

ODGELESS

dodgeless (etc.), *see* ODGE

ODGER

bodger podger lodger codger
dodger

ODGING

dodging lodging (etc.), *see* ODGE

ODICE, *see* **ODDESS**

ODIC

odic parodic melodic iodic
episodic spasmodic periodic methodic
exodic aesthesodic synodic rhapsodic
kinesodic hellanodic anodic sarcodic

ODING, OADING

loading foreboding (etc.), *see* OAD

ODISH, OADISH

modish show-dish toadish

ODLING, ODDLING

codling godling modeling toddling
coddling waddling swaddling twaddling

ODLY, *see* **ODDLY**

ODOUR, *see* **ODER**

ODOUS, ODUS

modus nodous

ODY (*short*), *see* **ODDY**

OELIESS, *see* **EW** *and* **O**

OEM

poem proem "know him" (etc.)

OER, OWER

crower	lower	sower	overthrower
goer	mower	slower	(etc.), *see* O,
grower	ower	thrower	*also possible*
knower	rower	bestower	*rhymes in*
			OAR

OET, *see* **OATE**

OFFEE

coffee	offee	spoffy

OFFER

coffer	offer	goffer	doffer
cougher	proffer	scoffer	golfer

OFFEST, *see* **OPHIST**

OFFICED, *see* **OPHIST**

OFFING

coughing	offing	scoffing (etc.), *see* **OFF**

OFTEN, ORPHAN

often	soften

OFTENER

oftener	softener

OFTY

lofty	softy

OGEY, OGI, OGUEY

bogey	jogi	roguey	bogie
voguey	fogey		

OGGISH

doggish	hoggish	"froggish"

OGGLE

boggle	coggle	joggle	toggle
goggle			

OGGY

boggy	doggy	soggy	froggy
cloggy	foggy	joggy	*pedagogy*
groggy			

Ogle

bogle ogle "fogle"

Ogress

ogress progress

Oguey, *see* **Ogey**

Ogy (*short*), *see* **Oggy**

Oic

stoic heroic melanochroic hypozoic benzoic dichroic azoic protozoic eozoic hylozoic dyspnoic

Oiceless

choiceless (etc.), *see* **Oice**

Oider

moider embroider voider "employed her" (etc.) avoider

Oiler

boiler (etc.), *see* **Oil**

Oily, *see* **Oyly**

Oilless

toilless (etc.), *see* **Oil**

Oiner

coiner enjoiner purloiner

Oing, Owing

owing foregoing (etc.), *see* **O**

Oinless

coinless (etc.), *see* **Oin**

Ointal, Ointel

pointel disjointal

Ointer

pointer anointer (etc.), *see* **Oint**

Ointless

pointless (etc.), *see* **Oint**

Ointment

anointment appointment disjointment disappointment

Oiseless
noiseless (etc.), *see* Oise

Oison

oison	poison	empoison	toison

Oister, Oyster

cloister	oyster	roister	moister
encloister	foister	hoister	

Oiter, Oitre

goitre	loiter	reconnoitre	adroiter
exploiter			

Oken

broken	bespoken	outspoken	unspoken
oaken	betoken	foretoken	free-spoken
spoken	fair-spoken	unbroken	soft-spoken
token	forespoken		

Oker, *see* Ochre

Okeless
jokeless (etc.), *see* Oak

Oky, *see* Ochee

Olar (*long*), **Oller, Owler**

bowler	scroller	doler	coaler
molar	roller	poler	droller
polar	solar	enroller	poller
circumpolar	stroller	comptroller	toller
consoler	cajoler	controller	troller
patroller			

Olar (*short*), *see* Ollar

Olden

bolden	golden	beholden	withholden
embolden	holden	olden	

Older, *see* Oulder

Oldier

soldier	"hold yer" (etc.)

Olding
molding (etc.), *see* Old

Oldless
goldless (etc.), *see* Old

Oldly
boldly coldly manifoldly

Oleful, Oulful, Owlful
bowlful doleful soulful

Olely, *see* Oaly

Olemn, Olumn
column solemn

Olen, *see* Ollen

Oler, *see* Ollar

Olesome
dolesome wholesome

Olfish, Ullfish
bullfish wolfish

Olic, Ollick
colic symbolic embolic melancholic
frolic bucolic metabolic epipolic
rollick alcoholic systolic eolic
vitriolic apostolic diabolic parabolic
diastolic bibliopolic hyperbolic variolic
epistolic

Olid
solid squalid stolid volleyed
jollied olid

Olish, Ollish
dollish abolish demolish tollollish
polish

Olkless
folkless (etc.), *see* Oak

Ollar, Olar (*short*), **Oler, Olour**
collar loller *squalor* sollar
dollar scholar

Ollard, Ollared

collared	dollared	pollard	Lollard
"scholard"	bollard		

Ollege, *see* **Owledge**

Ollen (*long*), **Olen, Olon**

colon	stolen	swollen	semicolon

Oller, *see* **Olar**

Ollet

collet	swallet	wallet

Olley, *see* **Olly**

Ollier

collier	jollier

Ollop

collop	escallop	wallop	lollop
dollop	trollop		

Ollow

collow	hollow	wallow	hollo
follow	swallow	Apollo	

Olly (*long*), *see* **Oaly**

Olly (*short*), **Olley, Ollie, Oly**

collie	melancholy	Molly	trolley
dolly	holly	folly	volley
golly	jolly	polly	loblolly

Olon, *see* **Ollen**

Olonel, *see* **Ernal**

Olour, *see* **Ollar** *and* **Uller**

Olster

bolster	holster	upholster

Olter, Oulter

bolter	coulter	revolter	jolter (etc.), *see* **Olt**

Oltest, Oulticed

poulticed	revoltest (etc.), *see* **Olt**

Oltish
coltish doltish

Oltless
coltless (etc.), *see* Olt

Olumn, *see* Olemn

Olver
solver, absolver, revolver, resolver (etc.), *see* Olve, "involve her" (etc.)

Oly, *see* Oaly *and* Olly (*short*)

Oma
coma, aboma, diploma, aroma, sarcoma, theobroma, zygoma

Omach, Ummock
hummock, stomach

Omachs, Ummocks, Ummax
flummax, hummocks, stomachs, "hummox"

Oman (*short*), **Omon, Owman**
gnomon, bowman, Roman, foeman, showman, yeoman

Ombless
combless (etc.), *see* Oam *and* Oom

Omeless
homeless (etc.), *see* Oam

Oment
foment (noun), moment, bestowment

Omer
homer, omer, misnomer (etc.), *see* Oam, beach-comber, gomer, roamer, vomer

Omet, Omit
comet, vomit, domet, grommet

Omic
comic, agronomic, entomic, nomic, astronomic, anatomic, diatomic, isonomic, stereotomic, economic, autonomic, dystomic, monatomic, triatomic, vomic

OMING (*long*)
roaming (etc.), *see* **OAM**

OMING (*short*), **UMMING**

coming	benumbing	becoming	forthcoming
humming		(etc.), *see* **UM**	unbecoming

OMISH, OAMISH

loamish	Romish

OMIT, *see* **OMET**

OMON, *see* **OMAN**

OMPASS, UMPUS

compass	rumpus	encompass	"stump us" (etc.)

OMPTER

compter	prompter	accompter	"prompt her" (etc.)

ONANT, *see* **ONENT**

ONDANT, *see* **ONDENT**

ONDAY, *see* **UNDAY**

ONDANT, ONDENT

fondant	despondent	co-respondent	frondent
respondent	correspondent		

ONDEL, *see* **ONDLE**

ONDER

bonder	corresponder	yonder	responder
fonder	squander	absconder	hypochonder
ponder	wander	desponder	condor

ONDLE, ONDEL

fondle	rondel

ONDLESS
bondless (etc.), *see* **OND**

ONDLING

bondling	fondling	rondeling

ONELESS
boneless (etc.), *see* **OAN**

Onely, Only

lonely	only		

Onent, Onant

conant	deponent	opponent	proponent
component	exponent	sonant	

Oner, *see* **Onner** *and* **Onor**

Onest

honest	dishonest	donnest	wannest (etc.),
connest	non est		*see* **On**

Oney (*long*), *see* **Ony**

Oney (*short*), *see* **Unny**

Onger

conger	longer	*prolonger*	*wronger*
stronger			

Ongeous, Ungeous

lungeous	spongeous		

Onging (*hard*)

wronging (etc.), *see* **Ong**		longing	

Onging (*soft*), *see* **Unging**

Ongless

prongless (etc.), *see* **Ong**

Ongueless

tongueless (etc.), *see* **Ung**

Ongly

longly	strongly	wrongly	

Ongy (*soft*)

lungy	plungy	spongy	

Onic

chronic	harmonic	symphonic	canonic
conic	ionic	Teutonic	crotonic
tonic	laconic	diatonic	draconic
euphonic	mnemonic	histrionic	ironic
telephonic	architectonic	acronyc	masonic
agonic	antiphonic	atonic	monophonic

ONIC—(*Cont.*)

parsonic	isotonic	colophonic	paratonic
sermonic	metonic	diaphonic	pulmonic
carbonic	neurotonic	hedonic	tectonic
cyclonic	platonic	jargonic	theogonic
geogonic	stratonic	monochronic	Housatonic

ONION, UNNION

onion	ronion	trunnion	munnion
brunion	bunion		

ONNISH, ONISH

donnish	admonish	astonish	wannish
premonish	tonnish		

ONKY, ONKEY

conky	donkey

ONKEY, UNKEY, UNKY

flunkey	monkey	spunky	funky
trunky	chunky		

ONKISH, UNKISH

drunkish	monkish	skunkish

ONLY, *see* ONELY

ONNER, ONER, ONOR

goner	wanner	dishonor	conner
honor	aleconner		

ONNET

bonnet	unbonnet	sonnet	"con it" (etc.)

ONOR, ONER, OWNER

donor	owner	atoner (etc.), *see* OAN	"known her" (etc.)

ONOR, *see* ONNER

ONSAL, ONSIL, ONSUL

consul	enconsal	proconsul	responsal
tonsil			

ONTEST

contest	wantest

ONTRACT

contract	entr'acte

Ony, Oney, Oni

bony, crony, parsimony, antimony, coney, pony, sanctimony, lazzaroni, macaroni, alimony, stony, patrimony, astony, drony, tony, testimony, matrimony, gony, phony, "aloney"

Ooby, Uby

booby, looby, ruby

Oodle, Eudal

boodle, feudal, noodle, udal, flapdoodle, paludal

Oodless

foodless (etc.), *see* Ood *and* Ud

Oody (*short*)

goody, woody, "could he" (etc.)

Oody (*long*)

moody (etc.), *see* Ood

Oofless

roofless (etc.), *see* Oof

Ookish (*long*)

flukish, spookish

Ookish (*short*)

bookish, rookish, "cookish" (etc.)

Ookless

cookless (etc.), *see* Ook

Ooky (*short*)

booky, cooky, hookey, hooky, rooky

Ooky (*long*)

fluky, spooky, "Aunt Suky"

Ooler

cooler (etc.), *see* Ool

Oolish, Ulish

coolish, foolish, mulish, schoolish

Oolless

school-less (etc.), *see* Ool

OOLLY, *see* **ULY**

OOMER, *see* **UMER**

OOMLESS
roomless (etc.), *see* **OOM**

OOMY, *see also* **UMY**

bloomy	gloomy	plumy	rheumy
broomy	roomy		

OONER; *see also* **UNAR** *for allowable rhymes*

schooner	spooner	sooner (etc.), *see* **OON**

OONFUL; *see* **UNEFUL** *for imperfect rhymes*

spoonful	"moon full"

OONY, UNY, UISNE

loony	puisne	spoony	tuny
moony	*puny*		

OOPER, UPER, OPOR

cooper	super	stupor	trooper (etc.), *see* **OOP**
hooper			

OORER, *see* **URER**

OORLY, *see* **URELY** *for imperfect rhymes*
poorly (etc.), *see* **OOR**

OOSELESS
gooseless (etc.), *see* **OOSE**

OOSELY, *see* **USELY** *for imperfect rhymes*
loosely (etc.), *see* **OOSE**

OOSER (*flat*), **UISER, OOZER**, *see also* **USER** *for imperfect rhymes*

boozer	chooser	cruiser	loser (etc.), *see* **OOSE**
bruiser			

OOTER; *see also* **UTER** *for imperfect rhymes*

mooter	freebooter (etc.), *see* **OOT**	"shoot her" (etc.)

OOTING
shooting (etc.), *see* **OOT**

OOTLE; *see also* **UTAL** *for possible rhymes*

brutal	footle	tootle	"boot'll" (etc.)

Ootless

bootless	fruitless (etc.), *see* Oot		

Ootling

footling	rootling		

Ooty, Ooti; *see also* Uty

booty	fruity	rooty	fluty
dhooti			

Ooveless

grooveless (etc.), *see* Oove

Oozer, *see* Ooser

Oozle, Ousel; *see also* Usal *for imperfect rhymes*

foozle	ousel	bamboozle	perusal

Oozler

foozler	bamboozler		

Oozy

boozy	oozy	*musy*	"shoosy"
bruisy	snoozy	woosy	"twosy"

Opal

copal	opal	nopal	

Opeless

hopeless (etc.), *see* Oap

Oper (*long*)

sloper	toper	groper	interloper
eloper			(etc.), *see* Oap

Oper (*short*), *see* Opper

Ophe, *see* Oafy

Opic

topic	microscopic	hydropic	canopic
tropic	spectroscopic	telescopic (etc.)	myopic (etc.)
acopic			

Oping

coping	soaping (etc.), *see* Oap		

Oplar, Oppler

poplar	toppler		

Opless

topless, (etc.), *see* Op

Opling, Oppling

fopling, toppling

Opper, Oper

copper, cropper, hopper, proper, stopper, improper, chopper (etc.), *see* Op, whopper, grasshopper, eavesdropper

Opping

chopping, topping, whopping (etc.), *see* Op

Oppy, Opy

choppy, copy, sloppy, droppie, moppy, soppy, poppy, shoppy, croppy, floppy, hoppy, loppy

Opsy

dropsy, Topsy, copsy, autopsy, dysopsy

Opter

propter, adopter, helicopter, phenicopter

Optic

coptic, optic, synoptic, autoptic

Option

option, adoption

Opy (*long*), **Oapy**

mopy, ropy, soapy, slopy

Opy (*short*), *see* **Oppy**

Orage, Orridge, *see also* **Ourage**

borage, gorage, shorage, *porridge*, storage

Oral (*long*)

choral, floral, chloral, horal, oral, sororal, thoral, auroral, trifloral

Oral (*short*), **Orral, Orrel, Aurel**

coral, laurel, moral, quarrel, sorrel, immoral

Oran, Oron
koran moron oxymoron "pour on" (etc.)

Orax
borax storax corax thorax
"show-racks"

Orbel
corbel warble

Orceless
forceless (etc.), *see* **Orce**

Orchard
orchard tortured

Orcher
scorcher torture

Order
border forder disorder rewarder (etc.),
order warder recorder *see* **Ord**

Ordial
cordial primordial

Ording
lording according (etc.), *see* **Ord**

Ordless
fordless (etc.), *see* **Oard**

Ordon
cordon warden

Ordship
lordship wardship

Ordure, *see* **Orger**

Ordy, *see* **Urdy**

Oreal, *see* **Orial**

Oreign, *see* **Orin**

Oreless
doorless (etc.), *see* **Oar**

ORER
borer (etc.), *see* OAR

OREST, ORREST

forest	borest	floorest	ignorest (etc.), *see* OAR

ORGAN

organ	gorgon	Morgan

ORGER

forger	gorger	ordure	disgorger

ORGES

forges	gorges	disgorges

ORGON, *see* ORGAN

ORIC

doric	historic	perchloric	chloric
metaphoric	paregoric	allegoric	roric
choric			

ORID, ORRID

florid	horrid	gloried	storied
torrid			

ORIN

florin	foreign	warren

ORIST, OREST

borest	florist	sorest (etc.), *see* OAR

ORKLESS
workless (etc.), *see* ERK *and* ORK

ORKY
porky (etc.), *see* ORK

ORMANT

dormant	informant

ORMER

dormer	warmer	performer	reformer (etc.), *see* ORM
former	informer		

ORMING

forming	house-warming (etc.), *see* ORM

Ormless
formless (etc.), *see* Orm

Ormly
warmly uniformly

Ormous
enormous informous "warm us" (etc.)

Orner
horner warner suborner (etc.), *see* Orn

Ornet
cornet hornet

Orney, *see* Ourney

Ornful
hornful mournful scornful

Orniced, Ornest
corniced warnest (etc.), *see* Orn

Orning
morning mourning scorning warning (etc.), *see* Orn

Ornless
hornless (etc.), *see* Orn

Orny
corny horny thorny

Orough
borough thorough burrow *burro*

Orous, *see* Orus

Orphan, *see* Often

Orpoise, *see* Orpus

Orpor
torpor warper

Orpus
corpus porpoise

Orral, Orrel, *see* Oral (*short*)

ORRENT

torrent	warrant	abhorrent

ORRER, *see* ORROR

ORRIDGE, *see* ORAGE

ORROR

horror	adorer	ignorer (etc.), *see* OAR	"bore her" (etc.)
abhorrer			

ORROW

borrow	morrow	sorrow

ORRY

quarry	sorry

ORRY (*as in* worry), *see* URRY

ORSAL, ORSEL

dorsal	foresail	morsel	torsel

ORSELESS

horseless (etc.), *see* ORSE

ORSION, *see* ORTION

ORSTED, IRSTED

thirsted	worsted	"bursted"

ORTAL, *see* ORTLE

ORTAR, ORTER

mortar	reporter	supporter	extorter (etc.), *see* ORT
quarter			

ORTEN

quartan	shorten

ORTHLESS

worthless (etc.), *see* EARTH

ORTIE, *see* ORTY

ORTION

portion	apportion	distortion	retortion
torsion	consortion	extortion	disproportion
abortion	contortion	proportion	

ORTLE

chortle	mortal	portal	immortal

Ortly, Ourtly

courtly	portly

Ortive

sportive	tortive	transportive	abortive

Ortment

assortment	disportment	deportment	transportment
comportment			

Ortress

fortress	porteress

Ortune

fortune	importune	misfortune

Orture, *see* **Orcher**

Ortured, *see* **Orchard**

Orty

forty	snorty	sortie	warty
rorty			

Orum

forum	quorum	variorum	"bore 'em"
jorum	indecorum		(etc.)

Orus, Orous

chorus	sonorous	pylorus	"before us"
porous	canorous	torous	(etc.)
decorous	imporous	torus	ictheosaurus

Ory, *see* **Oary**

Osel, *see* **Ozzle**

Oseless

roseless (etc.), *see* **Ose**

Osely, Ossly

closely	jocosely	morosely	verbosely
grossly			

Osen, *see* **Ozen**

Oser

poser (etc.), *see* **Ose**

OSET, OSIT
closet interposit posit reposit
deposit juxtaposit

OSHER
josher washer (etc.), *see* OSH

OSHY
boshy toshy sloshy swashy
squashy washy

OSIER, *see* OSURE

OSION
corrosion erosion ambrosion explosion
implosion

OSIT, *see* OSET

OSIVE
corrosive explosive erosive

OSLING
gosling *jostling* nozzling

OSSACKS
Cossacks trossachs

OSSAGE
bossage sausage

OSSING
bossing (etc.), *see* OSS

OSSLESS
bossless (etc.), *see* OSS

OSSLY, *see* OSELY

OSSOM
blossom opossum possum odontoglossum

OSSY
bossy flossy lossy posse
drossy glossy mossy tossy

OSTAL (*long*), OASTAL
coastal postal

Ostal (*short*), **Ostel, Ostil**
costal
hostel
postil
accostal
infracostal
intercostal
Pentecostal

Oster (*long*), *see* **Oaster**

Oster (*short*)
coster
foster
accoster
paternoster
imposter
kloster
Pentecoster
roster

Ostess
ghostess
hostess

Ostic, Austic
caustic
acrostic
agnostic
diagnostic
prognostic
ateostic
geognostic
gnostic
paracrostic
pentacostic

Ostle, Ossil, Assail
dossil
fossil
jostle
throstle
wassail
apostle
colossal
dosel
hypoglossal
tossel

Ostler
hostler
jostler
ostler
wassailer

Ostless
costless (etc.), *see* **Ost**

Ostly
ghostly
mostly

Ostrel, Ostril
costrel
nostril
lamellirostral
rostral

Ostrum
nostrum
rostrum

Osure, Osier
cosier
closure
crosier
hosier
osier
rosier
composure
disclosure
enclosure
exposure
discomposure
disposure
foreclosure
reposure

Osy, Ozy
dozy
nosy
posy
prosy
rosy
cosy

OTAL
dotal
sacerdotal
notal
sclerotal
total
anecdotal
rotal
teetotal
antidotal
extradotal

OTAN
oaten
Wotan
"verboten"

OTARD, OTORED
dotard
motored

OTCHER
botcher
blotcher
notcher
splotcher
watcher

OTCHET, OCHET
crochet
rochet

OTCHLESS
scotchless (etc.), *see* OTCH

OTCHY
blotchy
botchy
notchy
splotchy

OTELESS
boatless (etc.), *see* OAT

OTEM, *see* OTUM

OTER, OTOR
bloater
quoter
voter (etc.), *see* OAT
locomotor
motor

OTEST, OTICED, OTIST
noticed
protest
votest
wrotest (etc.), *see* OAT

OTHER
bother
pother
fother
father

OTHER (*as in* other)
brother
other
another
t'other
mother
smother

OTHING (*long*)
clothing
loathing
betrothing

OTHIE, OTHY
bothie
frothy
mothy

OTHLESS, *see* **OATH**

OTIC

chaotic	*anecdotic*	demotic	pyrotic
despotic	carotic	erotic	quixotic
exotic	culottic	glottic	sarcotic
hypnotic	neurotic	idiotic	zoötic
acrotic	osmotic	narcotic	zymotic
anaptotic	patriotic		

OTICED, *see* **OTEST**

OTION

lotion	potion	groschen	locomotion
motion	devotion	emotion	nicotian
notion	commotion	promotion	remotion
ocean			

OTIVE

emotive	votive	promotive	locomotive

OTLESS

cotless (etc.), *see* **OT**

OTLEY, OTLY

hotly	motley	squatly

OTOR, *see* **OTER**

OTTAGE

cottage	pottage

OTTAR, *see* **OTTER**

OTTEL, *see* **OTTLE**

OTTEN, OTTON

cotton	rotten	forgotten	misbegotten
gotten	begotten		

OTTER

clotter	rotter	blotter	jotter
ottar	totter	cotter	knotter
otter	trotter	dotter	spotter
plotter	bog-trotter	garotter	squatter (etc.),
potter	complotter	hotter	*see* **OT**

OTTIER

clottier	cottier	knottier	spottier

OTTISCHE, OTTISH

Scottish	schottische	sottish	

OTTLE, OTTEL

bottle	throttle	glottal	tottle
dottel	wattle	mottle	twattle
pottle			

OTTLING

bottling (etc.), *see* OTTLE

OTTO

grotto	motto	Otto	ridotto
lotto	fagotto	risotto	

OTTON, *see* OTTEN

OTTY

blotty	knotty	snotty	totty
clotty	potty	spotty	hotty-motty

OTUM, OTEM

quotum	totem	factotum	

OUBLE, UBBLE

bubble	grubble	rubble	trouble
double	knubble	stubble	

OUBLER

doubler (etc.), *see* OUBLE

OUBTLESS, OUTLESS

doubtless (etc.), *see* OUT

OUCHLESS

couchless (etc.), *see* OUCH

OUDER, *see* OWDER

OUDLESS

cloudless (etc.), *see* OUD

OUDLY

loudly	proudly		

OUDY, *see* OWDY

OUGHBOY, OWBOY

cowboy	ploughboy	"now, boy" (etc.)	

OUGHEN

roughen	toughen

OUGHLESS, *see* **OFF, UFF, OW, OCK**

OUGHLY, *see* **UFFLY**

OUGHTEN

foughten	wroughten	"boughten"

OUGHTY, *see* **AUGHTY** *and* **OUTY**

OULDER, OLDER

bolder	moulder	smoulder	older (etc.),
boulder	shoulder		*see* **OLD**

OULDERING

shouldering	mouldring	soldering	"gold ring"
smouldering			

OULING

fouling (etc.), *see* **OUL**

OULTICED, *see* **OLTEST**

OUNCELESS

bounceless (etc.), *see* **OUNCE**

OUNCIL, *see* **OUNSEL**

OUNDER

bounder	founder	pounder	sounder (etc.),
flounder	iron-founder	rounder	*see* **OUND**

OUNDING

bounding (etc.), *see* **OUND**

OUNDLESS

groundless (etc.), *see* **OUND**

OUNDLING

foundling	groundling

OUNDLY

roundly	unsoundly	profoundly

OUNDNESS

roundness (etc.), *see* **OUND**

OUNDARY, OUNDRY

boundary	floundery	foundry

OUNDSEL, *see* OUNSEL

OUNGLING, *see* UNGLING

OUNSEL

council	counsel	groundsel	

OUNTAIN

fountain	mountain	catamountain	"accountin'"

OUNTANT

mountant	accountant		

OUNTER

accounter	encounter	rencounter	surmounter
mounter			(etc.), *see* OUNT

OUNTLESS

countless (etc.), *see* OUNT

OUNTRIES, *see* UNTRESS

OUNTY

bounty	county	mounty	viscounty

OURAGE, URRAGE; *see also* ORAGE

borage	demurrage	discourage	encourage
courage			

OURI, *see* OWRY

OURISH, URRISH

currish	flourish	nourish	

OURLESS

hourless (etc.), *see* OUR, OOR, OAR

OURLY

hourly	sourly		

OURNEY, ERNY, ORNEY, URNEY

ferny	spurney	attorney	"churny"
journey	tourney	"burny"	(etc.)

OURSER

courser	coarser	hoarser (etc.), *see* OARSE	

OURSELESS

courseless (etc.), *see* ORCE

OURTEOUS, *see* URCHASE

OURTLY, *see* ORTLY

OUSAL, OUSEL

housel	towzle	espousal	ousel
nousel	carousal	crousal	spousal

OUSEL, *see* OOZLE *and* OUSAL

OUSELESS

houseless (etc.), *see* OUSE

OUSER

mouser	rouser	trouser	carouser (etc.), *see* OUSE
Towser	"arouse her" (etc.)		

OUSERS, *see* OUSER

OUSIN, *see* OZEN

OUSING

rousing (etc.), *see* OUSE

OUSY

lousy	drowsy	"sousey"	"carrousy"
mousy	blowsy		

OUTLESS

boutless (etc.), *see* OUT

OUTLY

stoutly	devoutly

OUTRE, UITOR, OOTER (etc.)

suitor	accoutre	shooter (etc.), *see* OOT

OUTY, OUGHTY

droughty	doughty	grouty	snouty
gouty			

OVAL

disapproval	reproval	approval	removal
disproval			

OVEL

grovel	hovel	novel

OVELESS

doveless (etc.), *see* OVE

OVEMENT

movement	approvement	improvement	

OVEN (*long*)

cloven	hoven	woven	interwoven
proven			

OVEN (*short*), **OVIN**

covin	oven	sloven	"shovin'" (etc.)

OVING

roving (etc.), *see* OVE

OVER (*long*)

clover	over	stover	moreover
drover	rover	trover	half-seas-over

OVER (*short*)

cover	plover	discover	uncover
glover	shover	recover	table-cover
lover			

OVETAIL

dovetail	love-tale		

OWARD

coward	flowered (etc.), *see* OUR		

OWARD (*long* O), *see* OARD

OWBOY, *see* OUGHBOY

OWDER, OUDER

crowder	powder	chowder	prouder (etc.), *see* OUD

OWDY, OUDY

cloudy	dowdy	rowdy	shroudy
crowdy	proudy		

OWEL

bowel	towel	vowel	semi-vowel
dowel	trowel	disembowel	avowal
rowel			

OWER (*long*)

sower	lower	mower, etc., *see* OW	

Owered
lowered etc., see Ower | *forward* | untoward | toward

Owing
flowing | knowing | cock-crowing (etc.), *see* O

Owledge, Ollege
college | knowledge | acknowledge | foreknowledge

Owler
bowler (etc.), *see* Olar *and* Oul

Owless
rowless (etc.), *see* O *and* Ow

Owling
bowling (etc.), *see* Oal *and* Oul

Owlless
goalless (etc.), *see* Oul *and* Oal

Owly, *see* Oaly

Owner, *see* Onor

Ownish
brownish | clownish | townish | downish

Ower, *see* Oer

Ownless
townless (etc.), *see* Own

Ownsman
gownsman | townsman

Owny
brownie
browny
downy
towny
frowny

Owry, Ouri, Owery, Oury
bowery
dowry
floury
flowery
houri
showery
towery
avowry
cowry
lowery

Owsy, *see* Owzy

Owy (ō)

blowy	showy	snowy	towy
doughy	glowy		

Owy (ŏ)

sloughy	"zowie"	"now he" (etc.)

Owzy, Owsy

blowzy	bowzy	frowzy	mousy
drowsy			

Oxen, Oxswain

coxswain	oxen

Oxy, Ocksy

cocksy	proxy	heterodoxy	foxy
doxy	orthodoxy	cacodoxy	paradoxy

Oyal

loyal	pennyroyal	disloyal	sur-royal
royal			

Oyalty

loyalty	royalty

Oyer

annoyer	destroyer	employer

Oyless

toilless (etc.), *see* **Oil** *and* **Oy**

Oyly, Oily

coyly	doily	oily	roily

Oyment

cloyment	enjoyment	chatoyment	deployment
employment	unemployment		

Ozen, Osen (*long*)

boatswain	frozen	hosen	rosen
chosen	squozen		

Ozen (*short*), **Ousin**

cousin	cozen	dozen

Ozzle, Osel

losel	nozzle	sozzle

Uage, Ewage

sewage escuage brewage

Ual, Ewal

dual pursual renewal subdual
eschewal reviewal

Uant, Uent

fluent truant pursuant

Ubbard, Upboard

cupboard lubbard blubbered rubbered

Ubber

blubber slubber grubber (etc.), *see* Ub "dub her" (etc.)
lubber landlubber
rubber indiarubber

Ubbish

clubbish grubbish rubbish tubbish
cubbish

Ubble, *see* **Ouble**

Ubbly

bubbly knubbly rubbly stubbly
doubly

Ubby

chubby scrubby fubby tubby
grubby shrubby stubby cubby
hubby

Ubeless

tubeless (etc.), *see* **Ube**

Ubless

cubless (etc.), *see* **Ub**

Ubtle, *see* **Uttle**

Uby, *see* **Ooby**

Uccour, *see* **Ucker**

Ucent, Usant

lucent adducent interlucent redusent
recusant conducent abducent traducent
relucent tralucent producent unlucent
translucent

Ucer
looser (etc.), *see* Oose (*hard*)

Ucial
crucial fiducial

Ucive, Usive

abusive	delusive	inclusive	confusive
allusive	diffusive	infusive	perfusive
collusive	effusive	intrusive	reclusive
conclusive	elusive	obtrusive	seclusive
conducive	exclusive	inconclusive	seducive
deducive	illusive		

Ucker, Uccor

mucker	succor	sucker	tucker (etc.), *see* Uck
pucker			

Ucking
ducking (etc.), *see* Uck

Uckle

buckle	knuckle	suckle	honeysuckle
chuckle	muckle	truckle	"luck 'll"
huckle	stuckle	unbuckle	(etc.)

Uckler

buckler	swashbuckler	knuckler	swingebuckler (etc.), *see* Uckle
chuckler			

Uckless
luckless (etc.), *see* Uck

Uckling
buckling duckling suckling (etc.), *see* Uckle

Uckold
cuckold suckled (etc.), *see* Uckle

Ucky

ducky	mucky	plucky	unlucky
lucky			

Ucre, Euchre, Uker

euchre	fluker	lucre	rebuker (etc.), *see* Uke

UCTER, *see* UCTOR

UCTION

fluxion
ruction
suction
abduction
affluxion
construction
deduction
defluxion
destruction
effluxion
induction
instruction
obstruction
production
reduction
seduction
introduction
misconstruction
reproduction
superstruction
superinduction
adduction
conduction
diduction
duction
influxion
manuduction
obduction
traduction

UCTIVE

constructive
deductive
destructive
inductive
instructive
adductive
conductive
traductive
obstructive
productive
reductive
seductive
introductive
reproductive
superstructive
superinductive

UCTOR

abductor
conductor
constructor
destructor
instructor
obstructer
adductor
ductor
eductor
monuductor

UDDER, OODER

dudder
pudder
scudder
flooder
rudder
shudder
udder

UDDING (*For rhymes to* budding *see* UD)

hooding
pudding

UDDLE

cruddle
cuddle
uddle
huddle
muddle
puddle
ruddle
buddle
nuddle
scuddle

UDDLY

cuddley (etc.), *see* UDDLE

UDDY, UDY

bloody
cruddy
cuddy
muddy
ruddy
studdy
study
puddy

UDELESS

foodless (etc.), *see* OOD

UDELY. *see* EWDLY

UDENESS
rudeness (etc.), *see* OOD

UDENT

prudent	imprudent	concludent	occludent
student			

UDER
ruder (etc.), *see* OOD

UDGELESS
smudgeless (etc.), *see* UDGE

UDGELING

cudgelling	drudgeling	judgeling

UDGEON

bludgeon	dudgeon	grudgeon	curmudgeon

UDISH

crudish	"new dish"	nudish	rudish
lewdish	(etc.)	prudish	shrewdish

UDLESS
mudless (etc.), *see* UD

UEL

crewel	duel	newel	jewel
cruel	fuel	gruel	tewel

UELESS
crewless (etc.), *see* EW

UELY, *see* ULY

UENT, *see* UANT

UET

cruet	*pewit*	suet	"knew it" (etc.)

UEY, EWY

bluey	dewy	fluey	viewy
cooee	gluey	*roué*	thewy
buoy			

UFFER, OUGHER

buffer	huffer	tougher (etc.),	snuffer
duffer	puffer	*see* UFF	suffer

Uffin

muffin	ragamuffin	"snuffin'" (etc.)	"enough in" (etc.)
puffin			

Uffing

puffing — stuffing (etc.), *see* Uff

Uffle

buffle	ruffle	unmuffle	snuffle
muffle	scuffle	shuffle	duffel
truffle			

Uffly

bluffly	roughly	shuffly	toughly
gruffly	ruffly	snuffly	truffly
muffly	scuffly		

Uffy

buffy	puffy	sloughy	fluffy
huffy	snuffy	stuffy	pluffy
bluffy	chuffy		

Ufti, Ufty

mufti — tufty

Ugal, *see* **Ugle**

Ugely

hugely — scroogely

Ugger

lugger	hugger (etc.), *see* Ug	rugger	hugger-mugger
drugger			

Uggest, Uggist

druggist — snuggest (etc.), *see* Ug

Uggle

guggle	juggle	struggle	snuggle
smuggle			

Uggler

smuggler (etc.), *see* Uggle

Uggly, *see* **Ugly**

Uggy

buggy	muggy	puggy	sluggy

UGLE, UGAL

bugle	frugal	fugal	fugle

UGLY, UGGLY

guggly	smuggly	struggly	snugly
juggly	smugly	snuggly	ugly

UICELESS, *see* OOSE (*hard*)

UICY

juicy	sluicy

UISANCE, USANCE

nuisance	usance

UISER, *see* OOSER

UITING
suiting (etc.), *see* OOT

UITER, *see* OOTER

UITLESS
fruitless, bootless (etc.), *see* OOT

UITY, *see* OOTY

UKER, *see* UCRE

ULELESS
ruleless (etc.), *see* OOL

ULER
ruler (etc.), *see* OOL

ULGAR

Bulgar	fulgor	vulgar

ULGENCE

effulgence	self-indulgence	refulgence	indulgence

ULGENT

fulgent	indulgent	refulgent	preofulgent
effulgent	circumfulgent	interfulgent	self-indulgent

ULGOUR, *see* ULGAR

ULKY

bulky	sulky	hulky

ULLAR, ULLER, OLOR

culler	duller	luller	guller
color	sculler	discolor	tricolor
cruller	annuller	medullar	

ULLET (*as in* bullet)

bullet	pullet

ULLET (*as in* gullet)

gullet	mullet	cullet

ULLEY, ULLY

bully	pulley	*beautifully*	*dutifully* (etc.),
fully	woolly		*see* ULL

ULLION

mullion	scullion	cullion	bullion

ULLY (*as in* bully), *see* ULLEY

ULLY (*as in* sully)

cully	gully	hully	sully
dully	beautifully, *and words in* ULL *for possible rhymes*		

ULSION

compulsion	emulsion	evulsion	appulsion
convulsion	expulsion	impulsion	divulsion
repulsion	revulsion	propulsion	pulsion
avulsion	demulsion		

ULSIVE

compulsive	emulsive	impulsive	divulsive
convulsive	expulsive	propulsive	revulsive
repulsive	appulsive		

ULTED

consulted (etc.), *see* ULT

ULTLESS

cultless (etc.), *see* ULT

ULTRY

sultry	adultery

ULTURE

culture	sepulture	horticulture	pisciculture
vulture	agriculture	aviculture	(etc.)

ULVER

culver pulver

ULY; *see also* OOLY

duly	newly (etc.), *see* EW	unduly	guly

UMAGE

fumage	plumage	*roomage*

UMAN, UMON, *see* OMAN

UMBAR, UMBER

lumbar	slumber	encumber	disencumber
lumber	umber	outnumber	cumber
number	cucumber		

UMBENT

accumbent	incumbent	recumbent	superincumbent
decumbent	procumbent		

UMBLE

bumble	fumble	scumble	rumble
crumble	grumble	jumble	bejumble
drumble	humble	mumble	umbel
stumble	tumble		

UMBLER

tumbler (etc.), *see* UMBLE

UMBLY (B *sounded*), *see* UMBLE

UMBLY (B *silent*), *see* UMLY

UMBO

gumbo mumbo-jumbo

UMBRATE

adumbrate	inumbrate	obumbrate

UMBROUS

cumbrous	penumbrous	slumbrous	unslumbrous

UMELESS

fumeless (etc.), *see* OOM

UMEN, *see* UMINE

UMER; *see also* OOMER *for imperfect rhymes*

humor	tumor	perfumer (etc.), *see* UME

Umid

fumid	humid	tumid	spumid

Umine, Umen

acumen	illumine	relumine	"assumin'"
bitumen	legumen	catechumen	(etc.)

Uming

fuming (etc.), *see* Ume

Umly, Omely

comely	numbly	humoursomely	troublesomely
dumbly	cumbersomely	mettlesomely	wearisomely
grumly	frolicsomely	quarrelsomely	

Ummer, Omer, Umber

comer	summer	scummer	newcomer
drummer	mummer	plumber	hummer (etc.),
dumber	mid-summer	grummer	*see* Um

Ummet, Ummit

plummet	summit	grummet

Umming, *see* Oming

Ummit, *see* Ummet

Ummock

hummock	stomach

Ummon

summon	"rum 'un"

Ummy

crummy	scrummy	plummy	rummy
dummy	gummy	scummy	tummy
crumby	lummy	mummy	thrummy

Umor, *see* Umer

Umous

fumous	humus	dumous	strumous
grumous	plumous	spumous	humous

Umnal

autumnal	columnal

UMPASS

compass	encompass	rumpus	"thump us" (etc.)

UMPER

bumper mumper thumper (etc.), *see* UMP

UMPET

crumpet	strumpet	trumpet	"thump it" (etc.)

UMPISH

dumpish	lumpish	plumpish	mumpish
frumpish	grumpish		

UMPKIN

bumpkin	*pumpkin*	lumpkin

UMPLE

crumple	rumple

UMPLING

crumpling	dumpling	pumpling	rumpling

UMPTION

gumption	assumption	presumption	subsumption
sumption	consumption	resumption	

UMPTIVE

assumptive	presumptive	resumptive	subsumptive
consumptive			

UMPUS, *see* OMPASS

UMPY

dumpy (etc.), *see* UMP

UMY; *see also* OOMY

fumy	spumy	"knew me" (etc.)

UNAR; *see also* OONER *for imperfect rhymes. Note on p.* 114

lunar	nonilunar	oppugner	communer
importuner	attuner	tuner	lacunar
impugner	interlunar	jejuner	plenilunar

UNBURNT

sunburnt	unburnt	"Hun burnt"

UNCHEON, UNCHION

luncheon	truncheon	puncheon	scuncheon
nunchion			

UNCLE

crunkle	uncle	carbuncle

UNCTION

function	compunction	punction	injunction
junction	conjunction	disjunction	inunction
unction	defunction	expunction	sejunction
adjunction	interjunction		

UNCTIVE

adjunctive	conjunctive	subjunctive	adjunctive
compunctive	disjunctive		

UNCTURE

juncture	puncture	conjuncture	ocupuncture

UNDANCE

superabundance	redundance	"sun dance" (etc.)

UNDANT

abundant	redundant	superabundant

UNDATE

fecundate	inundate	secundate

UNDAY, ONDAY

Monday	Fundy	Sunday	"one day"

UNDER, ONDER

blunder	thunder	asunder	dissunder
plunder	under	fecunder	"stunned her"
sunder	wonder	jocunder	(etc.)
refunder	rotunder	therunder	

UNDIT

pundit	conduit	"shunned it" (etc.)

UNDLE

bundle	rundle	trundle

UNDRY

sundry	thundry

UNEFUL, *see* **OONFUL** *for imperfect rhymes. Note, p.* 114

tuneful

UNELESS

tuneless (etc.); *see* UNE; *also* OON *for imperfect rhymes*

UNELY

tunely	jejunely	importunely	opportunely

UNER; *see also* OONER

tuner	propugner (etc.), *see* UNE		"impugn her" (etc.)
impugner			

UNGEON

dungeon	plungeon

UNGER (*soft* G)

lunger	blunger	spunger	expunger
plunger			

UNGER (*hard* G)

hunger	monger	ironmonger	younger (etc.), *see* UNG
enhunger			

UNGEST

youngest (etc.), *see* UNG

UNGLE

bungle	jungle

UNKARD—ERD

drunkard	dunkard	bunkered

UNKER

bunker	flunker	funker	"sunk her" (etc.)
junker	"punker"	plunker	
drunker			

UNKY

chunkey	funky	powder-monkey	"nunky"
flunkey	monkey	spunky	

UNNAGE

dunnage	gunnage	tonnage	"one age" (etc.)

UNNEL

funnel	runnel	tunnel	"one'll" (etc.)
gunwale	trunnel		

UNNING

cunning	dunning (etc.), *see* UN

UNNY

bunny	honey	sonny	tunny
funny	money	sunny	unsunny
gunny			

UNSTER

gunster punster

UNTAL

contrapuntal frontal gruntle disgruntle

UNTED

shunted (etc.), *see* UNT

UNTER

hunter bunter (etc.), *see* UNT and ONT

UNTING

bunting fronting (etc.), *see* UNT

UPPER

cupper	tupper	scupper	crupper
upper	supper		

UPPET

puppet "up it" "sup it"

UPPISH

puppish uppish

UPPLE

couple supple

UPLE

octuple	septuple	subduple	quadruple
quintuple	sextuple	pupil	scruple

UPTER

corrupter (etc.), *see* UPT

UPTING

erupting (etc.), *see* UPT

URA

amphidura	Cæsura	legatura	seisura
Angostura	datura	pietra-dura	velatura
appoggiatura	fissura	pleura	vettura
bravura	flexura	"cuta-cura"	

Ural

antemural	interneural	pleural	tellural
Cæsural	intramural	sinecural	crural
commissural	jural	"cure-all"	plural
extramural	mural	sural	rural
intermural	neural		

Urance

allurance	endurance	assurance	reassurance
durance	perdurance	insurance	

Urate

curate	jurat	"endure it" (etc.)

Urban

suburban	urban	turban

Urely; *see* Oorly *for imperfect rhymes. See Note, p.* 114

demurely	obscurely	purely	securely
maturely			

Urchase

purchase	*searches* (etc.)

Urement

abjurement	conjurement	obscurement	procurement
allurement	immurement		

Ureness; *see also* Oor *for imperfect rhymes*
demureness (etc.), *see* Ure

Urer

juror	nonjuror	furor	abjurer (etc.), *see* Ure

Urder

absurder	herder	self-murder	"heard her" (etc.)
engirder	murder	"thirder"	
girder			

Urest

jurist	purist	*tourist, see* Oor *for imperfect rhymes*	adjurest (etc.), *see* Ure

Ureth
abjureth (etc.), *see* Ure

Urgent

abstergent	assurgent	convergent (etc.), *see* Erge

Urgeon

burgeon	sturgeon	surgeon

Urgle

"burgle"	gurgle

Uric

hydrosulphuric	purpuric	sulphuric	telluric
hydrotelluric			

Urim

Purim	urim

Urin

burin	daturin	neurin

Uring; *see also* Oor *for imperfect rhymes*

abjuring (etc.), *see* Ure

Urist, *see* Urest

Urler

burler	hurler	"purler"	whirler
curler	pearler	twirler	skirler
furler			

Urlew

curlew	purlieu

Urly

burly	early	knurly	surly
churly	hurly-burly	pearly	whirly
curly			

Urrow

burrow	furrow	borough	thorough

Ursor

amercer	cursor	precursor	accurser (etc.)
ante-cursor	mercer	purser	

Uro

chiaroscuro	maduro

Urous

anurous	dolichurus	Eurus	urus
Arcturus			

Urry

burry	furry (etc.),	flurry	scurry
curry	*see* Ur	hurry	worry

Ury; *see also* **Erry**

de jure	fury	jewry	jury
ewry			

Usal

refusal	perusal

Useful

juiceful	useful

Useless

juiceless	useless	excuseless (etc.), *see* Use *and* Oose

Useness

abstruseness	looseness

User

abstruser	user	excuser (etc.), *see* Use *and* Oose	"you sir" (etc.)
accuser			

Usal, Usil

refusal	fusil	musal	hypothenusal *see also* Oozle
perusal	bamboozle		

Uses; *see also* Ooses *for imperfect rhymes*

abuses	uses	amuses	confuses
excuses	accuses	bruises	fuses

Usest

abstrusest (etc.), *see* Use, Uce *and* Oose

Useth

abuseth — amuseth (etc.), *see* Use, Uce, *and* Oose

Usil

fusil — protrusile, *see* Usal

Using

abusing — using, amusing (etc.), *see* Use, Uce, *and* Oose

Usion

abusion	effusion	perfusion	transfusion
affusion	elusion	pertusion	abstrusion
allusion	exclusion	preclusion	detrusion
circumfusion	fusion	profusion	extrusion
collusion	illusion	prolusion	intrusion
conclusion	inclusion	reclusion	obtrusion
confusion	infusion	refusion	protrusion
contusion	interclusion	retrusion	retrusion
delusion	interfusion	seclusion	trusion
diffusion	*Malthusian*	self-delusion	*Carthusian*
dissillusion	occlusion	suffusion	

Usive, *see* Ucive

Uscan

Della-cruscan	Etruscan	molluscan	Tuscan
dusken			

Uscate

coruscate	infuscate	obfuscate

Usher

blusher	flusher	husher	rusher
brusher	gusher	plusher	usher
crusher	"rush her" (etc.)		

Ushes

blushes (etc.), *see* Ush

Usker

husker	tusker

Usket

busket	musket

Usky

dusky	husky	musky	tusky

Usoe

Crusoe	whoso	"do so"	"knew so" (etc.)

USSET

gusset	russet

USSION

concussion	percussion	recussion	Russian
discussion	Prussian	repercussion	incussion

USSIVE

concussive	percussive	repercussive	succussive
discussive			

USSY

fussy	mussy	*hussy*

USTED

adjusted (etc.), *see* UST

USTER

adjuster	distruster	knuckle-duster	muster
bluster	duster	lack-luster	robuster
buster	filibuster	luster	thruster
coadjuster	fluster	lustre	truster
cluster	juster		

USTERED

blustered	clustered	flustered	mustard
bustard	custard	lustered	mustered

USTIC

fustic	rustic

USTION

adustion	combustion	fustian

USTLE

bustle	justle	mussel	rustle
hustle	muscle	opuscle	tussle

USTLER

bustler	hustler	rustler	tussler

USTLY

augustly	justly	robustly

USTMENT

adjustment	entrustment	enthoustment

USTRATE

augustate	illustrate	incrustate

Ustral

lacustral	lustral	palustral

Ustrous

blustrous	lustrous	lack-lustrous

Ustrum

flustrum	lustrum

Usty

dusty	gusty	musty	trusty
fusty	lusty	rusty	

Usum

usum (Latin)	*gruesome*	"blew some" (etc.)	"use 'em" (etc.)
bosom	*twosome*		

Usy, *see* **Izzy**

Utal, *see* **Utile**

Utches

clutches (etc.), *see* **Utch**

Utate

circumnutate	immutate	scutate

Utcher

scutcher	toucher

Uted

unsuited	comminuted	commuted (etc.), *see* **Ute** *and* **Oot**

Utement

confutement	imbrutement	recruitment

Uteness

absoluteness (etc.), *see* **Ute**

Uter, Euter

acuter (etc.), *see* **Ute** *and* **Oot**	neuter	suitor	*accoutre*
	pewter	tutor	

Utest

acutest (etc.), *see* **Ute** *and* **Oot**

Uteth

commuteth (etc.), *see* **Ute** *and* **Oot**

Uthful

ruthful	truthful	untruthful	youthful
toothful			

Uthless

ruthless	toothless	truthless	uncouthness

Utic, Eutic

diazeutic	maieutic	propædeutic	therapeutic
emphyteutic	pharmaceutic	scorbutic	toreutic
hermeneutic			

Utile, Utal; *see also* **Ootle**

futile	rutile	refutal	inutile
sutile			

Uting

commuting (etc.), *see* **Ute** *and* **Oot**

Ution

ablution	destitution	iminution	prosecution
absolution	devolution	insecution	prostitution
allocution	dilution	institution	redargution
attribution	diminution	interlocution	resolution
circumlocution	dissolution	involution	restitution
circumvolution	distribution	irresolution	retribution
collecution	elocution	Lilliputian	revolution
comminution	evolution	locution	solution
constitution	execution	persecution	substitution
contribution	imbution	pollution	volution
convolution			

Utist

flutist	lutist	pharmaceutist	therapeutist
hermeneutist			

Utive

coadjutive	indutive	persecutive	resolutive
constitutive			

Utor, *see* **Uter**

Uture

future	puture	suture

Utler

butler	guttler	subtler	sutler
cutler	scuttler		

UTTER

abutter, bread-and-butter, butter, clutter, cutter, flutter, gutter, mutter, nutter, pilot-cutter, putter, rebutter, scutter, shutter, splutter, sputter, strutter, stutter, utter, wood-cutter, "cut her" (etc.)

UTTAL

abuttal, cuttle, guttle, rebuttal, ruttle, scuttle, shuttle, subtle, suttle

UTTON

bachelor-button, button, glutton, mutton

UTTY

butty, gutty, jutty, nutty, putty, rutty, smutty, tutty

UTY; *see also* OOTY

duty, beauty, fluty, "cutey" (etc.), *see* UTE

UZZLE

bemuzzle, fuzzle, guzzle, muzzle, nuzzle, puzzle, unmuzzle

UZZLER

guzzler, muzzler, puzzler

UZZY

fuzzy, hussy, fuzzy-wuzzy, "does he"

THREE-SYLLABLE RHYMES

ABASIS

anabasis, metabasis

ABBIER

flabbier, shabbier, "gabbier"

ABBIEST

flabbiest, shabbiest

ABBILY

flabbily, shabbily

ABBINESS
flabbiness scabbiness shabbiness slabbiness

ABBLEMENT
babblement dabblement gabblement rabblement
brabblement

ABELER
gabeler labeler

ABIAN
Arabian Fabian Sabian Sorabian

ABICAL
Arabical monosyllabical polysyllabical

ABIDNESS
rabidness tabidness

ABIFY
dissyllabify labefy syllabify tabefy

ABINET
cabinet tabinet

ABITUDE
habitude tabitude

ABLATIVE
ablative bablative

ABLENESS
sableness stableness unstableness

ABOLA
metabola parabola

ABORER
laborer taborer

ABORING
laboring belaboring neighboring

ASABLE
chasable effaceable erasible ineffaceable
retraceable traceable evasible

ABULAR
confabular pabular tabular tintinnabular

ABULATE

"confabulate" tabulate

ABULIST

fabulist vocabulist

ABULOUS

fabulous pabulous sabulous tintinnabulous

ABULUM

acetabulum pabulum tintinnabulum

ACENCY

adjacency complacency interjacency

ACERATE

emacerate lacerate macerate

ACERY

embracery tracery

ACHIAN

batrachian eustachian Noachian

ACHRONISM

anachronism metachronism

ACIATE

emaciate glaciate ingratiate "way she ate" (etc.)

ACINATE

abbacinate assassinate deracinate exacinate fascinate

ACINESS

laciness raciness

ACIOUSNESS

audaciousness capaciousness contumaciousness disputatiousness edaciousness efficaciousness fallaciousness fugaciousness graciousness incapaciousness inefficaciousness loquaciousness mendaciousness ostentatiousness perspicaciousness pertinaciousness pugnaciousness rapaciousness sagaciousness tenaciousness ungraciousness veraciousness vexatiousness vivaciousness voraciousness

Acity
audacity
bellacity
bibacity
capacity
contumacity
dicacity
edacity
feracity
fugacity
incapacity
loquacity
mendacity
minacity
mordacity
opacity
"pass it, he" (etc.)
perspicacity
pertinacity
pervicacity
procacity
pugnacity
rapacity
sagacity
salacity
saponacity
sequacity
tenacity
veracity
vivacity
voracity

Ackery
hackery
knick-knackery
quackery
"hijackery"

Acketed
bracketed
jacketed
racketed

Acketing
bracketing
jacketing
racketing

Ackishness
brackishness
knackishness

Actible
compactible
attractable
contractible
detractible
distractible
extractible
infractible
intactable
intractable
refractable
retractable
tactable
tractable

Actedness
abstractedness
contractedness
distractedness
protractedness

Actical
didactical
practical

Actional
factional
fractional
pactional

Actiousness
factiousness
fractiousness

Activeness
abstractiveness
activeness
attractiveness
contractiveness
detractiveness
distractiveness
protractiveness
putrefactiveness
refractiveness

ACTORY

detractory	lactary	phylactery	satisfactory
dissatisfactory	manufactory	refractory	tractory
factory	olfactory		

ACTUAL

actual	factual	tactual	

ACTURING

fracturing	manufacturing		

ACULAR

opacular	piacular	supernacular	tentacular
oracular	spectacular	tabernacular	vernacular

ACULATE

bimaculate	immaculate	jaculate	maculate
ejaculate			

ACULOUS

miraculous	oraculous	piaculous	vernaculous
abaculus			

ADABLE

shadable	evadible	wadeable	tradeable
persuadable			

ADEDNESS

bejadedness	fadedness	persuadedness	shadedness
degradedness	jadedness		

ADIAN

Acadian	Barbadian	nomadian	Palladian
Arcadian	Canadian		

ADITIVE

traditive	additive		

ADIUM

palladium	radium	stadium	vanadium

AËRY

aëry	faëry		

AFTILY

craftily	draughtily		

AGEABLE

assuageable	gaugeable		

Ageousness
advantageousness disadvantageousness "rampageousness" umbrageousness
courageousness outrageousness

Aggedly
jaggedly raggedly

Aggedness
craggedness jaggedness raggedness

Aggerer
staggerer swaggerer

Aggering
staggering swaggering

Aggery
faggery raggery waggery zigzaggery
jaggery

Agginess
bagginess knagginess scragginess shagginess
cragginess

Agian
Brobdignagian magian pelagian

Agical
magical tragical

Agileness
agileness fragileness

Aginal
imaginal paginal

Aginous
cartilaginous lumbaginous octagynous voraginous
farraginous mucilaginous oleaginous

Agonism
agonism antagonism

Agrancy
flagrancy fragrancy vagrancy

Aical

algebraical, Hebraical, paradisaical, Pharisaical
archaical, laical

Aiety, Aity

gaiety, laity

Ainable

ascertainable, drainable, obtainable, strainable
attainable, explainable, ordainable, sustainable
constrainable, gainable, restrainable, trainable
containable, maintainable, retainable, unattainable
distrainable

Ainfulness

disdainfulness, gainfulness, painfulness

Ailable

assailable, exhalable, retailable, unassailable
available, mailable, saleable, unavailable
bailable

Ailery

nailery, raillery

Airiness

airiness, chariness, glariness, hairiness

Airable

bearable, declarable, unbearable, wearable
airable, repairable, unwearable

Aisable

praisable, raisable, suasible, persuasible

Akable

breakable, implacable, pacable, undertakable
impacable, mistakable, placable, unshakable

Akerism

Quakerism, Shakerism, "fakirism"

Akery

bakery, rakery, "fakiry"

Akiness

flakiness, quakiness, shakiness, snakiness

Algia

neuralgia, nostalgia, pleuralgia

ALIANISM

bacchanalianism
alienism
Episcopalianism
saturnalianism
sesquipedalianism
universalianism

ALIFY

alkalify
calefy
salify

ALINESS

dailiness
scaliness

ALITY

abnormality
accidentality
actuality
alamodality
animality
artificiality
banality
bestiality
biblicality
brutality
carnality
casuality
centrality
circumstantiality
classicality
comicality
confidentiality
congeniality
conjecturality
conjugality
connubiality
constitutionality
consubstantiality
conventionality
conviviality
cordiality
corporality
criminality
curiality
dextrality
duality
egality
elementality
ephemerality
essentiality
ethereality
eventuality
externality
exterritoriality
fantasticality
fatality
feminality
feudality
finality
finicality
formality
frugality
fundamentality
generality
geniality
graduality
gutturality
horizontality
hospitality
ideality
illegality
immateriality
immorality
immortality
impartiality
imperiality
impersonality
inconsequentiality
individuality
ineffectuality
informality
inimicality
instrumentality
integrality
intellectuality
intentionality
intrinsicality
irrationality
joviality
laicality
laterality
legality
liberality
lineality
literality
locality
logicality
magistrality
magnality
materiality
mentality
meridionality
mesnality
modality
morality
mortality
municipality
mutuality
nasality
nationality
naturality
neutrality
notionality
officiality
Orientality
originality
orthodoxality
parochiality
partiality
pedality
penality
personality
plurality
potentiality
practicality
preternaturality
primality
principality
prodigality
proportionality
provinciality
prudentiality
punctuality
radicality
rascality
rationality
reality

ALITY—(*Cont.*)

reciprocality
regality
rivality
rurality
sectionality
sensuality
sentimentality
septentrionality
seriality
sesquipedality
severality
sexuality
signality
sociality
sodality
speciality
spectrality
spirality
spirituality
substantiality
superficiality
supernaturality
technicality
temporality
theatricality
tonality
totality
traditionality
transcendality
triality
triviality
universality
unusuality
vegetality
venality
veniality
verbality
verticality
visuality
vitality
vocality
whimsicality

ALLIATE

palliate
malleate

ALLERY

gallery
raillery
salary

ALLIDNESS

impallidness
invalidness
pallidness
validness

ALLIER

dallier
rallier
sallier
tallier

ALLIUM

pallium
thallium

ALLOWER

callower
hallower
shallower
sallower
tallower

ALLOWEST

callowest
hallowest
shallowest
sallowest

ALLOWISH

sallowish
shallowish
tallowish

ALLOWNESS

callowness
fallowness
sallowness
shallowness

ALLYING

dallying
rallying
sallying
tallying

ALMISTRY

palmistry
psalmistry

ALOGISM

analogism	dialogism	paralogism	

ALOGIST

analogist	dialogist	mammalogist	penalogist
decalogist	genealogist	mineralogist	

ALOGIZE

analogize	dialogize	genealogize	paralogize

ALOGY

analogy	genealogy	mineralogy	pyroballogy
crustalogy	genethlialogy	paralogy	tetralogy
dianoialogy	mammalogy	petralogy	

ALYSIS

analysis	catalysis	dialysis	paralysis

AMABLE

blamable	irreclaimable	reclaimable	unblamable
claimable	namable	tamable	untamable

AMARY

mammary	gramary		

AMATIST

dramatist	grammatist	hierogram-matist	lipogrammatist
epigrammatist			melodramatist

AMATIVE

amative	exclamative		

AMATIZE

dramatize	epigrammatize		

AMBULATE

ambulate	funambulate	perambulate	somnambulate
deambulate			

AMBULISM

noctambulism	somnambulism		

AMBULIST

funambulist	noctambulist	somnambulist	

AMEFULNESS

blamefulness	shamefulness		

Amelessness
aimlessness namelessness shamelessness tamelessness
blamelessness

Ameron
Decameron Heptameron

Ameter
diameter octameter pirameter viameter
dynameter parameter pluviameter voltameter
hexameter pentameter tetrameter

Amical
amical balsamical dynamical

Amina
lamina stamina

Aminate
contaminate laminate

Amity
amity calamity

Ammerer
clamorer hammerer stammerer

Ammering
hammering clamoring stammering

Ammonism
Mammonism Shamanism

Ammonite
Ammonite Mammonite

Amorous
amorous clamorous

Amperer
hamperer pamperer scamperer tamperer

Ampering
hampering pampering scampering tampering

Ampion
campion champion tampion

Amulus
famulus hamulus ramulous

Anable
insanable
sanable
tanable

Anary
granary
panary

Andable
commandable
demandable
reprimandable
understandable

Anderer
meanderer
panderer
philanderer
slanderer

Andering
meandering
pandering
philandering
slandering

Anderous
panderous
slanderous

Andify
candify
dandify

Andiness
handiness
sandiness

Andrian
Alexandrian
meandrian
Menandrian

Anea
miscellanea
succedanea

Anefully
banefully
disdainfully
painfully

Aneous
absentaneous
antecedaneous
araneous
circumforaneous
circumterraneous
coëtaneous
constantaneous
contemporaneous
cutaneous
dissentaneous
extemporaneous
exterraneous
instantaneous
limitaneous
Mediterraneous
membraneous
miscellaneous
momentaneous
porcellaneous
simultaneous
spontaneous
subcutaneous
subterraneous
succedaneous
temporaneous
terraneous

Anery
chicanery
lanary
planary

Angency
plangency
tangency

ANGIBLE

frangible	intangible	refrangible	tangible
infrangible			

ANGLESOME

tanglesome	wranglesome	"angle some" (etc.)

ANGULAR

angular	quadrangular	slangular	triangular
octangular	rectangular		

ANIA

Anglo-mania	dipsomania	logomania	monomania
anthomania	eleutheromania	mania	pyromania
bibliomania	erotomania	metromania	succedanea
decalcomania	gallomania	miscellanea	Titania
demonomania	kleptomania		

ANIAL

cranial	domanial	subterraneal

ANIAN

Alcmanian	extemporanean	Sandemanian	Turanian
Equitanian	Iranian	subterranean	volcanian
circumforanean	Lithuanian	Transylvanian	Vulcanian
cyanean	Mediterranean		

ANICAL

botanical	charlatanical	mechanical	tyrannical
Brahmanical	galvanical	panicle	

ANIFY

humanify	insanify	sanify

ANIMUS

animus	multanimous	pusillanimous	unanimous
magnanimous			

ANISHING

banishing	planishing	vanishing

ANISHMENT

banishment	evanishment	vanishment

ANISTER

banister	canister	ganister

ANITY
aldermanity
Christianity
gigmanity
humanity
immanity
inanity
inhumanity
inorganity
insanity
inurbanity
mundanity
paganity
profanity
sanity
subterranity
urbanity
vanity
volcanity

ANIUM
cranium
geranium
pericranium
succedaneum
titanium
uranium

ANKERING
cankering
anchoring
encankering
hankering

ANKEROUS
cankerous
cantankerous

ANIKIN
manikin
pannikin

ANELLING
panelling
channelling

ANNERET
banneret
lanneret

ANERY
charlatanery
cannery
granary
panary
stannary
tannery

ANNULAR
annular
cannular
penannular

ANULATE
campanulate
annulate
granulate

ANOGRAPH
galvanograph
pianograph

ANOSCOPE
diaphanoscope
galvanoscope

ANSIVENESS
expansiveness
advanciveness

ANSOMER
ransomer
handsomer

ANSOMEST

ransomest	handsomest

ANTABLE

grantable	plantable

ANTERER

banterer	canterer

ANTERING

bantering	cantering

ANTHROPIST

misanthropist	philanthropist	psilanthropist	theophilanthropist

ANTHROPY

apanthropy	philanthropy	psilanthropy	theophilanthropy
lycanthropy	phobanthropy	theanthropy	zoanthropy
misanthropy	physianthropy		

ANTICIDE

giganticide	infanticide

ANTICNESS

franticness	giganticness	romanticness

ANULA

canula	granula

APABLE

capable	incapable	papable	shapeable
drapeable	escapeable	inescapeable	

APERER

caperer	paperer	vaporer

APERING

capering	papering	tapering	vaporing

APERY

apery	grapery	papery	vapory
drapery	napery		

APHICAL

autobiographical	bibliographical	cartographical	ethnographical
autographical	biographical	cosmographical	geographical
	calligraphical	diagraphical	glossographical

Aphical—(*Cont.*)

graphical
lexicographical
lexigraphical
orthographical
palæontographical
photographical
physiographical
phytographical
pterylographical
seraphical
topographical
typographical

Apidly

rapidly
sapidly
vapidly

Apidness

rapidness
sapidness
vapidness

Appier-est

happier
"sappier"
snappier

Appiness

happiness
sappiness
snappiness

Aqueous

aqueous
chylaqueous
subaqueous
terraqueous

Arable

arable
parable
comparible
incomparible

Arative

comparative
declarative
narrative
preparative
reparative

Arbering

barbering
harboring

Arcener

coparcener
larcener
parcener

Arceny

coparceny
larceny

Archical

archical
hierarchical
hylarchical
monarchical
tetrarchical

Ardian

guardian
pericardian

Ardiness

fool-hardiness
hardiness
tardiness

AREFULLY

carefully prayerfully uncarefully

AREFULNESS

carefulness sparefulness uncarefulness warefulness prayerfulness

ARIA

adversaria area caballaria calceolaria cineraria dataria digitaria malaria *pariah* wistaria

ARIAL

actuarial areal calendarial commissarial diarial glossarial malarial nectarial notarial ovarial puparial secretarial vicarial

ARIAN

abecedarian adessenarian agrarian alphabetarian altitudinarian anecdotarian antiquarian antisabbatarian antitrinitarian apiarian apollinarian aquarian Arian Aryan atrabilarian attitudinarian barbarian Bavarian Briarean Bulgarian Cæsarian centenarian diarian dietarian disciplinarian doctrinarian equalitarian estuarian experimentarian futilitarian grammarian humanitarian Hungarian Icarian Janizarian lapidarian latitudinarian libertarian librarian limitarian lunarian malarian Megarian millenarian miscellanarian necessarian necessitarian nectarian nonagenarian octagenarian ovarian Parian parliamentarian platitudinarian plenitudinarian predestinarian proletarian riparian sabbatarian sacramentarian sanitarian sectarian sententiarian septuagenarian sexagenarian societarian stipendarian sublapsarian supralapsarian tartarean tractarian trinitarian ubiquarian ubiquitarian unitarian utilitarian valetudinarian vegetarian veterinarian vulgarian

ARIANT

contrariant omniparient variant

ARIAT

commissariat proletariat prothonotariat secretariat

Ariate
variate
vicariate
"where he ate" (etc.)

Arier
charier
warier
See also Arrier

Aries
Aries
caries

Ariest
chariest
variest
wariest

Ariform
peariform
scalariform

Arify
clarify
saccharify
scarify

Ariness
arbitrariness
contrariness
salutariness
sanguinariness
sedentariness
solitariness
temporariness
tumultuariness
ubiquitariness
voluntariness
wariness

Aringly
daringly
glaringly
sparingly
flaringly

Ario
impresario
Lothario

Arious
arbitrarious
arenarious
Aquarius
atrabilarious
calcareous
contrarious
denarius
frumentarious
gregarious
hilarious
horarious
lutarious
malarious
multifarious
nectareous
nefarious
omnifarious
precarious
quadragenarious
retiarius
Sagittarius
sequarious
tartareous
temerarious
testudinarious
vagarious
valetudinarious
various
vicarious
viparious
"carry us" (etc.)

Aritude
amaritude
claritude

Arity
angularity
barbarity
cavity
charity
debonarity
circularity
clarity
disparity
dissimilarity
exemplarity
familiarity
fissiparity
gemmiparity
globularity
hilarity
imparity
insularity
irregularity
jocularity
molecularity

ARITY—(*Cont.*)

muscularity
omniparity
parity
particularity
peculiarity
perpendicularity
piacularity
polarity
popularity
pupilarity
rectangularity
rectilinearity
regularity
secularity
similarity
singularity
solidarity
titularity
triangularity
uncharity
vascularity
viviparity
vulgarity

ARIUM

aquarium
aqua-vivarium
columbarium
glaciarium
honorarium
sacrarium
sanitarium
tepidarium
termitarium
vivarium

ARLATAN

charlatan
tarlatan

ARMINGLY

alarmingly
charmingly

ARNISHER

garnisher
tarnisher
varnisher

ARNISHING

garnishing
tarnishing
varnishing

ARONITE

Aaronite
Maronite

ARASSING

harassing
embarrassing

ARASSMENT

harassment
embarrassment

ARRIER

barrier
carrier
farrier
marrier
tarrier
charier
"carry her" (etc.)

ARRINESS

starriness
tarriness

ARRIOR

warrior
sorrier
quarrier

ARROWER

harrower
narrower

Arrowest
harrowest narrowest

Arrowing
harrowing narrowing

Arrowy
arrowy marrowy

Arrying
carrying harrying marrying tarrying

Arterer
barterer charterer

Artering
bartering chartering

Artialism
martialism partialism

Article
article particle

Artiness
swartiness wartiness

Artizan
artizan bartizan partizan

Artlessly
artlessly heartlessly

Artlessness
artlessness heartlessness

Asable
chasable defaceable irreplaceable untraceable
effaceable replaceable traceable

Ashery
fashery haberdashery sashery

Ashiness
ashiness flashiness trashiness

Asia
Asia Aspasia aphasia paronomasia
acacia leucophasia euthanasia Australasia

ASIAN

Asian, Alsatian, Athanasian, Australalasian, Caucasian, Eurasian, Galatian, Hieraçian, Horatian, Latian, Pancratian, Rabelaisian, sefatian, Thracian

ASIVENESS

dissuasiveness, evasiveness, persuasiveness, pervasiveness, suasiveness

ASPINGLY

gaspingly, raspingly

ASSIA

cassia, Parnassia, quassia

ASSIAN

Circassian, Parnassian

ASSIBLE

impassible, irascible, passable, renascible, surpassable

ASSINESS

brassiness, "classiness", glassiness, "sassiness", grassiness, massiness

ASSIONING

compassioning, fashioning, passioning

ASSIVELY

impassively, massively, passively

ASSIVENESS

impassiveness, massiveness, passiveness

ASTARDY

bastardy, dastardy

ASTEFULLY

distastefully, tastefully, wastefully

ASTERING

beplastering, mastering, overmastering, plastering

ASTERSHIP

mastership, pastorship

Astery
dicastery mastery plastery self-mastery

Astical
ecclesiastical encomiastical fantastical orthodoxastical
elastical enthusiastical

Asticism
ecclesiasticism fantasticism monasticism scholasticism

Astily
hastily pastily tastily

Astrian
alabastrian Lancastrian Zoroastrian

Astrophe
catastrophe epanastrophe

Atable
abatable creatable dilatable regulatable
collatable debatable ratable translatable

Atchable
immatchable attachable matchable unmatchable
catchable detachable

Atefully
fatefully gratefully hatefully

Atefulness
fatefulness gratefulness hatefulness

Atellite
patellite satellite

Atency
latency patency

Ateran
cateran Lateran

Aterer
waterer slaughterer

Atering
watering slaughtering

Atherer

foregatherer	latherer	tax-gatherer	upgatherer
gatherer	"blatherer"		

Athering

"blathering"	gathering	upgathering	wool-gathering
foregathering	lathering		

Athesis

diathesis	parathesis

Athian

Carpathian	Sabbathian

Atiate

expatiate	glaciate	insatiate	satiate
emaciate	ingratiate	"way she ate" (etc.)	

Atible

compatible	combatable	incompatible	patible
"comeatable"	impatible		

Atica

dalmatica	sciatica	hypatica

Atical

abbatical	autocratical	emblematical	phantasmatical
acroamatical	automatical	emphatical	piratical
aërostatical	axiomatical	enigmatical	pragmatical
anathematical	bureaucratical	epigrammatical	primatical
anidiomatical	climatical	fanatical	schismatical
apophthegmatical	democratical	grammatical	separatical
	diplomatical	hebdomatical	Socratical
apostatical	dogmatical	idiomatical	spasmatical
aristocratical	dramatical	leviratical	statical
asthmatical	ecstatical	mathematical	vatical

Aticism

Asiaticism	fanaticism	grammaticism

Aticize

emblematicize	fanaticize	grammaticize

Atify

beatify	gratify	ratify	stratify

Atinate

gelatinate	Palatinate

ATINESS
slatiness weightiness

ATINIZE
gelatinize Latinize platinize

ATINOUS
gelatinous platinous

ATIONAL
international irrational national rational
associational dissertational imitational respirational
congregational educational inspirational rotational
conservational emigrational observational sensational
conversational gradational probational stational
creational gyrational relational terminational
denominational ideational representational
derivational

ATIONER
foundationer probationer reprobationer stationer
oblationer

ATIONIST
annexationist convocationist emigrationist repudiationist
annihilationist cremationist imitationist restorationist
annotationist degenerationist inflationist transmutationist
causationist educationist innovationist
conversationist emancipationist inspirationist

ATIONLESS
foundationless conversationless educationless imitationless
temptationless imigrationless inspirationless

ATITUDE
beatitude gratitude latitude platitude
attitude ingratitude

ATIVENESS
alliterativeness imitativeness nativeness penetrativeness

ATOMOUS
diatomous paratomous

ATOMY
anatomy atomy

ATRICAL
idolatrical theatrical

ATRICIDE
fratricide matricide patricide

ATRONAGE
matronage patronage

ATRONAL
matronal patronal

ATRONIZE
matronize patronize

ATTERER
batterer clatterer patterer smatterer
blatterer flatterer scatterer splatterer
chatterer

ATTERING
battering bespattering flattering smattering
beflattering blattering pattering spattering
bepattering chattering scattering splattering
bescattering clattering shattering

ATTERY
battery flattery shattery slattery
tattery

ATTINESS
chattiness fattiness nattiness

ATTLEMENT
battlement embattlement prattlement tattlement

ATULATE
congratulate gratulate spatulate

ATURATE
maturate saturate supersaturate

AUCITY
paucity raucity

ALLABLE
enthrallable recallable

ALTERER
alterer falterer palterer

ALTERING
altering paltering unaltering unfaltering
faltering

ALTIEST
saltiest faultiest

ALTINESS
saltiness faultiness maltiness

AUGHTIER
haughtier naughtier

AUGHTIEST
haughtiest naughtiest

AUGHTILY
haughtily naughtily

AUGHTINESS
haughtiness naughtiness

AUREATE
aureate baccalaureate laureate poet-laureate
"more he ate" (etc.)

AUREOLE
aureole laureole

AUTERY
cautery watery

AVAGER
ravager savager scavager

AVAGING
ravaging scavaging

AVANESE
Havanese Javanese

AVELER
raveler traveler unraveler

Aveling
graveling raveling traveling unraveling

Avender
chavender lavender

Averous
cadaverous papaverous

Avian
avian Belgravian Moravian Scandinavian
Batavian

Avishness
knavishness slavishness

Avisher
lavisher ravisher

Avishing
enravishing lavishing ravishing

Avishment
enravishment lavishment ravishment

Avity
cavity depravity pravity suavity
concavity gravity

Avorous
flavorous savorous

Avorer
favorer laverer quaverer waverer
flavorer

Avoring
favoring quavering unwavering wavering
flavoring savoring

Avory
savory gravery slavery unsavory
bravery

Awdiness
bawdiness gaudiness

Awdriness
bawdriness tawdriness

AWFULLY
awfully lawfully unlawfully

AWFULNESS
awfulness lawfulness unlawfulness

AWKILY
gawkily chalkily pawkily

AWKINESS
gawkiness pawkiness squalkiness talkiness
chalkiness

AWNIEST
brawniest tawniest

AYABLE
payable portrayable unpayable unswayable
conveyable repayable unprayable

AZINESS
craziness haziness laziness maziness

AXABLE
relaxable taxable

EABLE
agreeable decreeable feeable irremeable
creable disagreeable

EADERSHIP
leadership readership

EADIER
headier readier steadier unsteadier

EADIEST
headiest readiest steadiest unsteadiest

EADILY
headily readily steadily unsteadily

EADINESS
headiness steadiness unsteadiness unreadiness
readiness threadiness

EAGERLY
eagerly meagerly overeagerly

EAGERNESS

eagerness	meagerness	overeagerness	

EAKABLE

speakable	unspeakable		

EAKISHNESS

freakishness	cliquishness	sneakishness	

EALABLE

concealable	healable	repealable	revealable
congealable	inconcealable		

EALIZE

idealize	realize		

EALISM

idealism	realism		

EALIST

idealist	realist		

EALOUSLY

jealously	overzealously	zealously	

EALTHIER

healthier	stealthier	wealthier	

EALTHIEST

healthiest	stealthiest	wealthiest	

EALTHILY

healthily	stealthily	wealthily	

EALTY

fealty	realty		

EANISM

epicureanism	peanism	Pythagoreanism	Sabaeanism
Laodiceanism	plebeianism		

EASABLE

appeasable	feasible	indefeasible	squeezable
cohesible	freezable	infeasible	unappeasable
creasable	releasable	increasable	
defeasible	inappeasible	seizable	

EASANTRY

pheasantry	pleasantry		

Easoning
reasoning
seasoning
unreasoning

Eastiness
reastiness
yeastiness

Eastliness
beastliness
priestliness

Easurer
measurer
pleasurer
treasurer

Easuring
measuring
pleasuring
treasuring

Eatable
cheatable
eatable
entreatable
escheatable
uneatable

Eathering
feathering
leathering
tethering
weathering

Eathery
feathery
heathery
leathery
weathery

Eathlessly
breathlessly
deathlessly

Eathlessness
breathlessness
deathlessness

Eatiness
meatiness
peatiness
sleetiness

Ebrious
ebrious
funebrious
inebrious
tenebrious

Eccable
impeccable
insecable
peccable

Ecency
decency
indecency
recency

Ecently
decently
indecently
recently

Eachable
bleachable
impeachable
reachable
teachable
umimpeachable
unteachable

ECHEROUS

lecherous treacherous

ECHERY

lechery treachery

ECIOUSNESS

speciousness facetiousness

ECKONING

beckoning dead-reckoning reckoning

ECREMENT

decrement recrement

ECTEDNESS

abjectedness
affectedness
dejectedness
disaffectedness
infectedness
suspectedness
unsuspectedness

ECTIBLE

affectible
collectible
correctible
defectible
delectable
detectible
dissectible
effectible
erectable
expectable
indefectible
indelectable
objectable
perfectible
reflectible
rejectable
respectable
suspectable

ECTICAL

apoplectical dialectical

ECTIFY

objectify rectify

ECTIONAL

affectional
complexional
correctional
inflectional
insurrectional
interjectional
intersectional
protectional
sectional

ECTIONIST

insurrectionist perfectionist protectionist resurrectionist

ECTIONIZE

resurrectionize sectionize

ECTITUDE

rectitude senectitude

ECTIVENESS
collectiveness
defectiveness
effectiveness
ineffectiveness
objectiveness
prospectiveness
protectiveness
reflectiveness
subjectiveness

ECTORAL
electoral
pectoral
protectoral
rectoral
sectoral

ECTORATE
directorate
electorate
expectorate
protectorate
rectorate

ECTORY
correctory
directory
nectary
rectory
refectory
sectary

ECTUAL
effectual
ineffectual
intellectual
lectual

ECTURAL
architectural
conjectural

ECTURER
conjecturer
lecturer

ECULAR
molecular
secular
specular

ECULATE
peculate
speculate

ECUTIVE
consecutive
executive
subsecutive

EDABLE
exceedable
impedible
obedible
pleadable
readable

EDDITIVE
redditive
sedative

EDERAL
federal
hederal

EDFULNESS
heedfulness
needfulness
unheedfulness
unneedfulness

Edial

bimedial	medial	pedial	remedial
intermedial			

Edian

comedian	encyclopedian	median	tragedian

Edible

credible	dreadable	edible	incredible

Edical

medical	pedicle

Edicant

medicant	predicant

Edicate

dedicate	medicate	predicate

Edience

disobedience	expedience	inexpedience	obedience
ingredients	expedients		

Edient

disobedient	inexpedient	ingredient	obedient
expedient			

Edier

greedier	needier	seedier	weedier
beadier	reedier	speedier	

Ediest

greediest	neediest	seediest	weediest
beadiest	reediest	speediest	

Edily

greedily	needily	speedily

Ediment

impediment	pediment	sediment

Ediness

greediness	seediness	speediness	weediness
neediness			

Edinous

mucedinous	putredinous	rubedinous

EDIOUS
intermedious tedious

EDITED
accredited discredited edited miscredited
credited

EDITING
accrediting discrediting editing miscrediting
crediting

EDITOR
creditor editor

EDIUM
medium tedium

EDLESSLY
heedlessly needlessly

EDLESSNESS
heedlessness needlessness

EDULOUS
credulous incredulous sedulous

EERIER, *see* ERIOR

EFERENCE
cross-reference deference preference reference

EFERENT
deferent efferent

EFICENCE
beneficence maleficence

EFICENT
beneficent maleficent

EFINESS
beefiness leafiness

EGALISM
legalism regalism

EGALNESS
legalness regalness illegalness

Eggable
beggable
legable

Eggary
beggary
eggery

Egginess
dregginess
legginess

Egian
collegian
Fuegian
Norwegian

Egnancy
pregnancy
regnancy

Eity
contemporaneity
corporeity
deity
diathermaneity
extraneity
femineity
gaseity
hæcceity
hermaphrodeity
heterogeneity
homogeneity
incorporeity
instantaneity
multeity
omneity
personeity
plebeity
seity
simultaneity
spontaneity
sulphureity
terreity
velleity

Eivable
conceivable
achievable
perceivable
receivable
believable
cleavable
relievable
retrievable
deceivable
grievable
unbelievable
inconceivable
irretrievable
undeceivable

Ekily
cheekily
creakily
leakily
sleekily
sneakily
squeakily

Ekiness
cheekiness
creakiness
leakiness
sneakiness
squeakiness

Elegate
delegate
relegate

Elery
celery
stellary

Elfishness
elfishness
selfishness

Elian
Aristotelian
carnelian
Delian
Hegelian
Ismaelian
Machiavellian
Mephisto-
phelian
Mingrelian

Elical
angelical
bellical
evangelical
helical
pellicle

Elion
anthelion
aphelion
chameleon

Ellable
compellable
delible
expellable
fellable
gelable
indelible
ingelable
spellable
tellable

Ellative
compellative
correlative
relative

Ellian
Boswellian
Cromwellian
evangelian
selion

Ellical
bellical
pellicle

Ellishing
embellishing
relishing

Ellishment
cmbellishment
relishment

Ellower
bellower
mellower
yellower

Ellowest
bellowest
mellowest
yellowest

Ellowing
bellowing
mellowing
yellowing

Ellular
cellular
intercellular
stellular
unicellular

Elony
felony
melony

Elterer
shelterer
welterer

Eltering
sheltering weltering

Eltery
sheltery smeltery

Emable
esteemable redeemable

Ematist
emblematist theorematist schematist thematist

Embering
dismembering membering remembering unremembering
"Novembering" "Decembering"

Emerist
ephemerist euhemerist

Eamery
creamery dreamery

Emial
academial endemial gremial vindemial

Emian
academian Bohemian

Emical
academical chemical endemical polemical
alchemical electrochemical epidemical

Eamier
beamier creamier dreamier premier

Eamily
beamily creamily dreamily steamily

Eminal
feminal geminal seminal

Eminate
effeminate geminate ingeminate

Eaminess
creaminess dreaminess steaminess

Emion
anthemion
procemion

Emnity
indemnity
solemnity

Emone
Agapemone
anemone
Gethsemane

Emoral
femoral
nemoral

Emory
memory
gemmery

Emperor
emperor
temperer

Emulent
temulent
tremulent

Emulous
emulous
tremulous

Enable
amenable
convenable

Enary
centenary
decennary
denary
hennery
senary
venery

Encelessly
defencelessly
senselessly

Encelessness
defencelessness
senselessness

Endible
accendible
amendable
commendable
comprehendible
defendable
dependable
descendable
endable
extendible
invendible
lendable
mendable
recommendable
rendible
unascendable
vendible

Endancy
ascendancy
attendancy
dependency
equipendency
impendency
independency
intendancy
interdependency
resplendency
tendency
superintendency
transcendency
transplendency

Enderer

engenderer, slenderer, surrenderer, tenderer, renderer

Enderest

engenderest, slenderest, surrenderest, tenderest, renderest

Endering

engendering, rendering, surrendering, tendering, gendering

Enderly

slenderly, tenderly

Enderness

slenderness, tenderness

Endious

compendious, incendious

Endlessly

endlessly, friendlessly

Endlessness

endlessness, friendlessness

Endously

stupendously, tremendously

Eneous

ebeneous, genius, ingenious, primigenious, arsenious, heterogeneous, nitrogeneous, selenious, extrageneous, homogeneous, pergameneous

Enerate

degenerate, ingenerate, progenerate, venerate, generate, intenerate, regenerate

Enery

deanery, machinery, plenary, scenery, greenery

Enesis

parenesis, ontogenesis, paragenesis, phytogenesis, biogenesis, homogenesis, abiogenesis, polygenesis, eugenesis, organogenesis, parthenogenesis, psychogenesis, genesis, palingenesis, phylogenesis, xenogenesis, heterogenesis, pangenesis

ENIA

encenia	gardenia	neurosthenia	

ENIAL

congenial	genial	primigenial	venial
demesnial	menial	uncongenial	

ENIAN

Armenian	Cyrenian	Fenian	Madrilenian
Athenian	Estremenian	Hellenian	Ruthenian

ENICAL

arsenical	ecumenical	scenical	sirenical
catechumenical			

ENIENCE

convenience	inconvenience	lenience	

ENIENCY

conveniency	inconveniency	leniency	

ENIENT

advenient	inconvenient	introvenient	supervenient
convenient	intervenient	lenient	

ENISON

benison	denizen	endenizen	venison

ENITIVE

genitive	lenitive	primogenitive	splenitive

ENITUDE

lenitude	plenitude	serenitude	

ENITY

amenity	obscenity	serenity	terrenity
lenity			

ENIUM

proscenium	selenium		

ENNIAL

biennial	millennial	perennial	septennial
centennial	novennial	quadrennial	triennial
decennial	octennial	quinquennial	vicennial
duodecennial			

ENNIFORM

antenniform	penniform		

Ensative
compensative
condensative
defensative
dispensative
insensitive
intensative
pensative
sensitive

Ensible
comprehensible
condensable
defensible
deprehensible
dispensable
distensible
extensible
incomprehensible
incondensable
indefensible
indispensable
insensible
ostensible
reprehensible
sensible
subsensible
tensible

Ensical
forensical
nonsensical

Ensional
ascensional
conventional
descensional
extensional
intentional
preventional

Ensionist
extensionist
recensionist

Ensity
condensity
density
immensity
intensity
propensity
tensity

Ensiveness
comprehensiveness
expensiveness
extensiveness
inoffensiveness
intensiveness
offensiveness
pensiveness

Ensory
defensory
dispensary
incensory
ostensory
prehensory
sensory
suspensory

Entable
fermentable
frequentable
inventible
presentable
preventable
rentable
representable

Entacle
pentacle
tentacle

Entalism
accidentalism
elementalism
Orientalism
sentimentalism
transcendentalism

Entalist
experimentalist
instrumentalist
Orientalist
sentimentalist
transcendentalist

ENTALIZE
experimentalize Orientalize sentimentalize

ENTALLY
accidentally fundamentally incidentally sentimentally

ENTALNESS
accidentalness fundamentalness gentleness incidentalness instrumentalness sentimentalness ungentleness

ENTARY
accidentary alimentary complementary complimentary dentary elementary filamentary instrumentary integumentary parliamentary pigmentary placentary sacramentary sedimentary tegumentary tenementary testamentary unparliamentary

ENTATIVE
augmentative commentative complimentative experimentative fermentative frequentative presentative pretentative preventative representative tentative

ENTIARY
penitentiary residentiary

ENTIATE
essentiate licentiate potentiate

ENTICAL
authentical conventical conventicle denticle identical

ENTICULE
denticule lenticule

ENTIMENT
presentiment sentiment

ENTINAL
dentinal sentinel

ENTIOUSNESS
conscientiousness contentiousness licentiousness pretentiousness

ENTITY
entity identity nonentity

Entiveness

alimentiveness attentiveness inattentiveness retentiveness

Entously

momentously portentously

Entousness

momentousness portentousness

Entual

accentual adventual conventual eventual

Entuate

accentuate eventuate

Enuant

attenuant genuant

Enuate

attenuate extenuate tenuate "when you ate" (etc.)

Enuous

ingenuous strenuous tenuous disingenuous

Eperous

leperous obstreperous prestreperous streperous

Epily

creepily sleepily weepily

Epiness

creepiness sleepiness steepiness weepiness

Eptible

deceptible imperceptible perceptible susceptible
acceptable insusceptible receptible

Eptical

antiseptical protreptical receptacle sceptical

Erbalism

herbalism verbalism

Erbalist

herbalist verbalist

Erbial

adverbial proverbial suburbial

ERBULENT
herbulent turbulent

ERCIAN
Cistercian lacertian *Persian, see also* ERTION *(2 syllable)*

ERCULOUS
tuberculous surculus surculous

EReROR
verderor murderer

ERFLUOUS
subterfluous superfluous

ERFULLY
cheerfully fearfully tearfully

ERFULNESS
cheerfulness fearfulness tearfulness

ERGENCY
convergency divergency insurgency vergency
detergency emergency urgency

ERIA
diphtheria eleutheria hesperia icteria
Egeria etheria hysteria Valkyria

ERIAL
aërial diabaterial funereal magisterial
arterial ethereal immaterial managerial
cereal ferial imperial manerial
material presbyterial serial vizierial
ministerial rhinocerial siderial

ERIALISM
immaterialism imperialism

ERIALIST
immaterialist imperialist

ERIAN
abderian Hanoverian phalansterian Spenserian
Aërian Hesperian Pierian Valerian
Algerian Iberian Presbyterian Valkyrian
Celtiberian Keplerian Shakesperian Wertherian
Cimmerian Luciferian

Erical

alexiterical, climacterical, helispherical, rhinocerical, atmospherical, esoterical, hysterical, spherical, chimerical, exoterical, numerical, sphericle, clerical, heliospherical, phylacterical

Erides

Anterides, Hesperides, Pierides

Eries

congeries, series

Eriest

beeriest, cheeriest, eeriest, weariest, bleariest, dreariest

Erily

verily, merrily

Erion

allerion, criterion, embaterion, Hyperion

Erior

anterior, drearier, interior, ulterior, exterior, eerier, posterior, wearier, cheerier, inferior, superior

Erious

deleterious, ethereous, mysterious, sidereous, cereous, imperious, serious

Erishing

cherishing, perishing, unperishing

Erited

disherited, emerited, inherited, merited, disinherited, ferreted

Eriting

inheriting, meriting, ferreting

Erity

ambidexterity, clerity, insincerity, posterity, asperity, dexterity, legerity, procerity, austerity, indexterity, prosperity, sincerity, temerity, verity, severity

Erium

acroterium	apodyterium	megatherium	titanotherium
agnotherium	dinotherium	palæotherium	

Erjury

chirurgery	perjury	purgery	surgery

Erlessness

cheerlessness	fearlessness	peerlessness

Erminal

germinal	terminal

Erminant

determinant	germinant

Erminate

determinate	exterminate	indeterminate	terminate
germinate			

Erminous

coterminous	terminus	verminous

Ernalism

externalism	journalism	"infernalism"

Ernalist

eternalist	journalist

Ernalize

eternalize	externalize	journalize

Ernery

fernery	turnery

Ernian

Avernian	Falernian	Hibernian	Saturnian

Ernity

alternity	fraternity	modernity	sempiternity
diuternity	maternity	paternity	taciturnity
eternity			

Erpentine

serpentine	turpentine

Errable

conferrable	inferable	referable	transferable
demurrable			

Errancy

aberrancy	currency	inerrancy	recurrency
concurrency			

Erryman

ferryman	wherryman

Ersary

anniversary	bursary	cursory	precursory
aspersory	controversary	nursery	

Ersible

conversable	coercible	incoercible	reimbursable
amerceable	immersible	irreversible	reversible
conversible			

Ersiform

diversiform	ursiform	versiform

Ersionist

excursionist	immersionist	versionist

Ersiveness

detersiveness	coerciveness	discursiveness	excursiveness

Ertitude

certitude	incertitude	inertitude

Ervancy

conservancy	fervency

Ervative

conservative	enervative	preservative	reservative
curvative	observative		

Escency

acescency	defervescency	excrescency	quiescency
acquiescency	delitescency	incalescency	recrudescency
adolescency	effervescency	liquescency	rejuvenescency
aekalescency	efflorescency	pubescency	turgescency
convalescency	erubescency		

Escience

nescience	prescience

Eshiness

fleshiness	meshiness

ESIA

æsthesia	anæsthesia	magnesia	Silesia
amnesia	ecclesia	parrhesia	

ESIAN

geodesian	Megalesian	Melanesian	Peloponnesian
gynæcian			

ESIDENT

president	resident

ESIMAL

centesimal	millesimal	quadragesimal	sexagesimal
infinitesimal	nonagesimal	septuagesimal	

ESSARY

confessary	pessary	professory	successary
intercessory			

ESSIBLE

accessible	fermentescible	ineffervescible	redressible
compressible	impressible	inexpressible	repressible
concessible	imputrescible	insuppressible	supressible
concrescible	inaccessible	irrepressible	transgressible
effervescible	incessable	marcescible	vitrescible
expressible	incompressible	putrescible	

ESSIONAL

accessional	discretional	processional	sessional
confessional	expressional	progressional	successional
congressional	intercessional	recessional	transgressional
digressional	possessional	retrocessional	

ESSIONER

possessioner	processioner

ESSIONIST

progressionist	secessionist	successionist

ESSITY

necessity	obesity

ESSIVENESS

aggressiveness	expressiveness	inexpressive-ness	oppressiveness
depressiveness	impressiveness		progressiveness
excessiveness			

ESTERING

festering	pestering	westering

Estial
agrestial bestial celestial supercelestial

Estible
comestible detestable incontestable intestable
congestible digestible indigestible testable
contestable divestible

Estinal
destinal intestinal

Estinate
destinate festinate predestinate

Estiness
restiness testiness

Estiveness
festiveness restiveness suggestiveness

Estrial
pedestrial superterrestrial terrestrial trimestrial

Estrian
campestrian palestrian pedestrian sylvestrian
equestrian

Estrious
pedestrious terrestrious

Estural
gestural vestural

Etable
forgetable fetable regrettable

Etaline
petaline metalline acetiline

Etallism
bimetallism monometallism petalism

Etchiness
sketchiness tetchiness

Etfully
forgetfully fretfully regretfully

Etfulness
forgetfulness fretfulness regretfulness

Etian

Capetian	Epictetian	Venetian	Grecian, *see also* Esion (*2 syllable*)

Etical

æsthetical	apathetical	emporetical	homiletical
aloetical	apologetical	energetical	hypothetical
alphabetical	arithmetical	epithetical	noetical
anchoretical	catechetical	exegetical	planetical
antipathetical	cosmetical	heretical	poetical
antithetical	dietetical	hermetical	theoretical

Eticism

æstheticism	asceticism	athleticism	peripateticism

Eticule

poeticule	reticule

Etinue

detinue	retinue	"met anew" (etc.)

Etory

completory	depletory	repletory	secretory

Etrical

alkalimetrical	geometrical	metrical	pulviometrical
asymmetrical	gnomiometrical	obstetrical	stichometrical
barometrical	graphometrical	perimetrical	symmetrical
craniometrical	horometrical	planimetrical	trigonometrical
diametrical	isoperimetrical		

Etriment

detriment	retriment

Ettering

bettering	fettering	lettering

Ettiness

jettiness	pettiness	sweatiness

Ettishly

coquettishly	pettishly

Ettishness

coquettishness	pettishness

Eveller
beveller dishevelier leveller reveller

Evellest
bevellest dishevellest levellest revellest

Evelling
bevelling dishevelling levelling revelling

Evelry
revelry devilry

Evermore
evermore nevermore

Evelism
levelism devilism

Evelment
revelment devilment bedevilment

Eviate
abbreviate alleviate deviate

Evious
devious previous

Evishly
peevishly thievishly

Evishness
peevishness thievishness

Evity
brevity levity longevity

Evolence
benevolence malevolence

Evolent
benevolent malevolent

Evolute
evolute revolute

Everer
cleverer endeavorer severer

Everest
cleverest endeavorest severest

Exible
flexible, inflexible, nexible, reflexible

Exity
complexity, convexity, intercomplexity, perplexity, pexity, reflexity

Exiveness
perplexiveness, reflexiveness

Esian
artesian, cartesian, ecclesian, Ephesian, etesian, magnesian, Milesian, Polynesian, trapezian

Eveler
leveler, reveler, bedeviler, beveler

Ezily
breezily, easily, greasily, uneasily, wheezily

Eziness
breeziness, cheesiness, easiness, greasiness, queasiness, sleaziness, uneasiness, wheeziness

Ezingly
freezingly, appeasingly, pleasingly, teasingly, wheezingly

Iable
acidifiable, appliable, classifiable, compliable, deniable, diversifiable, electrifiable, exemplifiable, falsifiable, fortifiable, friable, impliable, justifiable, liable, liquefiable, magnifiable, modifiable, pacifiable, petrifiable, pliable, qualifiable, rarefiable, rectifiable, reliable, saponifiable, satisfiable, solidifiable, triable, tryable, undeniable, verifiable, viable, vitrifiable

Iacal
bibliomaniacal, cardiacal, demoniacal, elegiacal, encyclopediacal, heliacal, hypochondriacal, maniacal, monomaniacal, paradisiacal, prosodiacal, simoniacal, zodiacal

Iacism
demoniacism, hypochondriacism

IADES
hamadryades hyades pleiades

IANCY
riancy cliency compliancy pliancy

IANTLY
compliantly defiantly pliantly reliantly

IARCHY
diarchy triarchy

IARY (*see two-syllable rhymes*)

IARIST
diarist piarist

IASIS
elephantiasis hypochondriasis

IATER
archiater psychiater

IBABLE
bribable indescribable scribable undescribable
describable inscribable subscribable

IBIA
amphibia tibia

IBIAL
amphibial stibial tibial

IBIOUS
amphibious bathybius stibious

IBITIVE
exhibitive prohibitive

IBULAR
fibular infundibular mandibular vestibular

ICAMENT
medicament predicament

ICATIVE
abdicative exsiccative indicative siccative
desiccative fricative predicative

ICIALISM
judicialism officialism

ICIALLY
judicially officially prejudicially superficially

ICICLE
icicle bicycle tricycle

ICIENCY
alliciency beneficiency deficiency efficiency inefficiency insitiency insufficiency proficiency self-sufficiency sufficiency

ICIEST
iciest spiciest

ICILY
icily spicily

ICINAL
fidicinal medicinal officinal vaticinal vicinal

ICINESS
iciness spiciness

ICITNESS
explicitness illicitness implicitness licitness

ICITUDE
solicitude spissitude vicissitude

ICITY
accomplicity achromaticity authenticity benedicite caloricity evangelicity felicity historicity hygroscopicity immundicity impudicity inelasticity infelicity canonicity catholicity causticity centricity clericity lubricity mendicity multiplicity myonicity pepticity periodicity plasticity publicity complicity conicity domesticity duplicity eccentricity pudicity rubricity rusticity simplicity spasticity sphericity spheroidicity stoicity elasticity electricity electrotonicity ellipticity endemicity stypticity tonicity triplicity unicity verticity volcanicity vulcanicity

ICKENING
quickening sickening thickening

ICKETER
cricketer picketer

ICKETING
cricketing picketing ticketing

ICKETY
pernicketty rickety thickety

ICKILY
stickily trickily

ICKINESS
stickiness trickiness

ICKLINESS
prickliness sickliness

ICOLIST
agricolist ignicolist plebicolist

ICOLOUS
agricolous sepicolous terricolous

ICOMOUS
auricomous flavicomous

ICTIONAL
contradictional fictional frictional jurisdictional

ICTIVELY
restrictively vindictively

ICTIVENESS
restrictiveness vindictiveness

ICTORY
benedictory interdictory valedictory victory
contradictory

ICULA
canicula fidicula zeticula

Icular
acicular
adminicular
articular
auricular
calicular
canicular
clavicular
cubicular
cuticular
fascicular
follicular
funicular
lenticular
navicular
orbicular
ovicular
particular
pellicular
perpendicular
quinquarticular
radicular
reticular
spicular
subcuticular
vehicular
ventricular
vermicular
versicular
vesicular

Iculate
articulate
canaliculate
matriculate
monticulate
paniculate
denticulate
fasiculate
particulate
reticulate
funiculate
geniculate
spiculate
vehiculate
gesticulate
vermiculate
vesiculate

Iculus
dendiculus
denticulus
fasciculus
folliculous
meticulous
ridiculous
urbiculous
ventriculous
vermiculous
vesiculous

Iculum
curriculum
geniculum

Idable
decidable
dividable
providable

Iddenness
forbiddenness
hiddenness

Idingly
decidingly
dividingly
abidingly
deridingly

Idial
noctidial
presidial

Idian
antemeridian
Lydian
meridian
nullifidian
Numidian
obsidian
ophidian
Ovidian
postmeridian
quotidian
rachidian
solfidian

Idiate
dimidiate
insidiate

Idical
druidical
juridical
veridical

Idify

acidify
lapidify
solidify

Idinous

libidinous
pinguidinous

Idiom

idiom
iridium
peridium

Idious

avidious
fastidious
hideous
insidious
invidious
lapideous
ophidious
parricidious
perfidious
splendidious
stillicidious

Idity

acidity
acridity
aridity
avidity
cupidity
frigidity
insipidity
insolidity
intrepidity
invalidity
gelidity
gravidity
hispidity
humidity
hybridity
limpidity
liquidity
lividity
lucidity
marcidity
morbidity
pallidity
pavidity
pellucidity
putidity
putridity
quiddity
rabidity
rancidity
rapidity
rigidity
sapidity
solidity
squalidity
stolidity
stupidity
timidity
torpidity
torridity
trepidity
tumidity
turbidity
turgidity
validity
vapidity
viridity
viscidity
vividity

Idual

individual
residual

Iduate

assiduate
individuate

Idulate

acidulate
stridulate

Idulous

acidulous
stridulous

Iduous

assiduous
deciduous
prociduous
residuous
succiduous
viduous

Iery

briery
fiery
friary

Ietal

parietal	varietal	hyetal	

Ieted

dieted	disquieted	quieted	rioted

Ieter

dieter	proprietor	quieter	rioter

Ietest

dietest	quietest	riotest	

Ieting

dieting	disquieting	quieting	rioting

Ietism

pietism	quietism		

Ietist

dietist	quietist	pietist	

Iety

anxiety	impropriety	notoriety	satiety
contrariety	inebriety	nullibiety	sobriety
dubiety	insobriety	omniety	society
ebriety	luxuriety	piety	ubiety
filiety	mediety	propriety	variety
impiety	nimiety		

Iferous

acidiferous	conchiferous	foraminiferous	lactiferous
aliferous	coniferous	fossiliferous	lamelliferous
aluminiferous	coralliferous	frondiferous	laminiferous
ammonitiferous	cruciferous	frugiferous	lanciferous
antenniferous	diamantiferous	fumiferous	laniferous
argentiferous	diamondiferous	furciferous	laticiferous
armiferous	doloriferous	gemmiferous	lauriferous
astriferous	ensiferous	geodiferous	letniferous
auriferous	estiferous	glandiferous	ligniferous
balaniferous	fatiferous	glanduliferous	lucriferous
balsamiferous	ferriferous	graniferous	luminiferous
bulbiferous	filiferous	granuliferous	magnetiferous
calcariferous	flammiferous	guttiferous	maliferous
calciferous	fletiferous	gypsiferous	mammaliferous
carboniferous	floriferous	hederiferous	mammiferous
cheliferous	fluctiferous	herbiferous	margaritiferous
cirriferous	foliferous	igniferous	melliferous

IFEROUS—(*Cont.*)

membraniferous
metalliferous
monstriferous
mortiferous
multiferous
nectariferous
nickeliferous
nimbiferous
nitriferous
noctiferous
nubiferous
nuciferous
odoriferous
oleiferous
omniferous
oolitiferous
opiferous
ossiferous
ostriferous
ozoniferous
palmiferous
pestiferous
pistilliferous
plantiniferous
plumbiferous
polypiferous
proliferous
pruniferous
pulmoniferous
quartziferous
racemiferous
resiniferous
roriferous
sacchariferous
sacciferous
saliferous
saliniferous
salutiferous
sanguiferous
scopiferous
scutiferous
sebiferous
sensiferous
setiferous
siliciferous
somniferous
soniferous
soporiferous
spiciferous
spiniferous
spumiferous
stameniferous
stanniferous
stelliferous
stoloniferous
succiferous
sudoriferous
tentaculiferous
tergiferous
thuriferous
tuberiferous
umbelliferous
umbraculiferous
umbriferous
vaporiferous
vasculiferous
vaciferous
zinciferous

IFICAL

beatifical
delenifical
dolorifical
lanifical
specifical

IFICANT

insignificant
mundificant
sacrificant
significant

IFICATE

certificate
pontificate
significate

IFICENT

magnificent
mirificent
munificent

IFICER

artificer
opificer

IFLUOUS

dulcifluous
fellifluous
ignifluous
mellifluous
sanguifluous

IFRAGOUS

fedrifragous
ossifragous
saxifragous

IFTABLE

liftable
shiftable

Iftily
shiftily
thriftily

Iftiness
shiftiness
thriftiness

Iftlessness
shiftlessness
thriftlessness

Ifugal
centrifugal
febrifugal
vermifugal

Igamist
bigamist
polygamist
trigamist

Igamous
bigamous
digamous
polygamous
trigamous

Igamy
bigamy
digamy
polygamy
trigamy

Igenous
alkaligenous
coralligenous
epigenous
fuliginous
gelatigenous
ignigenous
indigenous
lantiginous
marigenous
melligenous
montigenous
nubigenous
omnigenous
oxygenous
polygenous
pruriginous
sanguigenous
terrigenous
uliginous
unigenous
vertiginous
vortiginous

Igerate
belligerate
frigerate
refrigerate

Igerent
belligerent
refrigerant

Igerous
aligerous
armigerous
belligerous
cirrigerous
coralligerous
cornigerous
crucigerous
dentigerous
immorigerous
lanigerous
linigerous
morigerous
navigerous
ovigerous
palpigerous
pedigerous
pennigerous
piligerous
plumigerous
proligerous
setigerous
spinigerous

Iggery
piggery
whiggery
wiggery

Ighlander
highlander
islander

IGHTINESS
almightiness flightiness mightiness

IGHTLINESS
knightliness spriteliness unsightliness

IGIAN
Cantabrigian Phrygian Stygian

IGIDLY
frigidly rigidly

IGIDNESS
frigidness rigidness

IGIOUSNESS
litigiousness prodigiousness religiousness

IGMATIST
enigmatist stigmatist

IGMATIZE
enigmatize paradigmatize stigmatize

IGNANCY
indignancy malignancy

IGNEOUS
igneous ligneous

IGNIFY
dignify lignify signify undignify
ignify malignify

IGNITY
benignity dignity indignity malignity

IGOROUS
rigorous vigorous

IGRAPHY
calligraphy lexigraphy poligraphy stratigraphy
epigraphy pasigraphy pseudepigraphy tachygraphy

IGULATE
figulate ligulate

IGUOUS
ambiguous contiguous exiguous irriguous

ILEFULLY
guilefully wilefully

ILEFULNESS
guilefulness wilefulness

ILFULLY
skilfully wilfully unskilfully

ILFULNESS
skilfulness wilfulness unskilfulness

ILIA
memorabilia notabilia sedilia

ILIAD
chiliad Iliad

ILIAN
Brazilian crocodilian perfectibilian secilian
Castilian Kurilian reptilian Virgilian
Cecelian lacertilian

ILIARY
atrabiliary auxiliary

ILIATE
affiliate domiciliate filiate humiliate
conciliate

ILICAL
basilical filical silicle umbilical

ILIFY
fossilify nobilify stabilify vilify

ILIO
pulvilio punctilio

ILIOUS
atrabilious bilious punctilious supercilious

ILITATE
abilitate habilitate militate rehabilitate
debilitate impossibilitate nobilitate stabilitate
facilitate

ILITY

ability
absorbability
accendibility
acceptability
accessibility
accountability
acquirability
adaptability
addibility
admirability
admissibility
adoptability
adorability
advisability
affability
affectibility
agility
agreeability
alienability
alterability
amenability
amiability
amicability
amissibility
anility
appetibility
applicability
assimilability
associability
attainability
attemptability
attractability
audibility
availability
capability
changeability
civility
cognoscibility
cohesibility
combustibility
communi-
cability
commutability
compatibility
comprehensi-
bility
compressibility
computability
conceivability
condensability
conducibility
conductability
conformability
confusability
contempti-
bility
contractibility
contractility
convertibility
corrigibility
corrodibility
corrosibility
credibility
creditability
crocodility
culpability
curability
damnability
debility
deceptibility
deducibility
defectibility
demisability
demonstra-
bility
deplorability
descendibility
despicability
desirability
destructibility
determinability
detestability
diffusibility
digestibility
dilatability
disability
dissolubility
dissolvability
distensibility
divisibility
docibility
docility
ductility
durability
edibility
educability
eligibility
equability
exchange-
ability
excitability
exhaustibility
expansibility
extensibility
facility
fallibility
feasibility
fermentability
fertility
fictility
flexibility
flucility
fluctability
fluxibility
formidability
fossility
fragility
frangibility
friability
fusibility
futility
generability
gentility
gracility
gullibility
habitability
hostility
humility
ignobility
illability
imbecility
imitability
immeability
immeasur-
ability
immiscibility
immovability
immutability
impalpability
impartibility
impassibility
impeccability
impenetrability
impercepti-
bility
imperdibility
impermeability
imperturb-
ability
imperviability
implacability
impossibility
impregnability
imprescripti-
bility
impressibility
impressiona-
bility
improbability
imputability
inability
inaccessibility
incivility
incogitability
incognosci-
bility
incombusti-
bility

ILITY—(*Cont.*)

incommensurability
incommunicability
incommutability
incompatibility
incomprehensibility
incompressibility
inconceivability
incondensability
incontrovertibility
inconvertibility
incorrigibility
incorruptibility
incredibility
incurability
indefatigability
indefeasibility
indefectibility
indelibility
indemonstrability
indestructibility
indigestibility
indiscerpibility
indiscerptibility
indispensability
indisputability
indissolubility
indivisibility
indocibility
indocility
inductility
ineffability
ineffervescibility
ineligibility
inevitability
inexhaustibility
inexorability
inexplicability
infallibility
infeasibility
infertility
inflammability
inflexibility
infrangibility
infusibility
inhability
inheritability
inimitability
innumerability
insanability
insatiability
insensibility
inseparability
insociability
insolubility
instability
insuperability
insurmountability
insusceptibility
intangibility
intelligibility
interchangeability
intractability
inutility
invendibility
invincibility
inviolability
invisibility
invulnerability
irascibility
irreconcilability
irreductibility
irremovability
irreparability
irresistibility
irresponsibility
irritability
juvenility
lability
laminability
laudability
legibility
liability
malleability
manageability
memorability
mensurability
miscibility
mobility
modifiability
modificability
motility
movability
mutability
navigability
negotiability
neurility
nihility
nobility
notability
nuvility
opposability
organizability
ostensibility
palpability
partibility
passibility
peccability
penetrability
pensility
perceptibility
perdurability
perfectibility
permissibility
persuasibility
perturbability
placability
plausibility
pliability
ponderability
ponibility
portability
possibility
practicability
precipitability
preferability
prescriptibility
preventability
probability
producibility
puerility
quotability
ratability
readability
receivability
receptibility
redeemability
reductibility
reflexibility
refragability
refrangibility
refutability
reliability
remissibility
removability
remunerability

ILITY—(*Cont.*)

renewability
reparability
repealability
resistibility
resolvability
respectability
responsibility
reversibility
revocability
risibility
saleability
salvability
sanability
satiability
scurrility
senility
sensibility
separability
servility
sociability
solubility
solvability
sportability
squeezability
stability
sterility
suability
subtility
suitability
susceptibility
suspensibility
tactility
tamability
tangibility
taxability
temptability
tenability
tensibility
tensility
tolerability
torsibility
tractability
tractility
tranquillity
transferability
transmissibility
transmutability
transportability
unaccountability
unbelievability
unutterability
utility
vaporability
variability
vegetability
vendibility
venerability
verisimility
vernility
versability
versatility
viability
vibratility
vindicability
virility
visibility
volatility
volubility
vulnerability
writability

ILKIER

milkier
silkier

ILKIEST

milkiest
silkiest

ILLABLE

distillable
syllable
tillable
fillable

ILLAGER

pillager
villager

ILLERY

artillery
capillary
cilery
codicillary
distillery
Hilary
phyllary
pillory
Sillery

ILLETED

billeted
filleted
unfilleted

ILLETING

billeting
filleting

ILLIANCY

brilliancy
resiliency
transiliency

Illiest			
chilliest	hilliest	silliest	stilliest
Illiness			
chilliness	hilliness	silliness	
Illingly			
thrillingly	willingly	trillingly	"killingly"
Ilogize			
epilogize	syllogize		
Ilogism			
epilogism	episyllogism	syllogism	
Illowing			
billowing	pillowing		
Illowy			
billowy	pillowy	willowy	
Ilobite			
tilobite	stylobite		
Ilogy			
antilogy	dilogy	palilogy	trilogy
brachylogy	fossilogy		
Iloquence			
blandiloquence	grandiloquence	somniloquence	vaniloquence
breviloquence	magniloquence	stultiloquence	
Iloquent			
flexiloquent	melliloquent	stultiloquent	vaniloquent
grandiloquent	pauciloquent	sauviloquent	veriloquent
magniloquent	sanctiloquent		
Iloquism			
gastriloquism	pectoriloquism	somniloquism	ventriloquism
Iloquist			
dentriloquist	gastriloquist	somniloquist	ventriloquist
Iloquize			
soliloquize	ventriloquize		
Iloquous			
grandiloquous	pectoriloquous	ventriloquous	somniloquous
magniloquous			

Iloquy
dentiloquy pectoriloquy somniloquy sauviloquy
gastriloquy soliloquy stultiloquy ventriloquy
pauciloquy

Imanous
longimanous pedimanous

Imary
primary rhymery sublimary

Imature
climature limature

Imbricate
fimbricate imbricate

Imerous
dimerous polymerous

Imeter
alkalimeter gravimeter polarimeter scimiter
altimeter limiter pulsimeter tasimeter
calorimeter lucimeter rhysimeter trimeter
dasymeter pelvimeter saccharimeter velocimeter
dimeter perimeter salimeter zymosimeter
focimeter planimeter

Imetry
alkalimetry calorimetry planimetry saccharimetry
asymmetry isoperimetry polarimetry symmetry
bathymetry longimetry

Imical
inimical homonymical metonymical mimical
alchymical

Iminal
criminal regiminal viminal

Iminess
griminess sliminess

Iminate
accriminate discriminate incriminate recriminate
criminate eliminate indiscriminate

Iminous

criminous	moliminous

Imini

nimini-pimini	postliminy	"gimminy"

Imity

anonymity	magnanimity	pseudonymity	sublimity
dimity	parvanimity	pusillanimity	unanimity
equanimity	proximity	sanctanimity	

Imperer

simperer	whimperer

Impering

simpering	whimpering

Imulate

assimulate	dissimulate	simulate	stimulate

Imulus

limulus	stimulus

Inable

combinable	definable	inclinable	indefinable
assignable	designable	indeclinable	signable
declinable	finable		

Inament

linament	liniment	miniment

Inative

combinative	finative

Indery

cindery	tindery

Inery

alpinery	finery	quinary	swinery
binary	pinery	refinery	vinery
finary			

Indicate

indicate	syndicate	vindicate

Ineal

consanguineal	gramineal	lineal	pineal
finial	interlineal	pectineal	stamineal

Ineous
cartilagineous
consanguineous
flamineous
fulmineous
gramineous
ignominious
minious
sanguineous
stamineous
stramineous
testudineous
vimineous

Ingency
astringency
contingency
refringency
stringency

Ingerer
fingerer
lingerer
malingerer

Ingering
fingering
lingering
malingering

Ingian
Carlovingian
Merovingian
Thuringian
Zingian

Ingily
dingily
stingily

Inginess
springiness
stringiness
"ringiness"

Inginess
dinginess
stinginess

Inian
Abyssinian
anthropophaginian
Arminian
Augustinian
Britinian
Carolinian
Carthaginian
Czarinian
Darwinian
Delphinian
Eleusinian
Hercynian
Justinian
Palestinian
Sardinian
serpentinian
Socinian
viraginian
Virginian

Iniate
laciniate
delineate
lineate
miniate

Inicle
adminicle
binnacle
binocle
Brahminical
clinical
cynical
dominical
finical
flaminical
pinnacle
sinical
synclinical

Inier
brinier
shinier
spinier
tinier

Iniest
briniest
shiniest
spiniest
tiniest

Iniform

actiniform	aluminiform	laciniform	

Inikin

finikin	minikin		

Inishing

diminishing	finishing		

Inister

administer	minister	sinister	

Inistral

ministral	sinistral		

Inity

affinity	femininity	peregrinity	trinity
alkalinity	infinity	salinity	vicinity
asininity	Latinity	sanguinity	viraginity
consanguinity	masculinity	satinity	virginity
divinity	patavinity		

Inkable

drinkable	undrinkable	unsinkable	unthinkable
thinkable	unshrinkable		

Inkiness

inkiness	kinkiness	pinkiness	"slinkincss"

Inlander

Finlander	inlander		

Innacle

binnacle	binocle	finnical	

Inoline

chinoline	crinoline		

Inquity

longinquity	propinquity		

Interest

interest	winterest	splinterest	

Intery

printery	splintery	wintery	

Inthian

absinthian	Corinthian	hyacinthian	labyrinthian

INUATE

continuate insinuate sinuate "whin you ate"

INUOUS

continuous sinuous

IOCENE

miocene pliocene post-pliocene

IOLA

variola viola Iola

IOLET

triolet violet

IOLIST

sciolist violist

IOLUS

gladiolus sciolus variolus

IOPE

Calliope myopy presbyopy

IPAROUS

biparous
criniparous
deparous
fissiparous
floriparous
sebiparous
frondiparous
fructiparous
gemelliparous
gemmiparous
larviparous
multiparous
omniparous
oviparous
ovoviviparous
polyparous
polypiparous
sudoriparous
tomiparous
uniparous
vermiparous
viviparous

IPATHIST

antipathist somnipathist

IPATHY

antipathy kinesipathy somnipathy

IPEDAL

equipedal solipedal

IPHONY

antiphony exyphony polyphony

IPLICATE

sesquiplicate triplicate

IPOTENCE

armipotence ignipotence omnipotence plenipotence

IPOTENT
armipotent ignipotent omnipotent plenipotent
bellipotent multipotent

IPPERY
frippery slippery

IPTEROUS
dipterous peripterous tripterous

IPTICAL
elliptical apocalyptical cryptical

IPULATE
astipulate manipulate stipulate

IQUITOUS
iniquitous ubiquitous

IQUITY
antiquity iniquity obliquity ubiquity

IRABLE
acquirable expirable requirable transpirable
desirable perspirable respirable untirable

IRACY
conspiracy deliracy

IRACY
piracy retiracy

IRCULAR
circular furcular tubercular

IRCULATE
circulate tuberculate

IREFULNESS
direfulness irefulness

YRIAN
Assyrian Styrian Syrian Tyrian

IRICAL
empirical lyrical miracle satirical

IRICISM
empiricism lyricism

Irious
delirious Sirius "weary us" (etc.)

Irium, Yrium, Yreum
collyrium delirium empyreum

Irony
irony gyronny

Irthlessness
mirthlessness worthlessness

Isable
advisable analysable crystallizable demisable despisable devisable electrolysable excisable exercisable magnetizable organizable oxidizable prizable realizable recognizable sizable vaporizable

Iscency
reminiscency reviviscency

Isian
Frisian Elysian Paradisean Parisian precisian

Isible
acquisible divisible indivisible invisible visible

Isical
metaphysical paradisical phthisical physical psychophysical

Isitor
acquisitor inquisitor requisitor visitor

Isively
decisively derisively incisively indecisively

Isiveness
decisiveness derisiveness incisiveness indecisiveness

Iskiest
friskiest riskiest

Isory
decisory derisory incisory spicery

Isory
advisory provisory revisory supervisory
irrisory

Issible
admissible amissible immiscible incommiscible irremissible miscible omissible permiscible permissible remissible scissible transmissible

Issimo
bravissimo generalissimo pianissimo prestissimo
fortissimo

Issory
admissory emissory remissory rescissory
dismissory

Istency
consistency distancy existency inconsistency persistency pre-existency subsistency

Istener
christener listener

Istening
christening glistening listening unlistening

Istical
agonistical alchemistical antagonistical antarchistical aoristical apathistical aphoristical artistical atheistical cabalistical Calvinistical casuistical catechistical characteristical chemistical deistical dialogistical egoistical egotistical eucharistical eulogistical euphemistical hemistichal linguistical methodistical mystical paragraph-istical pietistical puristical sophistical statistical theistical theosophistical

Isticate
dephlogisticate sophisticate

Istlessness
listlessness resistlessness

Istory
consistory history mystery

Itable
citable, excitable, ignitible, incitable, indictable, lightable, requitable, unitable, writable

Itative
excitative, incitative, writative

Itchery
bewitchery, michery, stitchery, witchery

Itchiness
itchiness, pitchiness

Itefully
spitefully, delightfully, frightfully, rightfully

Iterate
illiterate, iterate, literate, obliterate, reiterate, transliterate

Itherward
hitherward, thitherward, whitherward

Ithesis
antithesis, epithesis

Ithesomely
blithesomely, lithesomely

Ithesomeness
blithesomeness, lithesomeness

Itiate
initiate, maleficiate, novitiate, officiate, patriciate, propitiate, vitiate

Itical
Abrahamitical, acritical, anchoritical, cosmopolitical, critical, diacritical, electrolytical, hermitical, hypercritical, hypocritical, Jesuitical, Levitical, political, pulpitical, soritical, thersitical

Itigant
litigant, mitigant

Itigate
litigate, mitigate

Itional
additional
commissional
conditional
definitional
dispositional
disquisitional
inquisitional
intuitional
positional
prepositional
propositional
repetitional
suppositional
traditional
transpositional
volitional

Itioner
admonitioner
coalitioner
commissioner
exhibitioner
missioner
practitioner
traditioner

Itionist
abolitionist
coalitionist
exhibitionist
expeditionist
oppositionist
prohibitionist
requisitionist
traditionist

Itiousness
adventitiousness
auspiciousness
avariciousness
capriciousness
deliciousness
expeditiousness
fictiousness
flagitiousness
inauspiciousness
judiciousness
maliciousness
meretriciousness
perniciousness
propitiousness
seditiousness
superstitiousness
suspiciousness
viciousness

Ittable
admittable
fittable
irremittable
knittable
quittable
transmittable

Ittany
dittany
litany
"kitteny"

Itterest
bitterest
embitterest
fritterest
glitterest

Ittering
bittering
embittering
frittering
twittering
glittering
tittering

Ittily
grittily
prettily
wittily

Ittiness
flittiness
grittiness
prettiness
wittiness

Ittleness
brittleness
littleness

Itual
habitual
obitual
ritual

Ituate
habituate lituate situate

Itular
capitular titular

Ivable
forgivable givable livable unforgivable

Ivable (*long*)
contrivable deprivable derivable revivable

Ivalent
equivalent omnivalent trivalent univalent
multivalent quinquivalent

Ivancy
connivancy survivancy

Ivative
derivative privative

Iviller
civiller driveller sniveller

Iverer
deliverer quiverer shiverer

Ivering
delivering quivering shivering

Ivery
delivery jail-delivery rivery shivery
goal-delivery livery

Ivial
convivial oblivial quadrivial trivial
lixivial

Ividness
lividness vividness

Ivious
bivious lixivious multivious oblivious
lascivious

Ivity

absorptivity
acclivity
activity
captivity
causativity
cogitativity
collectivity
conductivity
declivity
festivity
impassivity
incogitativity
instinctivity
motivity
nativity
negativity
objectivity
passivity
perceptivity
positivity
privity
proclivity
productivity
receptivity
relativity
sensitivity
subjectivity

Ivocal

equivocal
univocal

Ivorous

carnivorous
equivorous
frugivorous
fucivorous
graminivorous
granivorous
herbivorous
insectivorous
omnivorous
ossivorous
panivorous
phytivorous
piscivirous
sanguinivorous
vermivorous

Ivory

ivory
vivary

Ixable

fixable
mixable

Ixity

fixity
prolixity
siccity

Izzier

dizzier
busier
frizzier

Izziest

dizziest
busiest

Izzily

dizzily
busily

Obbering

clobbering
slobbering

Obbery

bobbery
jobbery
robbery
slobbery
snobbery
stock-jobbery

Obinet

robinet
bobbinet

Obular
globular lobular

Ocalism
localism vocalism

Ocalize
focalize localize vocalize

Ocative
locative provocative

Ochromy
heliochromy metallochromy monochromy stereochromy

Ochronous
isochronous tautochronous

Ocinate
patrocinate ratiocinate

Ociousness
atrociousness ferociousness precociousness

Ockery
crockery mockery rockery

Ockiness
"cockiness" rockiness stockiness

Ocracy
aristocracy
arithmocracy
autocracy
cottonocracy
democracy
demonocracy
despotocracy
gernotocracy
gynæcocracy
hagiocracy
hierocracy
hypocrisy
idiocrasy
logocracy
mobocracy
monocracy
neocracy
nomocracy
ochlocracy
pantisocracy
pedantocracy
plantocracy
plousiocracy
plutocracy
shopocracy
slavocracy
snobocracy
stratocracy
theocracy
theocrasy
timocracy

Ocratism
democratism Socratism

Octorship
doctorship proctorship

Ocular
binocular, locular, ocular, vocular, jocular, monocular

Oddering
doddering, foddering

Odial
allodial, episodial, prosodial, thenodial, custodial, palinodial

Odian
custodian, Herodian, prosodian, Rhodian

Odical
codical, monodical, prosodical, spasmodical, episcodical, nodical, rhapsodical, synodical, methodical, periodical

Odify
codify, modify

Odious
commodious, incommodious, melodious, odious

Odity
commodity, incommodity, oddity

Odium
odium, sodium

Odular
modular, nodular

Offering
offering, peace-offering, proffering

Ogamist
deuterogamist, misogamist, monogamist, neogamist

Ogamous
endogamous, heterogamous, phænogamous, phanerogamous, exogamous, monogamous

Ogamy
cœnogamy, endogamy, misogamy, monogamy, deuterogamy, exogamy

Ogative
derogative, interrogative, prerogative

Ogenist

abiogenist
biogenist
beterogenist
misogynist
monogenist
philogynist

Ogenous

endogenous
exogenous
hydrogenous
hypogynous
lithogenous
nitrogenous
pyrogenous
thermogenous

Ogeny

abiogeny
anthropogeny
biogeny
embryogeny
ethnogeny
geogeny
heterogeny
histogeny
homogeny
hymenogeny
misogyny
monogeny
odontogeny
ontogeny
osteogeny
pathogeny
philogyny
photogeny
phylogeny
progeny
zoögeny

Ogeyism

bogeyism
fogeyism

Ogian

archæologian
astrologian
gambogian
geologian
mythologian
neologian
philogian
theologian

Ogical

aërological
amphibiological
amphibological
analogical
anthological
anthropological
archæological
astrological
bibliological
biological
bryological
chronological
climatological
conchological
cosmological
craniological
demagogical
deontological
dialogical
doxological
Egyptological
etiological
etymological
genealogical
geological
glossological
glottological
homological
hydrological
ichnological
ideological
illogical
lithological
logical
mazological
metalogical
meteorological
mythological
necrological
neological
neurological
nosological
odontological
organological
ornithological
orological
osteological
palæontological
pantological
paralogical
penological
perissological
petrological
philological
phraseological
phrenological
physiological
phytological
pneumato-
logical
pomological
psychological
selenological
semeiological
sinological
sociological
spectrological
symbological
synagogical
tautological
technicological
technological
teleological
teratological
terminological
theological
toxicological
tropological
universological
zoölogical
zoöphytological
zymological

Ognomy

craniognomy
pathognomy
physiognomy

Ogonist

cosmogonist
theogonist

Ogony

autogony
cosmogony
geogony
pathogony
physiogony
theogony
zoögony

Ographer

autobiographer
bibliographer
biographer
calcographer
cartographer
chartographer
chorographer
chronographer
cosmographer
cryptographer
crystallographer
ethnographer
geographer
glossographer
glyphographer
glyptographer
haliographer
heresiographer
hierographer
historiographer
horologiographer
hydrographer
hymnographer
iambographer
lexicographer
lichenographer
lithographer
logographer
mimographer
monographer
mythographer
nomographer
orthographer
osteographer
palæographer
petrographer
photographer
psalmographer
selenographer
sphenographer
stenographer
topographer
typographer
zylographer
zincographer
zoögrapher

Ographist

chirographist
lichenographist
mechanographist
metallographist
monographist
museographist
organographist
orthographist
palæographist
phonographist
photographist
psalmographist
selenographist
siderographist
sphenographist
steganographist
topographist
uranographist
zoögraphist

Ography

anthography
anthropography
autobiography
autography
balneography
bibliography
biography
cacography
calcography
chartography
chirography
chorography
Christianography
chromatography
chromophotography
chromotypography
chromoxylography
climatography
cosmography
cryptography
crystallography
dactyliography
demography
dendrography
epistolography
ethnography
galvanography
geography
glossography
glyphography
glyptography
gypsography
hagiography
haliography
heliography
heliotypography

OGRAPHY—(*Cont.*)

hematography
heresiography
hetersiography
hierography
histography
historiography
horography
horologiography
hyalography
hydrography
hyetography
hymnography
ichnography
ichthyography
iconography
ideography
isography
lexicography
lichenography
lithography
logography
mechanography
metallography
microcosmography
monography
neography
neurography
nomography
nosography
numismatography
odontography
ophiography
oreography
organography
orography
orthography
osteography
palæography
palæontography
paneiconography
pantography
perspectography
petrography
phantasmatography
pharmacography
phonography
photography
phycography
physiography
phytography
plastography
pneumography
pornography
potamography
psalmography
pseudography
psychography
pterylography
rhyparography
scenography
sciography
seismography
selenography
semeiography
siderography
sphenography
steganography
stelography
stenography
stereography
stereotypography
stratography
stylography
symbolæography
tacheography
thermography
topography
toreumatography
topography
uranography
xylography
xylopyrography
zincography
zoögraphy

OINTEDLY

disjointedly
pointedly

OISTERING

cloistering
roistering

OICAL

egoical
heroical
stoical

OKENLY

brokenly
outspokenly

OLABLE

consolable
controllable
rollable
tollable

OLARIZE

polarize
solarize

OLARY

bolary	polery	solary	volary
cajolery			

OLATER

bibliolater	iconolater	mariolater	pyrolater
heliolater	idolater		

OLATROUS

idolatrous	symbolatrous

OLATRY

anthropolatry	gyneolatry	litholatry	pyrolatry
astrolatry	heliolatry	lordolatry	symbolatry
bibliolatry	hierolatry	mariolatry	thaumatolatry
cosmolatry	ichthyolatry	necrolatry	topolatry
demonolatry	idiolatry	ophiolatry	zoölatry
geolatry	idolatry	physiolatry	

OLEFULNESS

dolefulness	soulfulness

OLEUM

linoleum	petroleum

OLIA

magnolia	melancholia

OLIAN

Æolian	Creolean	metabolian	Pactolian
capitolian	melancholian	Mongolian	

OLIATE

foliate	infoliate	spoliate

OLICAL

apostolical	catholical	hyperbolical	symbolical
bibliopolical	diabolical	parabolical	

OLICSOME

frolicsome	rollicksome

OLIDLY

solidly	squalidly	stolidly

OLIER

holier	lowlier	unholier

Oliest

holiest, lowliest

Olify

idolify, mollify, qualify

Oliness

holiness, lowliness, shoaliness, unholiness

Olio

folio, olio, portfolio

Olisher

abolisher, demolisher, polisher

Olishing

abolishing, demolishing, polishing

Olity

frivolity, equality, inequality, interpolity, isopolity, jollity, polity, quality

Olium

scholium, trifolium

Ollified

qualified, mollified, unqualified

Ollower

follower, hollower, swallower, wallower

Ollowing

following, holloing, hollowing, swallowing, wallowing

Ologer

astrologer, acknowledger, botanologer, etymologer, geologer, horologer, mythologer, osteologer, philologer, phonologer, phrenologer, physiologer, "sockdolager", theologer

Ologist

aërologist, agriologist, anthropologist, apologist, archæologist, Assyriologist, battologist, biologist, campanologist, chronologist, conchologist, cosmologist, craniologist, crustaceologist, demonologist, deontologist, dendrologist, dermatologist, ecclesiologist, Egyptologist, electro-biologist, embryologist, entomologist, ethnologist, ethologist, etymologist, galvanologist, geologist

OLOGIST—(*Cont.*)

glossologist
glottologist
gypsologist
hagiologist
hierologist
histologist
horologist
hydrologist
hymnologist
hypnologist
ichthyologist
ideologist
lexicologist
lithologist
mantologist
martyrologist
mazologist
meteorologist
monologist
morphologist
mycologist
myologist
necrologist
neologist
neurologist
noölogist
nosologist
numismatologist
oneirologist
onomatologist
ontologist
oölogist
ophiologist
orchidologist
ornithologist
orologist
osteologist
palæoethnologist
palæologist
palæontologist
palætiologist
pantheologist
pantologist
pathologist
petrologist
pharmacologist
philologist
phonologist
photologist
phraseologist
phrenologist
physiologist
phytolithologist
phytologist
phytopathologist
pneumatologist
pomologist
pseudologist
psychologist
pteridologist
pyrologist
quinologist
runologist
saintologist
sarcologist
seismologist
sinologist
sociologist
symbologist
tautologist
technologist
teleologist
teratologist
theologist
thereologist
therologist
toxicologist
universologist
vulcanologist
zoölogist

OLOGIZE

apologize
astrologize
battologize
doxologize
entomologize
etymologize
geologize
mythologize
neologize
philologize
tautologize
theologize

OLOGOUS

heterologous
homologous
isologous
tautologous

OLOGY

actinology
conchology
conchyliology
cosmology
craniology
cryptology
dactyliology
dactylology
demonology
dendrology
deontology
dermatology
desmology
dialectology
dicæology
dittology
dosology
doxology
ecclesiology
Egyptology
electro-biology
electrology
electro-physiology
embryology
emetology
emmenology
endemiology
enteradenology
enterology
entomology
entozoölogy
epidemiology
epistemology
eschatology
ethnology
ethology
etiology
etymology
filicology
fossilology
fungology
galvanology
gastrology
genesiology
geology
giantology
glossology

OLOGY—(*Cont.*)

glottology
gnomology
graphiology
gynæcology
gypsology
hagiology
heterology
hierology
histology
historiology
homology
horology
hydrology
hyetology
hygiology
hygrology
hylology
hymenology
hymnology
hypnology
hysterology
ichnolithnology
ichnology
ichorology
ichthyology
iconology
ideology
insectology
kinology
laryngology
leptology
lexicology
lichenology
lithology
liturgiology
macrology
malacology
mantology
martyrology
mastology
mateology
mazology
membranology
menology
meteorology
methodology
metrology
miasmology
microgeology
micrology
misology
monadology
monology
morphology
muscology
mycology
myology
mythology
necrology
neology
nephrology
neurology
neurypnology
nomology
noölogy
nosology
numismatology
oceanology
odontology
ology
oneirology
onology
onomatology
oölogy
ophiology
ophthalmology
orchidology
organology
orismology
ornithichnology
ornithology
orology
osmonosology
osteology
otology
ourology
ovology
palæothenology
paleology
palæontology
palæophytology
palæozoölogy
palætiology
pantheology
pantology
paradoxology
parasitology
parisology
paromology
parthenology
pathology
patronomatology
penology
periodology
perissology
petrology
pharmacology
pharology
pharyngology
phenomenology
philology
phlebology
phonology
photology
phraseology
phrenology
phycology
physiology
phytolithology
phytology
phytopathology
phyto-physiology
pneumatology
pneumology
pomology
ponerology
posology
potamology
protophytology
psilology
psychology
psychonosology
pteridology
punnology
pyretology
pyritology
pyrology
quinology
runology
sarcology
seismology
selenology
sematology
semeiology
sinology
sitology
skeletology
sociology
somatology
soteriology
spasmology
speciology
spectrology
spermatology
spermology
splanchnology
splenology
statistology
stoichiology
stromatology
symbology
symptomatology

OLOGY—(*Cont.*)

synchronology
syndesmology
systematology
tautology
taxology
technology
teleology
teratology
terminology
termonology
testaceology
thanatology
theology
thereology
thermology
therology
threpsology
tidology
topology
toreumatology
toxicology
tropology
typology
universology
uranology
urology
uronology
vulcanology
zoölogy
zoöphytology
zymology

OLUBLE

insoluble
soluble
voluble

OLUTIVE

evolutive
revolutive
solutive
supervolutive

OLVABLE

absolvable
dissolvable
indissolvable
insolvable
resolvable
solvable

OLVENCY

insolvency
revolvency
solvency

OMACHY

alectoromachy
alectryomachy
gigantomachy
iconomachy
logomachy
monomachy
psychomachy
sciomachy
theomachy

OMANY

bibliomany
erotomany
Romany

OMATHY

chrestomathy
philomathy
pharmacomathy

OMATISM

achromatism
chromatism
diplomatism

OMENA

antilegomena
paralipomena
phenomena
prolegomena

OMENON

phenomenon
prolegomenon

OMEROUS

glomerous
isomerous

OMETER

absorptiometer
barometer
chronometer
actinometer
altometer
astrometer
audiometer
bathometer
cephalometer
chartometer
chromatometer
clinometer
craniometer
declinometer
dendrometer
drosometer
dynamometer
echometer
electrometer
endosmometer
eudiometer
galvanometer
geometer
geothermometer
goniometer
graphometer
heliometer
horometer
hydrometer
hygrometer
hypsometer
lactometer
logometer
macrometer
magnetometer
micrometer
micronometer
monometer
nauropometer
odometer
oleometer
ombrometer
optometer
ozonometer
pantometer
pedometer
phonometer
photometer
piezometer
planometer
platometer
pluviometer
pneumatometer
pulsometer
pyrometer
radiometer
refractometer
rheometer
saccharometer
salinometer
seismometer
sepometer
sonometer
spectrometer
spherometer
stereometer
stethometer
stratometer
tachometer
tannometer
thermometer
tribometer
trochometer
udometer
vinometer
volumenometer
zymometer

OMETRY

barometry
biometry
chronometry
craniometry
eudiometry
galvanometry
gasometry
geometry
goniometry
helicometry
horometry
hydrometry
hygrometry
hypsometry
Mahometry
micrometry
odometry
orthometry
ozonometry
pathometry
photometry
planeometry
phanometry
pneumometry
polygonometry
pyrometry
rheometry
saccharometry
seismometry
stereometry
stichometry
stoichiometry
trigonometry

OMICAL

agronomical
amphidromical
astronomical
atomical
comical
coxcombical
domical
economical
iconomical
tragi-comical

OMINAL

abdominal
cognominal
nominal
prenominal
surnominal

OMINANCE

dominance
predominance
prominence

OMINANT

dominant
prominent
subdominant
superdominant
predominant

OMINATE

abominate
comminate
nominate
predominate
agnominate
denominate
ominate
prenominate
annominate
dominate

OMINY

hominy
dominie

OMINOUS

abnominous
hypomenous
ominous
prolegomenous
dominus

ONABLE

lonable
tonable
unatonable

ONDERER

ponderer
squanderer
wanderer

ONDERING

pondering
squandering
unwandering
wandering

ONIA

Adonia
aphonia
bryonia
valonia
ammonia
begonia
pneumonia

ONIAC

demoniac
simoniac

ONIAL

baronial
demonial
monial
sanctimonial
ceremonial
intercolonial
oxygonial
testimonial
colonial
matrimonial
patrimonial

ONIAN

Amazonian
Chelonian
Gorgonean
Newtonian
ammonian
Ciceronian
Grandisonian
Oxonian
Aonian
colophonian
halcyonian
Patagonian
Ausonion
Cottonian
Heliconian
Plutonian
Babylonian
Daltonian
Ionian
Pyrrhonian
Baconian
demonian
Johnsonian
Sardonian
bezonian
Devonian
Laconian
Serbonian
Caledonian
Draconian
Livonian
Simonian
Cameronian
Etonian
Macedonian
Slavonian
Catonian
Favonian
Myrmidonian
Thessalonian

ONICA
harmonica
veronica

ONICAL
antichronical
antiphonical
architectonical
Babylonical
canonical
chronicle
conical
diaphonical
euphonical
geoponical
harmonical
iconical
ironical
Sorbonnical
synchronical
tautophonical
thrasonical
tonical
uncanonical

ONICISM
histrionicism
laconicism
Teutonicism

ONICON
chronicon
harmonicon

ONIOUS
acrimonious
alimonious
ceremonious
erroneous
euphonious
felonious
harmonious
inharmonious
matrimonious
parsimonious
querimonious
sanctimonious
simonious
symphonious
ultroneous

ONISHING
admonishing
astonishing
monishing

ONISHMENT
admonishment
astonishment
premonishment

ONIUM
harmonium
pandemonium
pelargonium
stramonium
zirconium

ONOGRAPH
chronograph
monograph

ONOMIST
agronomist
autonomist
demonomist
economist
eponymist
gastronomist
synonymist

ONOMIZE
astronomize
economize

ONOMY
agronomy
astronomy
autonomy
dactylonomy
Deuteronomy
economy
gastronomy
geonomy
heteronomy
isonomy
morphonomy
nosonomy
phytonomy
taxonomy
toponomy
zoönomy

Onymous

anonymous	heteronymous	paronymous	pseudonymous
autonomous	homonymous	polyonymous	synonymous
eponymous			

Onymy

homonymy	paronymy	polyonymy	synonymy
metonymy			

Ookery

bookery	cookery	rookery

Oominess

gloominess	roominess

Oonery

buffoonery	cocoonery	pantaloonery	poltroonery

Ootery

freebootery	fruitery	rootery

Opathist

allopathist	hydropathist	hylopathist	somnopathist
homœopathist			

Opathy

allopathy	hydropathy	monopathy	theopathy
enantiopathy	ideopathy	neuropathy	somnopathy
heteropathy	isopathy	psychopathy	leucopathy
homœopathy			

Opery

popery	ropery

Ophagi

androphagi	cardophagi	hippophagi	Lotophagi
anthropophagi	heterophagi	lithophagi	sarcophagi

Ophagist

galactophagist	hippophagist	ichthyophagist	pantophagist
geophagist			

Ophagous

androphagous	hippophagous	ophiophagous	sarcophagous
batrachophagous	hylophagous	pantophagous	sarcophagus
galactophagous	lithophagous	phytophagous	xylophagous
geophagous	necrophagous	saprophagous	zoöphagous
	œsophagous		

Ophagy
anthropophagy hippophagy pantophagy xerophagy
chthonophagy ichthyophagy phytophagy

Ophical
philosophical theosophical trophical

Ophilism
bibliophilism necrophilism Russophilism

Ophilist
bibliophilist Russophilist zoöphilist

Ophonous
cacophonous hydrophanous megalophonous pyrophanous
homophonous hygrophanous monophanous

Ophony
cacophony microphony photophony tautophony
homophony orthophony satanophany theophany
laryngophony

Ophorous
actinophorous galactophorous mastigophorous pyrophorous
adenophorous isophorous phyllophorous zoöphorous
electrophorous

Opia
Ethiopia myopia presbyopia Utopia

Opian
Esopian Ethiopian Fallopian Utopian
Carnopean

Opical
allotropical metoposcopical misanthropical topical
extropical microscopical subtropical tropical

Opiness
ropiness soapiness dopiness

Opishness
mopishness popishness

Opolis
acropolis metropolis necropolis

Opolist
bibliopolist monopolist pharmacopolist

Opolite
cosmopolite metropolite

Oppery
coppery foppery

Oppiness
choppiness sloppiness soppiness

Opsical
dropsical mopsical

Opterous
lepidopterous macropterous orthopterous

Optical
autoptical optical

Opulate
copulate populate

Orable
adorable deplorable explorable restorable

Orative
explorative restorative

Orceable
divoreable enforceable forcible

Ordering
bordcring ordering

Ordial
cordial exordial primordial

Ordinate
co-ordinate insubordinate ordinate subordinate
foreordinate

Ordian
Gordion accordion

Organize
organize gorgonize

Oria
aporia infusoria scoria victoria
dysphoria phantasmagoria

ORIAL

accessorial
accusatorial
adaptorial
admonitorial
amatorial
ambassadorial
ancestorial
arboreal
armorial
assessorial
auditorial
authorial
boreal
censoria
commentatorial
compromis-
sorial
compurgatorial
consistorial
corporeal
cursorial
dedicatorial
dictatorial
directorial
disquisitorial
editorial
electorial
equatoreal
executorial
expurgatorial
exterritorial
factorial
fossorial
gladiatorial
grallatorial
gressorial
gubernatorial
historial
immemorial
imperatorial
improvisatorial
incorporeal
infusorial
inquisitorial
insessorial
intercessorial
inventorial
legislatorial
manorial
marmoreal
mediatorial
monitorial
motorial
oratorial
phantasma-
gorial
pictorial
piscatorial
preceptorial
prefatorial
proctorial
procuratorial
professorial
proprietorial
protectorial
purgatorial
raptorial
rasorial
rectorial
reportorial
risorial
sartorial
scansorial
sectorial
seigniorial
senatorial
sensorial
spectatorial
sponsorial
speculatorial
suctorial
territorial
textorial
tinctorial
tonsorial
tutorial
uxorial
victorial
visitatorial

ORIAN

amatorian
Bosphorian
censorian
consistorian
dictatorian
Dorian
gladiatorian
Gregorian
hectorian
historian
hyperborean
marmorean
nestorian
oratorian
prætorian
purgatorian
salutatorian
senatorian
stentorian
valedictorian

ORIATE

excoriate
professoriate

ORICAL

allegorical
categorical
coracle
historical
metaphorical
oracle
oratorical
pictorical
rhetorical
tautegorical

ORIFY

glorify
historify
scorify

ORINESS

desultoriness
dilatoriness
goriness
hoariness
peremptoriness

ORIOLE

gloriole
oriole

ORIOUS

amatorious
arboreous
censorious
circulatorious
desultorious
expiatorious
expurgetorious
glorious
inglorious
inquisitorious
laborious
lorious
lusorious
meritorious
notorious
oratorious
purgatorious
raptorious
saltatorious
scorious
senatorious
stentorious
stertorious
suctorious
uproarious
ustorious
uxorious
vainglorious
victorious

ORIOUSLY

gloriously
ingloriously
laboriously
meritoriously
notoriously
stentoriously
uproariously
uxoriously
vaingloriously
victoriously

ORITY

anteriority
authority
deteriority
exteriority
inferiority
interiority
juniority
majority
meliority
minority
posteriority
priority
seniority
superiority
sorority

ORIUM

aspersorium
auditorium
digitorium
emporium
prætorium
sanatorium
scriptorium
sensorium
sudatorium
thorium
triforium

ORMATIVE

afformative
dormitive
formative
informative
reformative
transformative

ORMITY

abnormity
conformity
deformity
enormity
inconformity
multiformity
nonconformity
uniformity

OROUSLY

decorously
porously
sonorously

ORRIDLY

horridly
floridly
torridly

ORRIFY

horrify	torrefy

ORROWER

borrower	sorrower

ORROWING

borrowing	sorrowing

ORTICAL

cortical	vortical

ORTIFY

fortify	mortify

ORTLINESS

portliness	courtliness	uncourtliness

ORTUNATE

fortunate	importunate

OSCOPIST

metoposcopist	oneiroscopist	stereoscopist	stethoscopist
microscopist	ornithoscopist		

OSCOPY

cranioscopy	horoscopy	oneiroscopy	stereoscopy
geloscopy	meteoroscopy	organoscopy	stethoscopy
geoscopy	metoposcopy	ornithoscopy	uranoscopy
hieroscopy	omoplatoscopy	retinoscopy	

OSIA

ambrosia	symposia

OSIAL

ambrosial	roseal

OSIER

crosier	hosier	osier	"nosier"
cosier	prosier	rosier	

OSIEST

cosiest	prosiest	rosiest	"nosiest"

OSILY

cosily	prosily	rosily	"nosily"
			"dosily"

OSINESS
cosiness
doziness
prosiness
rosiness
"nosiness"

OSITY
actuosity
anfractuosity
angulosity
animosity
anonymosity
aquosity
atrocity
caliginosity
callosity
carnosity
curiosity
docity
dubiosity
ebriosity
fabulosity
ferocity
foliosity
fuliginosity
fumosity
furiosity
gemmosity
generosity
gibbosity
glandulosity
glebosity
globosity
glutinosity
grandiosity
gulosity
gummosity
hideosity
impecuniosity
impetuosity
ingeniosity
inunctuosity
libidinosity
litigiosity
lugubriosity
luminosity
monstrosity
muscosity
musculosity
nebulosity
negotiosity
nervosity
nodosity
oleosity
otiosity
pilosity
plumosity
pomposity
ponderosity
porosity
preciosity
precocity
pretiosity
reciprocity
religiosity
ridiculosity
rimosity
rugosity
sabulosity
saporosity
scirrhosity
scrupulosity
sensuosity
serosity
sinuosity
speciosity
spicosity
spinosity
tenebrosity
torosity
tortuosity
tuberosity
tumulosity
unctuosity
varicosity
velocity
verbosity
viciosity
villosity
vinosity
virtuosity
viscosity
vitiosity
vociferosity

OSIVENESS
corrosiveness
explosiveness

OSOPHER
philosopher
psilosopher
theosopher

OSOPHIST
chirosophist
deipnosophist
gymnosophist
philosophist
theosophist

OSOPHIZE
philosophize
theosophize

OSOPHY
gymnosophy
philosophy
theosophy

OSPHORUS
Bosphorus
phosphorus

Ossiness
drossiness glossiness mossiness

Otable
potable quotable notable votable
floatable

Otalism
sacerdotalism teetotalism

Otany
botany bottony cottony monotony

Otary
notary rotary votary

Otative
connotative denotative rotative

Otedly
devotedly bloatedly notedly

Otherhood
brotherhood motherhood

Othering
brothering mothering smothering

Otherlike
brotherlike motherlike

Otherly
brotherly southerly unbrotherly unmotherly
motherly

Othery
mothery smothery

Otian
Bœotian Nicotian notion (*see* Otion, *2 syl. rhymes*)

Otical
anecdotical despotical exotical zealotical
bigotical erotical

Otional
devotional emotional notional

Otomist
ichthyotomist phlebotomist phytotomist zoötomist

Otomy
apotomy bronchotomy dermotomy dichotomy encephalotomy ichthyotomy phlebotomy phytotomy scotomy stereotomy tracheotomy zoötomy

Ottery
lottery pottery tottery

Ottiness
dottiness knottiness spottiness

Oughtiness
doughtiness droughtiness goutiness

Oundable
compoundable soundable unsoundable

Oundedness
astoundedness confoundedness dumfoundedness unboundedness ungroundedness

Oundlessly
boundlessly groundlessly soundlessly

Oundlessness
boundlessness groundlessness soundlessness

Ountable
countable discountable insurmountable mountable surmountable unaccountable

Ourishing
flourishing nourishing

Ovable
approvable immovable irremovable movable provable reprovable

Ovelling
grovelling hovelling

Ovial
jovial synovial

Ovian
Cracovian Jovian

Owable

allowable, avowable, endowable

Owdedness

crowdedness, overcrowdedness, cloudedness, uncloudedness

Owdiness

dowdiness, cloudiness, rowdiness

Owdyism

dowdyism, rowdyism

Owering

cowering, dowering, empowering, flowering, glowering, lowering, overpowering, overtowering, showering, towering

Owery

bowery, dowery, flowery, lowery, showery, towery

Owlery

owlery, prowlery

Owziness

drowsiness, frowziness

Oyable

employable, enjoyable

Oyalism

loyalism, royalism

Oyalist

loyalist, royalist

Oyally

loyally, royally

Oyalty

loyalty, royalty, viceroyalty

Oxical

orthodoxical, paradoxical, toxical

Uable

pursuable, renewable, reviewable, suable, subduable

Ubbiness
chubbiness scrubbiness stubbiness shrubbiness
grubbiness

Uberous
protuberous suberous tuberous

Ubian
Danubian rubian

Ubilate
enubilate jubilate obnubilate volubilate

Ubrious
insalubrious lugubrious salubrious

Ucean
caducean Confucian

Ucible
adducible educible producible seducible
conducible inducible reducible traducible
deducible irreducible

Ucidly
ducidly deucedly mucidly pellucidly

Uckering
puckering succouring

Uckily
luckily pluckily

Uctible
conductible destructible indestructible instructible

Uctional
constructional fluxional inductional instructional

Uctionist
constructionist destructionist fluxionist

Uctively
constructively destructively instructively productively

Uctiveness
constructiveness destructiveness instructiveness productiveness

Uctory
conductory introductory reproductory

Uculent
luculent muculent

Uddery
duddery shuddery studdery

Uddily
muddily bloodily ruddily

Uddiness
ruddiness bloodiness muddiness

Udency
concludency pudency

Udible
eludible includible

Udinize
attitudinize platitudinize

Udinous
fortitudinous multitudinous platitudinous vicissitudinous
latitudinous paludinous solicitudinous

Udious
preludious studious

Udity
crudity rudity nudity

Ueller
dueller fueller jeweller

Uelling
duelling bejewelling fuelling

Uffiness
fluffiness huffiness puffiness stuffiness

Uggery
snuggery puggerie

Uginous
lanuginous salsuginous

UINESS

dewiness	gluiness

UINOUS

pruinous	ruinous

UITOUS

circuitous	fortuitous	gratuitous	pituitous
fatuitous			

UITY

acuity	contiguity	ingenuity	strenuity
ambiguity	continuity	innocuity	suety
annuity	discontinuity	perpetuity	superfluity
assiduity	exiguity	perspicuity	tenuity
circuity	fatuity	promiscuity	vacuity
conspicuity	gratuity		

ULEAN

herculean	Julian

ULITY

credulity	incredulity	sedulity

ULKINESS

bulkiness	sulkiness

ULLERY

gullery	medullary	scullery

ULMINANT

culminant	fulminant

ULMINATE

culminate	fulminate

ULSIVELY

convulsively	impulsively	repulsively

ULSIVENESS

compulsiveness	convulsiveness	impulsiveness	repulsiveness

ULTERY

adultery	consultary

ULTURISM

agriculturism	vulturism

Ulverin
culverin pulverin

Umberer
cumberer lumberer numberer slumberer
encumberer

Umbering
cumbering lumbering outnumbering unslumbering
encumbering numbering slumbering

Umbery
slumbery umbery

Umbingly
benumbingly becomingly numbingly unbecomingly

Umeral
humeral numeral

Umerous
humorous humerus numerous tumorous

Umery
perfumery plumery

Uminate
acuminate catechumenate illuminate luminate

Uminous
aluminous fluminous luminous voluminous
bituminous leguminous

Ummery
flummery nummary summary summery
mummery plumbery

Umulate
accumulate tumulate

Umulous
tumulous cumulus

Umpishness
dumpishness frumpishness lumpishness mumpishness

Umptiously
bumptiously "scrumptiously"

UNABLE
tunable
expugnable

UNDERSONG
undersong
wonder-song

UNDER-WORLD
under-world
wonder-world

UNDITY
fecundity
jocundity
jucundity
profundity
rotundity
rubicundity

UNGERING
hungering
mongering

UNICATE
communicate
excommunicate
tunicate

UNIFORM
cuniform
luniform
uniform

UNITIVE
punitive
unitive

UNITY
community
immunity
importunity
impunity
inopportunity
intercommunity
jejunity
opportunity
triunity
unity

UNNERY
gunnery
nunnery

UNNILY
funnily
sunnily

UNTEDLY
stuntedly
affrontedly
unwontedly
wontedly

UPERATE
recuperate
vituperate

URABLE
curable
durable
endurable
incurable
procurable
securable
assurable
insurable

URALISM
pluralism
ruralism

Uralist

pluralist	ruralist		

Urative

curative	maturative		

Urdily

sturdily	wordily		

Urgical

chirurgical	demiurgical	liturgical	theurgical
clergical	energical	surgical	

Urial

augurial	figurial	mercurial	purpureal

Urian

Asturian	Etrurian	scripturian	silurian
centurian			

Urient

esurient	paturient	scripturient	

Uriate

infuriate	luxuriate	muriate	parturiate

Urify

purify	thurify		

Urious

curious	injurious	perjurious	sulphureous
furious	luxurious	spurious	usurious
incurious	penurious	strangurious	

Urity

demurity	insecurity	obscurity	purity
immaturity	maturity	prematurity	security
impurity	naturity		

Urliest

burliest	curliest	pearliest	surliest
churliest	earliest		

Urliness

burliness	earliness	pearliness	surliness
curliness			

Urlishly

churlishly	girlishly		

Urlishness
churlishness
girlishness

Urnable
burnable
discernible
indiscernible
learnable
overturnable
returnable

Urnisher
burnisher
furnisher

Urnishing
burnishing
furnishing

Urrier
furrier
currier
hurrier
worrier

Urriest
furriest
hurriest
worriest

Urrying
currying
flurrying
hurrying
scurrying
worrying

Uscular
bimuscular
corpuscular
crepuscular
muscular

Usculous
corpusculous
crepusculous
musculous

Usible
fusible
confusable
diffusible
amusable
excusable
inexcusable
infusible
transfusible
usable

Usiveness
abusiveness
allusiveness
conclusiveness
conduciveness
delusiveness
diffusiveness
effusiveness
exclusiveness
illusiveness
inconclusiveness
inobtrusiveness
intrusiveness
obtrusiveness

Uskily
duskily
huskily
muskily

Usory
collusory
conclusory
delusory
elusory
exclusory
illusory
lusory
prelusory
reclusory

Ustering

blustering	clustering	flustering	mustering

Ustfully

distrustfully	lustfully	mistrustfully	trustfully

Ustible

adjustable	combustible	incombustible	dustable

Ustiest

crustiest	fustiest	lustiest	rustiest
dustiest	gustiest	mustiest	trustiest

Ustily

crustily	fustily	lustily	rustily
dustily	gustily	mustily	trustily

Ustiness

crustiness	fustiness	lustiness	rustiness
dustiness	gustiness	mustiness	trustiness

Ustrious

illustrious	industrious		

Utable

commutable	executable	mutable	transmutable
computable	immutable	permutable	inscrutable
confutable	imputable	refutable	mootable
disputable	incommutable	suitable	scrutable

Utative

commutative	disputative	putative	sternutative
confutative	imputative	sputative	

Uteous

duteous	luteous		

Uthfully

ruthfully	truthfully	youthfully	

Uthfulness

truthfulness	youthfulness		

Uthlessly

ruthlessly	truthlessly		

Utical

latreutical	pharmaceutical	scorbutical	therapeutical
cuticle			

Utiful

beautiful	dutiful		

Utinous

glutinous	mutinous	velutinous	

Utional

circumlocu-tional	constitutional	institutional	substitutional
	evolutional		

Utioner

executioner	resolutioner	revolutioner	

Utionist

circumlocu-tionist	constitutionist	evolutionist	revolutionist
	elocutionist	resolutionist	

Utlery

cutlery	sutlery		

Utterer

flutterer	splutterer	stutterer	utterer
mutterer	sputterer		

Uttering

buttering	guttering	spluttering	uttering
fluttering	muttering	sputtering	stuttering

Uttony

buttony	gluttony	muttony	

Uvial

alluvial	diluvial	exuvial	postdiluvial
antediluvial	effluvial	fluvial	

Uvian

antediluvian	Peruvian	postdiluvian	Vesuvian
diluvian			

Uzziness

fuzziness	muzziness	"wuzziness"	

Y *see* I

Appendix

Prymers for Rhymers

But prime the pump and it will keep on flowing

The training of a rhymester is like the training for any other artistic skill: subjection to rule, and constant practice. But practicing can become so monotonous as to lose value, as any young pianist will admit, or any singer who is exercising his vocal chords up and down the scales. To avoid such monotony in the practice of verse writing there are games which provide entertainment as well as training.

The Game of Limericks

For more than two centuries limericks (or British nonsense rhymes) have been built around the names of persons or places. Let each member of the assembled company be assigned the name of one of his associates. He may use the surname or given name or nickname; any name in fact which is identifying. He must, within a limited time, compose a limerick built around that name. This means it must be the final word in the first line of that limerick and, if the pattern of Lear's "nonsense rhymes" is followed, the final line must end with that word. (The task is made a little harder if the name is not repeated in the final line, but a rhyme for it is used.)

The winner is that one who first completes his limerick without flaw in rhyme or meter. A prize may also go to the one who composes the cleverest. The game may be varied by assigning to each the name of a place instead of a person. But the game has little disciplinary value if there is not insistence upon a time limit, and upon accuracy of rhythm and rhyme; although perfection of rhyme might be balanced by ingenuity of rhyming, as for instance in the following:

There was a young woman in Grinnich
Who had a great weakness for spinach.
  When it slipt down her chin
  She would lap it all in,
Initch by initch by initch.

The compiler of this book has accumulated five limericks having as many perfect rhymes for Schenectady.

If the company is capable of it, the winning limerick should be sung in chorus to a simple tune which has been traditional for many generations.

THE GAME OF SONNETS

As noted earlier in this book there have been many variations in the form of the sonnet. The most ancient, the Petrarchan, is best for the purpose for rigidity's sake and because of tradition. The rhyme-scheme may be found on page 38 of this book.

It is only fair to warn the company that the rhyme-sounds ending the first two lines are repeated three times in the sonnet so that the first two words dictated should be simple words having many rhymes.

Each player should be provided with pencil and paper and should write down in a column all the words as they are dictated. The first person in order proposes a word, such as "boy"; the second must suggest a word which does not rhyme with boy, as for instance "house." The third person must suggest a word which rhymes with house, such as "mouse." The next a word rhyming with boy, such as "joy." The fifth a word rhyming again with boy, such as "ahoy." The sixth another word rhyming with house, such as "louse." And so on, until there are fourteen words following the Petrarchan rhyme scheme—abbaabbacdecde.

Words may be challenged by any member of the company on the ground that they are unrhymable or, as in the case of "louse," that they limit the range of fancy for all the players. However, even that word might be defended on the ground that Bobby Burns wrote a serious poem on the subject. When all have their word lists, they retire into their several corners or nooks and fill in their sonnets.

The following samples prove that such a poetic achievement is not out of the reach either of a young student or a professional who ordinarily approaches his task in different fashion.

Set of words dictated by students themselves in a certain classroom:

Whole-sweet-greet-goal-role-feet-neat-soul-sleep-pass-know-deep-alas-go. Resulting sonnet, from a student, chosen at random:

This world, if we survey it as a whole
  Is quite as full of bitter as of sweet.
  So learn to laugh and love; and learn to greet
Each passing phase, though it is not the goal.
I play my part as if it were a role;
  The path which I must tread beneath my feet
  Is thorny sometimes, sometimes smooth and neat
And soothes that spirit which I call my soul.
So, if I am awake or if I sleep,
  From phase to phase I am required to pass.
I know no reason why, nor do you know;
I taste the froth, and then must I drink deep—
  Of sorrow more than happiness alas;
And thus through life we all of us must go.

The same set of words sent to Louis Untermeyer, the poet, who responded by return mail:

Let's kiss and say it's over. On the whole
  It wasn't bad—but that is life, my sweet.
  You've had your last of me; I'm glad to greet
The last of you. With freedom as my goal
The time has come for me to pack my roll
  And learn once more how to employ my feet.
  Shake hands and laugh: let's keep the ending neat—
Remember how we joked at "Body—Soul"?
Now what they call the soul has gone to sleep
  And the poor body's scarcely worth a pass.
    We never knew the things we ought to know;
We were afraid, we said, to get in deep.
  So here we are—too late to cry "Alas!"
    For when you gotta go, you gotta go.

The same words sent to Arthur Guiterman, the poet, who made instant response:

To him who builds a sonnet, on the whole
  The needful toil is arduous, if sweet:
  Though neither laurels nor applauses greet
The poetaster at his lyric goal.

He takes delight in choosing words that roll,
In finding rhymes and smooth Iambic feet,
In coining metaphors correct and neat
And giving meter everything but soul.

Yes, Homer nods, the Muses often sleep
And dabblers boast "That's good enough to pass!"
But "good enough" let every dabbler know
Is ten times damned, ten billion fathoms deep,
Beyond the seventh tier of Hell. Alas,
No farther down the sorry thing can go.

Another set of words dictated by students in a classroom:

Sonnet by a young student:

When I was but a tiny thoughtless boy
I wandered idly through the meadow hay,
To watch the soaring, dipping larks at play
And find a rusty trap, a passing toy,
And baby rabbits, curious and coy.
My mother'd warned me that I must not stay,
But cloud-ships beckoned down the airy way
And air-born voices challenged me "Ahoy!"
The world drew in, the heavens swelled with rain,
Shot darts of steel down toward the valley floor.
I fled back stumbling through the soaking grass;
The rusty trap jaws snapped, I howled with pain,
But somehow found my way to that kind door
Where home was, in the town of Reading, Mass.

Sonnet with the same words, required of the teacher:

As irresponsible as any boy
Who turns a somersault upon the hay
I tossed these words to you, and bid you play
As merry rhymesters with a new-found toy.
But some of you have found the muse too coy
Who at your call would neither stop nor stay;
While some have sailed along the Milky Way
And to the Pleiades have cried "Ahoy!"
And some have walked unwitting in the rain
And some with measured beat have trod the floor;

And some in frenzy rolled upon the grass.
And when I hear their sonnets, wrought with pain,
In deep remorse I seek some holy door,
Beg absolution, and attend a mass.

The Game of Capping Rhymes

In the days when English literature was approaching the height of its glory, it was a fad among cultured folk to play at "capping rhymes" and familiar quotations. Apparently, when any such company had got together, if one of them contributed to the conversation some familiar bit of verse, or some classic quotation, it was a challenge to any other member of the company to "cap" it by quoting some other equally notable lines which must begin with the same initial letter. An impromtu line of verse was also acceptable.

One of the first references to this social custom is dated 1588, and it seems to have been continued in the coffee houses and at private banquets and social gatherings down through the centuries, and is said still to survive in the classrooms of some British Latin schools.

Conversation was a fine art throughout those Shakespearean days, and the capping of rhymes was a flowering of that art. Whether it might be revived in prosaic America remains to be seen. All it requires is a social group assembled around a dinner table, and aware that they are about to revive a historic custom. They must not be thrown into awkward self-consciousness by the realization that if any member of the company happens to quote a familiar line of poetry someone is expected to cap it.

If, let us assume, the host is about to sever a drumstick from the duck, some guest remarks "Woodman, spare that tree!" some other guest must remark "What ugly sights of death within mine eyes!" (Shakespeare). Since both quotations begin with W, he is triumphant. But with no quotation at hand, an impromptu line of verse would have served, as for instance "Whoever carves a duck is like to run amuck"—for the initial is still imperative.

From small beginnings great events are born; and who knows but that a revival of forgotten Shakespearean pastimes may bring us again to Shakespearean achievement.

Parody

Parody deserves place in this handbook though it is not any single poetic form but plays with all forms. The serious-minded poet might think of it as a poor relation of poetic writing and even a disreputable one, were it not for the fact that there are famous parodies handed down to us through the years written by poets or versifiers of high repute.

The worth of a parody depends upon the closeness of its resemblance to the poem which it mimics; its skill is measured by the extent to which it can make use of the exact words of the original and completely alter their meaning.

The wickedness of parody lies in the fact that it can so completely distort a beautiful poem and do it so cleverly that one may find it hard ever again to read the original without smiling at the memory of the distorted version.

A famous example is a parody by J. K. Stephen which is not only a burlesque but a bit of sharp criticism, parodying Wordsworth's sonnet "Two Voices Are There." This parody first appeared in *Punch* and may be found in the article on "Parody" in the *Encyclopaedia Britannica.*

Two voices are there: one is of the deep;
It learns the storm-cloud's thunderous melody,
Now roars, now murmurs with the changing sea,
Now bird-like pipes, now closes soft in sleep:

And one is of an old half-witted sheep
Which bleats articulate monotony,
And indicates that two and one are three,
The grass is green, lakes damp and mountains steep;

And, Wordsworth, both are thine: at certain times
Forth from the heart of thy melodious rhymes,
The form and pressure of high thoughts will burst:

At other times—Good Lord! I'd rather be
Quite unacquainted with the A B C
Than write such awful twaddle as thy worst.

Despite a tendency toward rowdyism, parody has all the dignity of age. A parody in ancient Greek is ascribed to Homer himself; Shakespeare was parodied by Marston, and Dryden by Buckingham, and so on, to our own times. Owen Seaman, editor of *Punch*, was a master of the art; and many of the verses in *Alice's Adventures in Wonderland* are parodies of serious British poetry. As for parodies in prose, nothing can surpass those condensed novels by Thackeray and by Bret Harte.

The writing of parody is good practice for the versifier, for it forces him to fit his thoughts into accepted patterns of rhyme and rhythm, though it may make a satirist of him, or a disrespecter of sacred things.

The following parody of Mrs. Hemans' deathless lines may serve as a warning.

The gnashing teeth bit hard
  On a firm and rib-bound roast,
And boarders 'gainst a table scarred
  The leaden biscuit tossed.

And they frowned with inward storm
  As they scanned the dishes o'er
And recognized in a chowdered form
  The things they'd seen before.

Not as the conqueror comes,
  Stirred by the trumpet's yell,
They came at the call of empty tums,
  And the sounding supper bell.

Amid the meal they sang
  Small tales of tardy ones,
And eyed with ill-concealed pang
  Each other's sauce and buns.

A dame in watered silk
  Who sat beside the urn
Smiled coldly as she thinned the milk
  And doled to each in turn.

There were men with hoary hair
  Amid that hungry group,
Why had they come to wither there
  And mumble o'er their soup?

There was woman's hungry eye
  Seeking an extra roll;
There was manhood's brow serenely high
  Guarding the sugar bowl.

What sought those reaching arms?
  Fat pickings 'mid the dearth?
The wealth of seas, the spoil of farms?
  They sought their money's worth.

Save here a stain of broth
  And there a gravy trace,
They left a barren crumbless cloth
  Within that boarding place.

—B. J.

ARTIFICIAL RHYMES

Scattered throughout this dictionary are a few manufactured or artificial rhymes of the more obvious sort; but no attempt has been made to assemble many of them. They are a product of the ingenuity of any skilled rhymester who makes a necessary rhyme by putting two or three small words together, or by shameless but recognizable mispronunciation. Generally they add to the humor of humorous verse, but would be offensive in serious poetry.

W. S. Gilbert plays with them in the opening song of The Major General in *The Pirates of Penzance: din afore* and *Pinafore; sat a gee* and *strategy; javelin* and *ravelin'*; *commissariat* and *wary at.*

The rhymester who is ambitious to write humorous verse would do well to familiarize himself with that British classic written more than a century ago, *The Ingoldsby Legends*, and with the ingenious and delightful rhyming distortions of Ogden Nash. And he might add to his rhyming games an interchange of challenges to find rhymes for the unrhymable!

"MORE POETS YET!"

"More Poets yet!"—I hear him say,
    Arming his heavy hand to slay;—
  "Despite my skill and swashing blow,
  They seem to sprout where'er I go;—
I killed a host but yesterday!"

Slash on, O Hercules! You may.
Your task's, at best, a hydra-fray;
  And though *you* cut, not less will grow
      More Poets yet!

—AUSTIN DOBSON